Samuel Cox

The Genesis of Evil

And other Sermons, mainly expository

Samuel Cox

The Genesis of Evil
And other Sermons, mainly expository

ISBN/EAN: 9783337160753

Printed in Europe, USA, Canada, Australia, Japan

Cover: Foto ©Lupo / pixelio.de

More available books at **www.hansebooks.com**

THE GENESIS OF EVIL

AND OTHER SERMONS

MAINLY EXPOSITORY

BY

SAMUEL COX

AUTHOR OF 'SALVATOR MUNDI,' AND EDITOR OF 'THE EXPOSITOR'

LONDON
C. KEGAN PAUL & CO., 1, PATERNOSTER SQUARE
1880

TO MY CONGREGATION,

WITH MY LOVE.

PREFACE.

It is my happiness, as it is that of many Nonconformist ministers, to preach to a Congregation composed of personal friends, who have been gradually gathered round me, in the slow lapse of years, by community of thought or sentiment. Hence I can speak to them at once more confidentially and more colloquially than I could to an audience of comparative strangers: more confidentially, because any allusion I make to my own experience of Truth, or of the difficulties which stand in the way of receiving it, is pretty sure to awaken an instant response in their minds; more colloquially, because one of the feelings we have in common is a desire to see the technical and theological terms which have come down to us loaded with associations, often misleading, replaced by the simple homely phrases which plain men use and understand. The Editor of Canon Mozley's thoughtful 'Parochial and Occasional Sermons' apologizes, I observe, for leaving in them 'some homelinesses of expression' which he believes 'the Author would not have allowed to pass,' rather than substitute for them 'the conventional phrases which suggest themselves in their place.' I doubt whether he is right in believing that so able and experienced a Preacher as Canon Mozley would not have allowed his homeliest phrases to pass. I am sure that homely phrases carry more weight and leave a sharper impression than the conventional terms which have been worn smooth and light by constant handling. In the pulpit above all other places men like to hear a spade called a spade; and that mainly, I suppose, because, despite certain appearances to the contrary, they sincerely long to have the truths of Religion brought down into the common round of thought and conduct. And if sermons are to be preached, not for the glory of the Preacher, but for the benefit of his hearers, we need not lament 'the decay of pulpit eloquence,' popular as that theme is with certain Essayists, but should rather rejoice that, for the stately, and sometimes stilted, and often conventional eloquence of bygone years, we now so commonly get no eloquence beyond that of good talk. 'He who spake as never man spake' used the simplest words, the homeliest illustrations. There is nothing in the form of the Sermon on the Mount to make it hard to the most unlettered of men. And if He, before whom even Socrates and Aurelius and Epictetus must veil their faces, habitually employed a simplicity of speech which they could compass only in their best and highest moods, why should any servant of his apologize for 'homelinesses of expression'? Homely expressions come home: and, to my mind, the best sermon is that which most closely resembles the best conversation of educated and thoughtful men.

There is another point in which, I take it, a sermon should, so far as possible, resemble good conversation. 'Coward's castle' is often uncomfortable to its occupant, if at least he be a sensible man, precisely because he is aware that, say what he will in it, no one has the right of reply, nor can so much as start a difficulty or ask a question. Hence, a fair-minded man, who desires that only truth should prevail, ought, I think, to speak for his Congregation as well as for himself; ought, that is, to look at the subjects he handles from their point of view as well as from his own, and to state any objections or difficulties they are likely to entertain as frankly and forcibly as he can. This conception of the Preacher's duty is so strong in me that I often seem to myself to be listening and replying to the thoughts of my hearers rather than uttering my own; and I hope it will be found that in many of these Sermons I take a conversational tone, and try to do justice to the *other* side of the dialogue.

I say all this, not in apology for these discourses, but rather as explaining and justifying what may seem peculiar and unconventional in them. Nor do I plead in excuse for publishing them, though I too might urge the plea if I cared, the urgent requests of friends. I publish them because I heartily believe in the value of the truths which they enforce, and because, as I know they have been helpful to the friends who heard them, I hope they may also be useful to a still wider audience. One of the greatest preachers of the day has recently boasted that he has 'no sympathy with doubt.' I do not know that I have any sympathy with *doubt,* but I have a very keen sympathy with those who are tried by doubts they cannot solve. And if any of these tried but unknown neighbours of mine should gather helpful suggestions from any words printed here, I shall get for the labour bestowed on this book the wage and reward I most prize.

I had named this volume, which contains nearly all the Sermons that ill-health has allowed me to preach during the past year, 'The *Origin* of Evil,' &c., after the first two sermons contained in it; but when it was already in the press the publishers discovered that that title had been recently appropriated: hence we had to fall back on a less familiar, but still, I hope, sufficiently suggestive, phrase.

NOTTINGHAM,
    Christmas Day, 1879.

CONTENTS.

SERMON I.
THE ORIGIN OF EVIL.
FIRST PART.

  PAGE
'I am the Lord, and there is none else. I form the light, and create darkness; I make peace and create evil: I, the Lord, do all these things.'—Isaiah xlv. 6, 7 1

SERMON II.
THE ORIGIN OF EVIL.
SECOND PART.

'I am the Lord, and there is none else. I form the light, and create darkness; I make peace and create evil: I, the Lord, do all these things.'—Isaiah xlv. 6, 7 21

SERMON III.
THE HEAVENLY TREASURE AND THE EARTHEN VESSELS.

' But we have this treasure in earthen vessels.'—2 Corinthians iv. 7 42

SERMON IV.

GOD UNKNOWN YET KNOWN.

'Seek ye the Lord while he may be found, call ye upon him while he is near: Let the wicked forsake his way, and the unrighteous man his thoughts; and let him return unto the Lord, and he will have mercy upon him; and to our God, for he will abundantly pardon. For my thoughts are not your thoughts, neither are your ways my ways, saith the Lord. For as the heavens are higher than the earth, so are my ways higher than your ways, and my thoughts than your thoughts.'
—Isaiah lv. 6–9 61

SERMON V.

THE INCREDIBLE MERCY OF GOD.

'Seek ye the Lord while he may be found, call ye upon him while he is near: Let the wicked forsake his way, and the unrighteous man his thoughts: and let him return unto the Lord, and he will have mercy upon him; and to our God, for he will abundantly pardon. For my thoughts are not your thoughts, neither are your ways my ways, saith the Lord. For as the heavens are higher than the earth, so are my ways higher than your ways, and my thoughts than your thoughts.'
—Isaiah lv. 6–9 77

SERMON VI.

ALL THINGS OURS.

'All things are yours; whether Paul, or Apollos, or Cephas, or the world, or life, or death, or things present, or things to come: all are yours, and ye are Christ's, and Christ God's.'
—1 Corinthians iii. 21–23 91

SERMON VII.

THE TOO GREAT PROMISE.

PAGE

'All things are yours; whether Paul, or Apollos, or Cephas, or the world, or life, or death, or things present, or things to come: all are yours, and ye are Christ's, and Christ God's.' —1 CORINTHIANS iii. 21–23 106

SERMON VIII.

LED BY A CHILD.

FIRST PART.

'The wolf also shall dwell with the lamb, and the leopard shall lie down with the kid; and the calf and the young lion and the fatling together: and a little child shall lead them.'— ISAIAH xi. 6 122

SERMON IX.

LED BY A CHILD.

SECOND PART.

'The wolf also shall dwell with the lamb, and the leopard shall lie down with the kid; and the calf and the young lion and the fatling together: and a little child shall lead them.'— ISAIAH xi. 6 135

SERMON X.

THE LIVING GOD OF LIVING MEN.

'But that the dead rise, even Moses implied at the evergreen thornbush, when he calleth the Lord the God of Abraham, and God of Isaac, and God of Jacob. But he is not the God of dead men, but of living men; for all live unto him.' —ST. LUKE xx. 37, 38 148

SERMON XI.

DEATH AN EXODUS.

'And, behold, there were talking with him two men, who were none other than Moses and Elijah; who appeared in glory, and talked of his exodus which he should accomplish at Jerusalem.'—St. Luke ix. 30, 31 163

SERMON XII.

ON SERVING GOD WITH ONE SHOULDER.

'For then will I turn to the nations a pure lip, that they may all invoke the name of the Lord, and serve him with one shoulder.' —Zephaniah iii. 9 178

SERMON XIII.

WHY WE SUFFER.

'No doubt this man is a murderer whom, though he hath escaped the sea, Justice suffereth not to live.'—Acts xxviii. 4 . . 196

SERMON XIV.

AARON'S APOLOGY.

'I cast it into the fire, and there came out this calf.'—Exodus xxxii. 24 212

SERMON XV.

THE PARABLE OF THE TALENTS.

'The kingdom of heaven is as a man travelling into a far country, who called his own servants and delivered unto them his goods. And unto one he gave five talents, to another two, and to another one; to every man according to his several ability: and straightway took his journey,' &c., &c., &c.— St. Matthew xxv. 14–30 228

SERMON XVI.
THE PARABLE OF THE SHEEP AND THE GOATS.

'When the Son of Man shall come in his glory, and all the holy angels with him, then shall he sit upon the throne of his glory; and before him shall be gathered all nations; and he shall separate them one from another, as a shepherd divideth his sheep from the goats: and he shall set the sheep on his right hand, but the goats on the left,' &c., &c., &c.—St. Matthew xxv. 31–46 248

SERMON XVII.
THE PARABLE OF THE TEN VIRGINS.

'Then shall the kingdom of heaven be likened unto ten virgins, who took their lamps, and went forth to meet the bridegroom. And five of them were wise, and five were foolish,' &c., &c., &c.—St. Matthew xxv. 1–13 263

SERMON XVIII.
ST. PETER'S SIFTING AND CONVERSION.
1.—THE PROLOGUE IN HEAVEN.

'And the Lord said, Simon, Simon, behold Satan hath desired to have you that he may sift you as wheat; but I have prayed for thee, that thy faith fail not: and when thou art converted, strengthen thy brethren.'—St. Luke xxii. 31, 32 . . . 280

SERMON XIX.
ST. PETER'S SIFTING AND CONVERSION.
2.—THE SCENE ON EARTH.

'And the Lord said Simon, Simon, behold Satan obtained you that he may sift you like wheat; but I prayed for thee, that thy faith fail not: and when thou art converted, strengthen thy brethren.'—St. Luke xxii. 31, 32 298

SERMON XX.

ST. PETER'S SIFTING AND CONVERSION.

3.—THE SCOPE AND FUNCTION OF EVIL AS ILLUSTRATED BY THE SIFTING OF ST. PETER.

PAGE

Simon, Simon, behold Satan obtained you, that he may sift you like wheat; but I prayed for thee, that thy faith fail not: and when thou art converted, strengthen thy brethren.'—ST. LUKE xxii. 31, 32 317

SERMON XXI.

ST. PETER'S SIFTING AND CONVERSION.

4.—CONVERSION AS ILLUSTRATED BY THE CONVERSION OF ST. PETER.

When thou art converted, strengthen thy brethren.'—ST. LUKE xxii. 32 332

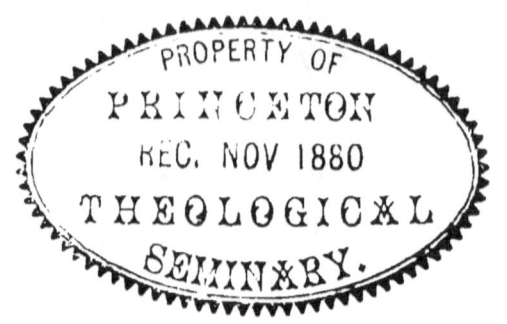

SERMONS.

I.

THE ORIGIN OF EVIL.

FIRST PART.

'I am the Lord, and there is none else. I form the light, and create darkness; I make peace, and create evil: I, the Lord, do all these things.'—ISAIAH xlv. 6, 7.

From my earliest years, or at least from the earliest in which I drew 'thoughtful breath,' I have been puzzled and perplexed by these words. And I suppose this bold unqualified affirmation that the Source of all Light is also the Fountain of Darkness, that evil as well as good is the work of God, must task and perplex every thoughtful mind. Dazed and confused by it as I was, however, I was always glad when this Chapter happened to be one of the lessons for the day, if only for the sake of another surprise and perplexity it used to quicken within me. Nor do I see how any intelligent lad who has begun to read ancient history can fail to be struck and impressed by its opening words: '*Thus saith the Lord to his Anointed, to Cyrus.*' The mere fact that Cyrus is brought into the Bible at all, that the history of the sacred race is thus suddenly invaded by the history of the general heathen world, is of itself not a little startling and impressive to a mind accustomed to think of the two as divided from each other by a great and wellnigh impassable gulf. And how can such an one fail to be still further astonished and impressed at hearing that God, who spake at sundry times and in divers manners to the Hebrew prophets, also spoke to a heathen, to a hero and king associated in his thoughts with such famous names as Alexander and Cæsar? That a secular hero, a famous conqueror and prince, should be admitted on any terms to tread the sacred stage and listen to the Divine Voice is sufficiently surprising; but how the surprise grows and deepens when we hear Jehovah calling him to assume the part of 'my Anointed,' that is, '*my Messiah*'! By what possible compromise and modification of Hebrew and Biblical ideas, such an one asks, can a Persian conqueror be called the Messiah of the Lord, and be set before us as a type, or image, of the Christ of the Gospels?

Thus two difficulties, and difficulties provocative of thought, meet us in the first seven Verses of the

Chapter: the one, God's imperative and absolute claim to be the Creator of evil; and the other, that God Himself should salute a Persian soldier as his Messiah. And these two difficulties are much more closely related to each other than they seem to be. Let us deal with the easier of them first.

'The character of Cyrus has been admitted by both ancient and modern writers to have been singularly noble. Greek authors for the most part represent him to have been energetic and patient, just and prudent, magnanimous and modest, and of a religious mind. Æschylus calls him "kindly" or "generous." Xenophon selected him as a model prince for all races. Plutarch says that "in wisdom and virtue and greatness of soul he appears to have been in advance of all kings." Diodorus makes one of his speakers say that Cyrus gained his ascendancy by his self-command and good feeling and gentleness.' The most humane and virtuous of conquerors, he hated the cruel and lascivious idols most men served, and worshipped one sole God, 'the God of heaven.' There is none like him in the ancient world, or none among the kings and princes of that world. And when, at his conquest of Babylon, he discovered in the captive Jews a race who also hated idols, and served one Lord, and knew a law of life at least as pure as his own; when he broke their bands asunder, set them free to return to their native land, and aided them to rebuild the temple and resume the worship of the God of their fathers, we cannot wonder that in this rare and noble nature, in this virtuous and religious Prince, they saw a 'Servant of Jehovah,' a man 'raised up in righteousness,' or even a partial and shadowy resemblance to that Divine Prince and Redeemer for whose advent they had long been taught to look. It was but natural that to the Prophets of the restored Israel the Persian hero should seem to be—as they called him and even made Jehovah call him—the 'Servant,' the 'Shepherd,' the 'Messiah' of the Lord of hosts.

If we bear in mind that Cyrus was *a Persian*, and the very flower and crown of the Persian race, and that the Prophet here represents Jehovah as addressing Himself to Cyrus, we shall find a key to our second and greater difficulty; we shall understand why, in speaking *to him*, Jehovah claims to be the Creator of darkness and evil no less than of goodness and light. For the creed of Cyrus and the Persians, though singularly pure and noble, had one grave defect. They believed in one God, indeed, and thought of Him so nobly that their symbol for Him was a circle with wings,—the circle to denote the completeness, the perfection, the eternity of God; and the wings to denote his all-pervading Presence. But while they believed in one only God, the Maker of all that was good, they also, and out of reverence for One to whom they dared not attribute any wrong, believed in an anti-god whom they made responsible for all that was evil. Ahriman (Angrô-mainyus), as they called this evil Spirit, was not perhaps the equal of Ahura-mazda, the good creative Spirit, but he was independent of Him and his perpetual rival. He was not made by God, nor was he subordinate to Him: and it was he, not God, to whom all that was evil in Nature and in human life was to be attributed. In short, they sacrificed the omnipotence of the God of heaven to his righteousness, and to save his goodness curtailed his power.

Cyrus held this creed. Nor, pure and thoughtful as he was, need we marvel that he held it when even to the pure keen intellect of John Stuart Mill, who died but the other day, it seemed to be the only rational solution of the moral enigma of the universe. Mill expressly affirms that in this respect the only 'difference between popular Christianity and the Persian religion is that the former pays its good Creator the bad compliment of having been the Maker of the Devil, and of being at all times able to crush and annihilate him and his evil deeds and counsels, which nevertheless He does not do.' His conclusion of the whole matter is that, if in an universe in which there is so much that is sinister, disastrous, bad, we are to believe in God at all, we must limit either his goodness or his power; and of the two he prefers to limit his power, thinks it less irrational to believe in a God who cannot do all that He would than to believe in a God capable of tolerating evil or originating it.

This conclusion, however, is impossible to us if we accept the teachings of the Bible. Cyrus held the very creed of Mill; and the Prophet represents Jehovah Himself as indignantly rejecting it. 'I am Jehovah,' He says again and again—the perpetual iteration of this phrase in the Chapter* indicating the immense emphasis laid on this point—'and there is none else; there is no God beside me. I form the light, and create darkness; I make peace, and create evil: I, Jehovah, do all these things.' It is as if He had said: 'I am the good creative Spirit in whom you believe; but I have no such rival and antagonist as you suppose. Ahura-mazda *is;* but Ahriman is *not.* I claim to be the sole Lord and Ruler of the universe. All that *is* is mine. I am responsible for the darkness as well as for the light. Evil is my servant, my creature, no less than good.'

Soften it down as we will, it is a tremendous

---

* Isaiah xlv. 5, 6, 7, 14, 18, 21, 22.

claim, a claim which plunges our thoughts into impenetrable mysteries, and suggests problems we cannot solve. We may say, and say fairly, that every word of this poetic passage must not be pressed as if it were part of a legal statute or a mathematical demonstration; and that we are not bound to assume from it, therefore, that all the evil in the universe is caused, or created, by God. We may fairly say that, since these words were addressed to a Persian, their main purpose was achieved if they conveyed to him the thought that the universe was not governed by two rival Powers, but by one Supreme Person, ever in harmony with Himself, who tolerated and controlled the evil forces of the universe no less than the good, though He did not originate them. But, soften and modify it as we will, the claim is so tremendous, and involves mysteries so profound, that it cannot but astonish and perplex our labouring thoughts.

And yet, it must also be admitted, that it meets and satisfies the cravings both of intellect and heart as no easier, no dualistic, theory does or can do. The universe is so obviously one that the intellect demands unity, and will be satisfied with nothing short of one Sovereign Lord, one Supreme Governor of the Universe. And how can our hearts be at rest until we know and are sure that God rules over the kingdom of darkness as well as in the kingdom of light, that the evils which befall us are under his control no less than the blessings which enrich and gladden us; that wherever we wander, and through whatever sorrowful changes we pass, we are never for a single moment out of his hand? A God who could not follow us into the darkness in which so much of our life has to be spent, who could not sustain us under our losses, comfort us in our sorrows, and redeem us from our sins, and shew us a path of life through the obscurity of death, would be little better than no God to us: we could not worship Him for long, and still less could we love and trust Him with all our soul and strength. He would be absent from us just when we most wanted Him, impotent just when we were most in need of a helping hand.

To believe in a Good Being to whom we owe all that we love in life, and in an Evil Being to whom we might attribute all that we hate, would be a very simple and easy creed, no doubt, and would relieve our thoughts of many problems by which they are tasked and baffled: but have you yet to learn, my brethren, that obvious theories are rarely true, that easy theories seldom satisfy us long? Is a simple and easy theory of this vast complex universe likely to be a correct and adequate theory, likely to cover all its facts and solve all its problems? Would it even be well for us that we should be altogether relieved of the difficulties by which our minds are braced and stimulated as well as taxed and perplexed?

Assuredly nothing can be more monstrous and unreasonable than the way in which men often treat the great problem, the ultimate mystery, of the universe. In nothing are they at once more like, and more unlike, themselves. A man will give his whole life to the study of a single class of plants, or of a single family of insects, or of the geological formations of a single district, and deem his life well spent if, in these several narrow fields of inquiry, he can glean a few facts unreaped by his predecessors, or add a few items to the sum of human knowledge. And yet you shall find many a patient inquirer in other paths of science who will gravely tell you he cannot believe in Religion unless the whole of this immense and complex science be compressed into a tiny portable theory which he can master and verify in a few hours, if even he will give so much as a few hours to the study of the most profound and far-reaching problems that can engage his thoughts! I have had men say to me in a flippant tone, or a tone of triumph even, as if they knew beforehand that I should be hopelessly posed: 'But how are you going to *prove* God?' who would not give as much real laborious thought to that great question as they would cheerfully give to the examination and classification of a plant they had never seen before? I have heard men say: 'But how can you reconcile the goodness of God with the existence of evil?' as if that were a question of no more difficulty and importance than, What is the best formula for combining oxygen with carbon? And I have seen them reject the Christian Faith as an outworn fable simply on the ground of the insoluble mysteries it involves when they cannot take, and know that they cannot take, a single step on any path of inquiry without being confronted by the insoluble mysteries of Force, and Life, and Thought.

To treat the deepest and gravest problems open to us thus is simply puerile; there is an intellectual dishonesty in it of which, however, those who are guilty of it cannot be always or fully conscious. No man can hope to reach the solution of any difficult problem without earnest and protracted labour. No man has ever solved a difficult problem without finding that his very solution of it started questions still more difficult or ran up into problems which wit of man can never solve. If we are going to study religious questions at all, let us confess at the outset that of necessity these great questions must be encompassed by mysteries we cannot hope to penetrate; let us at once assume that these mysteries will never become credible to us except as the mysteries of

Energy, Life, Thought become credible to us, by patient and stedfast mental toil.

On these terms, though on no other, the mystery here announced by Isaiah—that darkness as well as light, evil as well as good, are under the control of God, and must therefore be consistent both with his power and his goodness—will, I believe, become credible to us. We shall not penetrate that mystery in all directions indeed, and much less shall we dissipate it. How can *we* hope to do that? we who are a mystery, and even a whole series of insoluble mysteries, to ourselves; we in whose complex nature all the mysteries of the universe, all the unsolved problems of matter and of mind, of energy and thought, are compendiously summed up. But we may so approach it as to believe, on perfectly reasonable grounds, that one supreme Lord reigns throughout the universe, and governs all the forces, whether evil or good, which give shape and purpose to our life. 'And this will we do, if God permit.'

I am the Lord, and there is none else. I form the light, and create darkness; I make peace, and create evil: I, the Lord, do all these things. That is to say: 'There is no Ahriman, no rival god, no anti-god. The universe is one, with one Creator and Ruler. I, Jehovah, hold myself responsible for all that *is*. Even evil is under my control, and was, in some sense, created or originated by me.' In short, God here assumes the entire responsibility of evil,—a responsibility which we should never have dared to cast on Him; a responsibility which, as we have seen, the human mind, here in England, as well as in ancient Persia, *shrinks* from casting on Him. Obviously the words open up the whole question of the existence, the permission, the origination of evil; and so, in a manner, compel us, in Foster's phrase, to knock our heads against the great black wall that runs all round the universe of thought. And in considering this question it will be well for us to determine, first of all, what, and how much, of the evil that exists we ourselves can honestly attribute directly and immediately to God our Maker.

(1.) For, obviously, much of the evil within and around us is of *our own* making. I as I look back on my life, and you as you look back on yours, can see clearly enough that a large proportion of the pain, loss, and moral defeat of which we have been conscious, and are still conscious, has sprung from our own follies and faults. We have made mistakes; we have neglected opportunities; we have wilfully taken wrong courses; we have broken laws which we acknowledge to be good laws, and which we could have kept if we had tried: and these follies and mistakes are responsible for much of our past suffering and for much from which we suffer to this day. After making all due allowance for hereditary bias, for unhappy and unfavourable conditions, for almost irresistible conspiracies of opportunity with inclination, we are conscious of many faults and sins which we might have avoided and ought to have avoided. Most of *us* probably would admit that we are responsible for *most* of the disasters which have weakened and crippled us, and feel that we cannot honestly attribute them to God. He forbad the sins into which we fell. His Spirit strove to hold us back from them. We *would* give in to them, as we now confess with penitent shame. We exonerate Him, candour compels us to exonerate Him, from all responsibility for the sufferings they have produced. We humbly confess that the responsibility, the guilt, of them rests with us.

(2.) But if much of the evil that has lowered and afflicted our lives has been of our own making, much has also been of *our neighbours'* making. We inherited, with much that was good, some evil bias from our fathers. We have often had to breathe an atmosphere charged with moral infections which sprang from the corrupt habits of the world around us. Our education was not good, or was not wholly good and wise. We have had to live and trade, to work and play, with men whose influence on us, if often beneficial, has also been often injurious. The laws, maxims, customs of the little world in which we have moved have done much to blunt and lower our moral tone, to encourage us in self-seeking or self-indulgence, to countenance us in yielding to our baser passions and desires. Servants have been unfaithful to us, or masters unjust. The men of business with whom we have dealt have wronged and robbed us, or set us on taking an unfair advantage of others. Those whom we have trusted have not justified our trust in them; those whom we loved have been untrue to us. And thus our moral ideal has been lowered, our character tarnished, our lot marred and made painful to us. As we look back and think of all that we have lost and suffered, it is probable that we attribute far more of the evils which have fallen on us to *men* than to God. Our distrust of them, our righteous indignation against those who have wronged us, proves that it is they whom we hold to be responsible, not their Maker and ours. If conscience be healthy and active within us, we no more charge *their* offences on Him than we charge Him with our own. We say: 'I should have done well enough, I should have had little of which to complain, had I and my fellows kept his law and yielded to the motions of his Spirit.'

Now here already is an immense deduction to be

made from the sum of evils which we can fairly attribute to God. Take away all the wrongs, pains, losses, temptations, sins, which might and would have been avoided had both we and our neighbours done our best to obey the law of Conscience even, and how much do we leave? Very much less than we commonly assume.

(3.) For much that *seems* evil to us is not really evil, or is not necessarily evil, or is not altogether evil. Cyrus and his Persians had such evils as noxious plants and animals, excessive heat and cold, famine, drought, earthquake, storms, disease, and sudden death in their minds mainly when they spoke of the works of Ahriman, the eternal and malignant antagonist of God. But, as we know, *these* apparent ills are not necessarily ills at all, or they are the products of causes which work for good on the whole, or they carry with them compensations so large that the world would be the poorer for their loss. To take but a few illustrations. The storms, that wreck a few ships and destroy a few lives, clear and revivify the air of a whole continent, and carry new health to the millions in populous cities pent. The constant struggle for existence among plants and animals is a necessary condition of the evolution of their higher and more perfect species. To variations of heat and cold, and even to excessive variations, we owe the immense variety of the climates and conditions under which we live; and to these variations of climate the immense variety and abundance of the harvests by which the world is fed. Famine, as we are beginning to learn in India, has at least this compensation for its horrors—that it is the only sufficient check to excessive increase, the only adequate means of saving a race from sinking to levels of existence too low and squalid to be maintained. Pain is often a warning of danger, disease a rebuke to habits which imperil health and a hint to amend them. The sudden and cruel end of birds and beasts that fall a prey to their fellows moves us to pity; but if the choice lie between that and the lingering agony of starvation, as it commonly does, of the two it is surely better to be stung or struck to death in an instant which is not so painful as it seems if we are to credit those who have been bitten by a cobra, or shaken in a lion's mouth, or struck down by the tiger's paw. *We* pray against 'sudden death' for ourselves and for our neighbours; but to the Hebrew poets to be smitten down from the top of happy prosperous days, in place of being condemned to the long slow agony of age with its manifold and growing infirmities, seemed a fate so enviable that they murmured and complained if it were accorded to the wicked, holding that it should be reserved exclusively for the righteous. Is labour a curse, or the necessity which spurs us to labour? The world holds both health and wealth by the sole tenure of labour; while necessity is not only 'the mother of invention' but of a whole brood of offspring as excellent as its firstborn. Is adversity an evil? It is to the struggle with adversity that we owe many of our highest virtues, much of our strength; and as the men we most reverence are those who dared all things and endured all things, and who could take Fortune's buffets and rewards with equal thanks, with what face can we complain if God should grant us an opportunity of shewing that we too belong to the same heroic strain? And as we are driven to toil by the sting of want, and trained to courage by the assaults of adversity, so also we are moved to thought by the perplexities of life, and to trust and patience by its sorrows and losses and cares.

In fine, much that we call evil is not necessarily evil, or is not wholly evil. Much of it is even designed and adapted to call our attention to the true order of human life, and to the benign end to which all things round. Just as 'we take no note of time but by its loss,' so we forget, or should forget, the calm and beauty of Nature but for its storms and failures, its partial and occasional refusals to minister to our wants. We should not observe that health is the rule, or feel how sweet and good it is, save for the sicknesses which at once deprive us of it and teach us its value. We should not notice that on the whole our life is tranquil and happy if at times we were not summoned to confront pain and strife. We should not know the worth of love, or how much love is lavished on us, but for partings,—if we never lost, or feared to lose, the friends who love us. We should not realize how much of good there is in our lives if the current of our days were never vexed by ill winds.

Those who are too conscious of the evils that men suffer, or are driven towards pessimism by dwelling too much and too heavily upon them, could hardly do better than rouse themselves to look on human life as a whole. We have only to extend our view till it embraces the whole universe and all the generations of time in order to recognize and be impressed by the fact, that much which we call evil is not really, or is not necessarily, evil, only evil, and that continually. God sits in heaven, all worlds circling around his feet, all the generations of men rising and falling beneath his glance. And how shall there be a harmony meet for his ear unless there be discords in it? how a spectacle meet for his eye unless there be shadows in it? Nay, what should we ourselves care for our life if it were as a mere succession of sweet sounds, without any of the severer chords or dissonances apart from which the noblest harmony is impossible, or if it were as a picture untoned and unrelieved by any tender depths of shadow? When *we* stand in the shadow, or form part of the discord, we may find that life has suddenly grown hard and difficult to us; but the universe is wide, eternity long, God infinite. In his ear our discord may be blended with tones taken from past generations or distant worlds, and may run into a harmonious sequence which as yet we cannot catch. In his eye our shadow may lend new depth and meaning and pathos to a picture too vast for us to grasp as yet. But if one day we should sit down with Him in heavenly places, we too, as we gaze on the large perfect scene and listen to the mighty and complete harmony, may confess that He hath done all things well.

I am very far from denying that much which is really and painfully and frightfully evil enters into our life,—much even for which we ourselves are not altogether responsible. And, next Sunday, I will try to shew you in what sense God claims to be responsible for such evils as these, in what sense we may reverently attribute all evil to Him. But for the present let us be content to see that much which we think evil is not necessarily or wholly evil, but subserves the finest and noblest ends of discipline, raising the life it appears to lower, enriching the life it seems to impoverish. Let us humbly confess that the evils from which we ourselves suffer, in so far as they spring from violations of Divine Law, are of our own making, or of our neighbours' making, not of God's; that it is *we* who are responsible for them, although He here generously takes the whole responsibility of them on Himself, and bids us leave them with Him.

II.

THE ORIGIN OF EVIL.

SECOND PART.

'I am the Lord, and there is none else. I form the light and create darkness; I make peace, and create evil: I, the Lord, do all these things.'—ISAIAH xlv. 6, 7.

HERE, in so many words, the good God claims evil as his creature and work, and the Father of Lights proclaims Himself the Fountain of Darkness. How shall we explain and defend this singular claim? Easily enough—up to a certain point. For Jehovah is addressing Himself to Cyrus the Persian. And the Persians, while they believed in one only God, the Creator of all that is good, also believed in an antigod, the Author of all that is evil. 'I have no such rival as you imagine,' says Jehovah to Cyrus. 'I am the sole Lord of the universe. All that *is* is mine. I am God, and besides me there is none else.' The words do not necessarily mean more than this, therefore;—that the Persian theory of the universe, the dualistic hypothesis of two dominant Powers working independently and antagonistically, was an erroneous theory; that there is but one Supreme Power ruling over all. In their first intention, they are simply an assertion, conveyed in poetic forms which must not be too closely pressed, of the universal rule of the God of Israel.

But though, considering the general intention of the passage, we should not care to press such phrases as 'I *create* darkness,' 'I *create* evil,' yet does not this very intention itself raise the whole question of the origin and function of evil quite as effectually as this phrase or that?

'All God meant by the words was to disclaim and reject the dualistic theory of the universe held by the Persians, and to assert his sovereign sway, his sole supremacy, over all that is.'

Granted. But, then, *evil is*. And if we are forbidden to trace the existence of evil to any rival or subordinate Power, have we any alternative save to trace it to God Himself? Assuredly this is our only alternative: and so the very mystery which, by the help of Cyrus and his Persians, we have thrust out at the back door of this passage comes back upon us through the front window, and we have to face it at last as best we can.

And this mystery is a living, a present, mystery. It tasks and perplexes the thoughts of men *now* as much as ever, perhaps more than ever. Under its pressure John Stuart Mill and his school have even reverted to the old Persian theory, the dualistic hypothesis of the universe. They doubt whether there is a God, indeed, though they advise us to lean to that conclusion as hard as we can; but they are quite sure that, if there is a God, a God who rules over this sorrowful and afflicted world, He must be limited either on the side of his goodness or on the side of his power. And as a God not perfectly good would be much the same as no God, they incline to the alternative that his power is limited by the activity of some rival being or force,—a something not ourselves, and not Himself, which makes for *un*righteousness.

To meet our own wants, therefore, or the wants of our own time, we are obliged to consider what may be involved in the claim which the Prophet here puts into the mouth of Jehovah, the claim to be the sole Creative Power in the universe, the claim to be responsible for all that exists, and therefore for all the evil that exists.

It is quite true that in considering this question we approach a problem which the wise of all ages have pronounced insoluble; and hence it becomes us to move with diffidence, and to bear in mind that the most we can hope to attain is a working hypothesis which will commend itself to our reason, not a final solution of the mystery. That spirit is not an altogether unhealthy one which prompts us to say: 'We know so little of man and so much less of God, so little of time and so much less of eternity, that we can never hope to penetrate a mystery so great.' But you will observe that, after all, the question with *us* is not of what we can discover, but of what God has revealed, of how we are to explain and vindicate a claim which He Himself asserts. And surely it is but a poor tale if, with a Divine Revelation in our hand, we are not prepared to shew that the dualistic hypothesis of Mill and the Persians is inadequate and irrational, and to replace it with an hypothesis more consonant at once with Reason and with Holy Writ. Who is to 'find words for God,' and for the claims of God, if we cannot?

There *is* an hypothesis, my brethren, a theory of the origin, and function, and end of Evil suggested by Scripture which seems to me an eminently reasonable one; a theory which confirms the claim of God to be the Creator and Lord of evil, and disposes of that dualistic hypothesis which recognizes two rival and opposed Powers at work in the world around us and in the mind of man. And this hypothesis, if you will not grudge a little close attention, I will proceed to lay before you as clearly and as briefly as I can.

When we contemplate the universe of which we form part, the first impression made on us is of its immense variety; but, as we continue to study it, the final and deepest impression it makes upon us is that, under this immense and beautiful variety, there lies an all-pervading unity. As it is with us, so it has been with the race at large. At first men were so profoundly impressed by the variety of the universe that they split it up into endless provinces, assigned to each its ruling spirit, and worshipped gods of heaven and of earth, gods of mountains and plains, of sea and land, of air and water, of rivers and springs, of fields and woods, trees and flowers, of hearth and home, of the individual, the clan, the nation, the empire. Yet even then there hung in the dark background of their thoughts some conviction of the underlying unity of the universe, as was proved by their conception of an inscrutable Destiny or Fate, to which gods and men were alike subject, and by which all the ages of time were controlled. This conviction grew and deepened as the world went spinning down the grooves of change, until now Science herself admits that, by a thousand different paths of investigation and thought, it is led to the conclusion that, if there be a God at all, there can be but one God; that, if the universe had a Maker, it could have had but one Maker: that if human life is under rule, there can be but one Ruler over all. The same forces are at work everywhere; the same laws run and hold everywhere; all things on earth and all in heaven are bound together so intimately and in so many ways that it is no longer possible to believe in gods many and lords many. There may be one God,—*that*, to Science, is still an open question; but there cannot be more than one,—*that* question is closed, and Science herself stands to guard the way to it as with a sword in her hand.

But if there be only one supreme Lord, there cannot of course be any rival Power to his, any power that introduces alien forces or works by other laws. There may be subordinate powers; and at times these may seem to oppose Him, to contend against Him. But one Power, or Will, is supreme; for, as the very word itself suggests, the *universe* is an *unity*, —a vast complex of many forces perhaps and many laws, but still a single and organized whole. In reverting to the Persian hypothesis of two antagonistic Powers, therefore, Mill sinned against the most settled conclusion of modern thought. And it is both curious and inexplicable that while Science is so convinced of the unity of the universe that it is seeking to resolve all forms of matter, animate and inanimate, into one protoplasmic substance, all forces into one force unnamed as yet, and to reduce all the processes of creation and growth under the law of evolution, this great champion of Science should have fallen back on an hypothesis which runs right in its teeth.

Now if we either believe in one Supreme Creator and Lord, or, following Mill's advice, lean to that conclusion as hard as we can, our next step is to conceive, as best we may, what this first great Cause, this creative and ruling Power, is like. Accordingly, we look around us to find that which is highest in the universe, sure that in that which is highest we shall find that which most resembles the Most High. And in the whole visible creation we find nothing so high as man, no force of so divine a quality and temper as the will of man, when once that will is guided by wisdom and impelled by love. Even the material and vital forces of Nature flower in man; while to these are added the still higher forces of thought, affection, will. As Pascal put it: 'The possession of the whole earth would not add to my greatness. As to space, the universe encloses and absorbs me as a mere point; but by thought I embrace the whole universe.' And, again: 'Were the whole universe to rise against him (to slay him), man is yet greater than the universe, since man *knows* that he dies. The universe knows nothing of its power.' Nor is it only by force of thought that man rises to the top of creation and puts all things under his feet, but also by force of will. To him alone of all visible creatures is the strange power accorded of consciously and intentionally arresting or modifying the action of the great physical forces, of conquering Nature by obeying her, of changing her course by a skilful application of her own laws.

So that even though the Bible did not assure us that man was made in the image of God, Reason would compel us to conclude that, since the Creator of all things must include in Himself all the forces displayed in the work of his hands, and since we must see most of Him in the highest of his works, we must see most of Him in man, and in that which is highest in man,—viz., Thought, Will, Affection. Reason *has* reached this conclusion in that ancient oracle: '*Would you know God? Look within.*'

We have got our God, then; in some sense we may even be said to have *proved* God, since, so far, we have been following the guidance of Reason rather than of Inspiration : and, in God, we have the creative and supreme Spirit, Maker of all things, the Fountain of all force, the Administrator of all laws, of whom we frame our highest conception when we think of Him as the Source of all that is noblest in man,—as the Infinite Mind, the pure Eternal Will, the absolute Love.

And, now, we are prepared to take our next step,

and ask: How evil came to be? and how, if God is responsible for it, we can reconcile it both with his perfect goodness and his perfect power. We take this step, then, and inquire, (1) How did evil arise? and (2) How may it be justified?

(1.) For *the origin* of Evil we must go back to the creation of all things, and be content to use words which, though quite inadequate to the subject, may nevertheless convey true impressions of it.

If the conception of God we have just framed be a true one, and it seems to answer to the demands of Reason, then there must have been a time when the Great Creative Spirit dwelt alone. And in that Divine solitude—that infinite light which may seem to us an unbounded darkness, that infinite fulness which may seem to us an unrelieved emptiness—the question arose whether a creation, an universe, should be called into being, and of what kind it should be. Or, perhaps, we may rather say, that, just as the intelligent and creative spirit of man *must* work and act, must disclose itself in deeds, so the creative Spirit of God urged *Him* to commence 'the works of his hands.' However we may conceive it or phrase it, let us suppose the physical universe determined upon as the stage on which active intelligences were to play their part; and then ask yourselves what is implied in the very nature of active intelligent creatures such as we are, and whether anything less than such creatures could satisfy the Maker and Lord of all.

Would you have God surround Himself with a merely inanimate world, or tenant that world with mere automata, mere puppets, with no will of their own, capable indeed of reflecting his own glory back on Him, but incapable of a voluntary affection, a spontaneous and enforced obedience? Would it have been worthy of Him, even such as you can conceive Him to be, would it have given scope and verge to his energies and affections to make mere *marionettes*, even though he gave them wings and called them angels? Why, even you yourselves cannot gain full scope for your powers until you are surrounded, or surround yourselves, with beings capable of loving you freely, and obeying you with a cheerful and unforced accord, beings whose wills are their own and who yet make them yours? How much less, then, can you imagine that God should be content with a purely mechanical obedience, with a purely physical and necessary accord with the determinations of his will, with anything short of a voluntary obedience and affection? According to the best conception of Him we can frame, it was inevitable that He should surround Himself with life, thought, affection, with beings resembling Himself and capable of freely becoming one with Him in mind and heart and will.

But if you admit so much as this, consider, next, what is implied in the very nature of creatures such as these. If free to think truly, must they not be free to think untruly? if free to love, must they not be free not to love? if free to obey, must they not be free to disobey? You cannot get a voluntary affection and obedience from creatures incapable of withholding obedience and love. If my heart is not my own, I cannot give it to you. If my will is not mine, I cannot make it yours. And what is all that but to say, *that the very creation of beings in themselves good involves the tremendous risk of their becoming evil?* What is it but to say that in such an universe as we know, culminating in myriads of beings capable of ascertaining and obeying the righteous and kindly will of God, there must be a constant danger of some of them falling away from their true blessedness, by violations of the law which they are free to disobey, in order that they may be free to obey it?

Nay, if we consider the matter a little more closely we shall find, I think, that there was more to be confronted than the mere *risk* of the introduction of evil. To me it seems a dead *certainty*, a certainty which must have been foreseen and provided for in the eternal counsels of the Almighty, that in the lapse of ages, with a vast hierarchy of creatures possessed of freewill, some among them would assert and prove their freedom by disobedience. How else could man, for instance, assure himself that he *was* free, that his will was in very deed his own? He found himself in a vast natural world or order in which all creatures but himself rendered a necessary and involuntary obedience to their Maker and Lord. He was himself part of Nature. He was taken from the dust and had affinities with the dust; the animal life breathed in his nostrils and pervaded his frame. Was he no more than rocks and streams, plants and trees, birds and beasts? What meant, then, these motions of a higher and less restricted life of which he was conscious, this sense of freedom to do or to forbear from doing? Was he, after all, bound in the same chain of necessity as the creatures around and beneath him; or, if he dared, could he snap that chain, and be as free, though not so strong, as God Himself?

When once that question arose in the mind of man, as sooner or later it was sure to arise, how long do you think it would be before he risked an experiment, before he put his freedom to the touch, before he ventured to try whether disobedience was as possible to him as obedience? The poet Cowper says: 'I could sit at ease and quiet in my chamber all day long; but the moment I knew the door was locked upon me, I should try to get out at all risks.'

And is not that a feeling which awakens an immediate response in all our breasts? Is not the craving for liberty, for freedom of action and movement, common to man? Should we not any one of us try to get out of any chamber, however large and however exquisitely furnished for our pleasure and convenience, in which we felt that we were shut in, even though we knew we should gain no advantage and might even suffer by the change?

Are we not impatient of any *law* even by which we are bound, or suspect that we are bound, however good the law may be in itself? 'I was alive without the law once,' says St. Paul; 'but when the law came sin sprang into life, and I died;' yet, as he confesses, 'the law was holy, and just, and good.' And, again: 'I had not known concupiscence if the law had not said, "Thou shalt not covet."' Look at your little child. Consider how no sooner is a thing forbidden him than he hankers after it, and tries to get it or to do it. Why? Simply because he is of a depraved nature? Not at all. But simply because human nature, creature nature, is strong in him; because he is impatient of restraint; because he wants to prove and assert his freedom; because he has an intellectual curiosity to see what will come of *not* doing as he is bid.

Free creatures, again, creatures with intelligence, will, passion, are *active* creatures: and there is something, as all observers are agreed, in the very nature of activity which blunts and weakens our sense of inferiority, dependence, accountability. 'A messenger employed in his master's service becomes, in the very act of serving him, forgetful of him,' apt to exceed his commission, to assert and glorify himself by acting on his own motion, following his own impulse, assuming a power and an authority beyond his own.

Considering all this we cannot but conclude that the very creation of beings free to love and to obey their Maker involved, not the risk merely, but the certainty that sooner or later some of these beings would fall from their first estate; and that God must have foreseen and prepared for this certainty. Weakening their sense of dependence by their incessant activity, impatient of restraint, even of the wholesome restraints of a just and good law, who can wonder if they determined to prove that their powers *were* theirs by using them, to assure themselves of their freedom by transgressing their proper limits, to prove that their wills were their own by acts of selfwill?

The Bible affirms that what Reason might have anticipated actually took place. It tells us that both in heaven and on earth the creatures God had made *did* thus fall away from Him, doing their own will instead of his, taking their own course instead of the course marked out and hedged in for them by his pure and kindly laws. It asserts that, free to obey, they chose to disobey. And it moreover asserts, in full accordance with the teachings of Philosophy and Science, that, by their disobedience to the laws of their being and happiness, they jarred themselves into a false and sinister relation to the material universe; that, by introducing moral evil into the creation, they exposed themselves to those physical ills from which we suffer to this day.

On this point, the deduction of physical evils—such as pain, loss, decay—from moral offences, I cannot now dwell, and indeed need not dwell. For surely it must be obvious to every reflective mind that if the whole physical universe was created by the Word of God, if it is animated by his Spirit and ruled by his Will, then as many as disobey that high Will must put themselves out of harmony with all that obey it, must find the very forces which once worked for them turned against them. They are at war with the Will which pervades and controls the universe: how, then, can the universe be at peace with them? They have opposed themselves to the Creative Spirit which quickens and rules the whole realm of Nature; and hence, though no change should pass on heaven or earth, *they* are so changed that, for them, the fertile earth is cursed with barrenness, and the very stars in their courses fight against them. Any creature who quarrels with his whole environment turns that which was meant to feed and gratify and develop him into a mere apparatus of pain, hostility, and death: how much more, then, the creatures who quarrel with the quickening and shaping Spirit of their environment!

If, then, we now repeat the question with which we started: In what sense may we reverently attribute evil to God? in what sense can we concede his claim to be responsible for evil as well as for good, for darkness no less than for light? our reply must be that, in creating beings capable of loving and serving Him of their own choice, He created the possibility of evil, ran the risk of its existence, and even knew beforehand that it would certainly enter in and mar the work of his hands.

(2.) How, then, we ask finally, can we *justify* evil? how can we reconcile it at once with his perfect goodness and unbounded power?

On our hypothesis we reconcile it with his *power* by the plain and obvious argument that even Omnipotence cannot at once create freewill and not create it; that, when once He has created it, even the Almighty cannot interfere with it, cannot coerce and arrest it, without destroying it? If God made me free to choose evil, how can He possibly *compel* me to be good except by taking away my freedom of choice and action; *i.e.* by reducing me from a man to an automaton, a mere puppet of which He pulls the wires?

But if we would reconcile the existence of evil with the *goodness* of God—and this is by far the more difficult achievement—we must take the *whole* theory of human life and destiny taught by the Bible, and not merely a part of it. This theory let me put before you in the very briefest form, not staying to vindicate it—I am much mistaken if it will not vindicate itself—but only indicating it that you may see how it bears on our present argument.

As I read it, then, the Bible teaches what human reason had conjectured and hoped apart from the Bible,—that the lines of human life and destiny are to be produced beyond the grave, and wrought out to their final result in other worlds than this. It teaches us that while, in large measure, men do receive the due reward of their deeds here and now, yet, since justice is but imperfectly administered here, a more exact retribution will be meted out to us in the world into which we pass at death,—a more abundant reward for all that has been good in us, a more searching and cleansing punishment of what is evil. It teaches us that, as the result of this exacter retribution, this keener and more stimulating discipline, the good will be strengthened, settled, stablished, in righteousness, while the bad will be purged from their old sins by pangs that will turn them from darkness to light, from evil to good.

Now if all this be true—and as yet I do not ask you to affirm that it is true, I say only *if* it be true—is it any longer difficult for us to reconcile the permission of evil, or even the *creation* of it, if we must use that word, with the perfect goodness of the Creator? As we have seen, He could only surround Himself with beings capable of a voluntary, *i.e.* a real, goodness by leaving them free to choose evil if they would. And if, when those whom He had formed for obedience sinned against the law of their own being and well-being, He had left them to bear the doom which they themselves had pronounced on themselves, we could hardly have impeached his justice with any show of reason. But if it be true that even we who have abused our free will to our own hurt are—not to have our wills forced and coerced, but—to be taught by experience the evil of self-will, and the blessedness of living for others rather than for ourselves; if we are to be taught, whether in this or in other worlds, that then only are we free when we obey, and then alone strong when our wills are one with the best and purest Will; if evil has come in only that by tasting the loss and pain it involves we may rise to larger and more permanent forms of righteousness, and be established in them for ever beyond all danger of falling, who then can reasonably impeach the goodness which is leading us up, by stairs that 'slope through darkness,' to the light of an unclouded and everlasting day?

As I believe, all this *is* true, though even yet the half has not been told. For the Bible goes on to teach us that, in his pity and in his compassion, the great Father of our spirits came down to us his sinful children, virtually saying to us: 'I might much more reasonably attribute the evils from which you suffer to *you* than you to Me; for you owe them to your disobedience and self-will. But, see, I freely take them all on Myself. *I* claim to be responsible for them all. And since you cannot drive it away, *I* take away the sin of the world by a Sacrifice so great and so far-reaching, by an Atonement so potent, so cleansing, so divine, that you can but apprehend it afar off, and must not hope to fathom its full virtue and force and extent. To brace you for your daily strife with evil, I foretell a final and complete victory over it; I promise you that in the end I will sweep the evil that harasses and afflicts you clean out of the universe it has marred and defiled. And, meantime, it shall have no power to hurt or harm you if you will but put your trust in Me. All that is painful in it, all the sting of it, I take on Myself. For you, if you will but meet it wisely and trustfully, it shall be nothing but a helpful discipline, a training in vigour, in holiness, in charity.'

This, in brief, is the teaching of the Bible on the origin, function, and end of evil: this, at least, is the teaching which I have found in it after devoting nearly forty years to the study of the Bible. And it is with no misgiving, it is with the strongest conviction that you cannot but grant all which I demand, that I put it to you: Whether you believe in the teaching of the Bible or do not, is not this at least a reasonable theory of the origin and end of evil? Does it not commend itself to your judgment as far more consonant even with the teachings of modern thought and science than the dualistic theory of Mill and the Persians? Does it not commend itself to your hearts as affording you the very courage you need as you wage your own daily conflict with evil, and the very consolation you need as you groan under the burdens it inflicts on your fellow men? At the very lowest, do you know, can you conceive, of any 'working hypothesis' of this great mystery more reasonable, more probable, more welcome, if only it be true?

Assuredly those of you who accept it and rest in it will no longer find any great difficulty in the impressive pathetic words: 'I am the Lord, and there is none else: I form the light and create darkness; I make peace and create evil: I, the Lord, do all these things.'

NOTE.—If ever 'Evolution' should be proved to be not merely one of the laws which govern and control both the physical universe and the story of man, but the ruling and supreme law, it would only necessitate a slight modification of the theory suggested in this Discourse. For, in that case, instead of affirming that man fell from his original goodness, so giving evil an early triumph over him and it, we should have to affirm that from the very first evil is subordinated to good, 'and sin itself is but *the dark shadow cast by human free will as it emerges from animal instinct;* a fall indeed in appearance, but in reality an ascent from the innocence of ignorance to the righteousness that is bred by repentance and faith.' But despite the confident temper of its advocates, I doubt whether Evolution will succeed in making good this claim to supreme power, at least in the genesis and development of man. For, not to insist on the difficulties which still encompass the evolution of mind, spirit, conscience, I do not see how this hypothesis is ever to explain the great social and religious revolution wrought by the Christian Faith.

III.

THE HEAVENLY TREASURE AND THE EARTHEN VESSELS.

'But we have this treasure in earthen vessels.'—2 COR. iv. 7.

IF I were to begin my Sermon by saying: 'No, Paul, the vessels are pure heavenly as well as the treasure, and in calling them "earthly" you are bringing in a "damnable heresy,"' you would all be very much and very justly shocked. Have no fear: it is quite impossible for me to say anything so profane, except hypothetically, and in order to suggest to you the folly and presumption of certain self-elected champions of Religion who denounce 'modern criticism' and 'modern speculation,'—meaning thereby any speculation or criticism which does not jump with their own. 'All light is from God,' affirms St. Paul; 'and, above all, that revelation of Himself, which shines from the face of Jesus Christ. But we who seek to convey and interpret that light, we who are but the organs and media of Revelation, *we* are human, not divine, earthly and not heavenly.' This is the teaching of an inspired Apostle, although, according to certain modern authorities, it is 'flat blasphemy' on your lips or mine. 'The truth itself,' affirms St. Paul, 'the divine substance of the Revelation, is like gold and silver; but the men and the words that convey it are like the great earthenware jars in which ancient princes stored up their gold and silver coin.' Or, in the Rabbinical variation of the figure, the truth of God is like precious wine; while the men and the words that hold and convey it are like the earthen jars in which of old time wine was kept. But *we* cannot so much as hint that the jars are of a different and inferior quality to the wine or the coin without being denounced by men who affect to love the Bible more than we do, and to defer to its teaching more humbly. According to them, let St. Paul say what he will, the vessels are not earthly but heavenly. And not only the *original* vessels; but when the heavenly wine has been decanted from the Hebrew and Greek into English vessels, even these English vessels are pure heavenly too! Nay, still more strangely, even when the heavenly treasure has been poured out from the original and the secondary jars, when it has been melted in the dogmatic crucible, and recast into words and formulæ not to be found in the Bible, even these *doctrinal* vessels are as sacred and divine as the Scriptural, and you can only detect any flaw in them at your own proper peril!

Now to handle the Bible in this mechanical and slavish spirit, to reduce all its writers to a common level, to assert that they are all, and all equally, infallible, is not to honour the Bible, but to dishonour it; it is not to defer to its own account of itself, but to decline to defer to it: it is not to prepare the way for its acceptance, but to ensure its rejection. For, beyond all reasonable doubt, there are physical theories in the Bible—in the Book of Job, for instance—which are not scientifically accurate; there are historical statements which, to say the least of it, lie open to grave question,—as when Moses is contradicted by St. Stephen: there are moral precepts even which, though greatly in advance of the ethics of their time, are nevertheless not perfect, since, as our Lord Himself affirms, they were concessions to the hardness of their hearts who received them, or were to be superseded by the more spiritual and penetrating morality of his own commandments: and there are disclosures of spiritual realities which are not final and complete, since even the Great Teacher had many things to say which the men to whom He spoke were not able to hear. Had one taken these errors and defects to St. Paul, no doubt he would have replied: 'We have this heavenly treasure in earthen vessels, and of nothing earthly must you expect perfection.' But if we take them to those who hold the vessels to be as heavenly as the treasure itself, what can they do but flatly deny that any such defects exist, and go on denying it whatever the evidence we adduce, and at last try to stop our mouths with the anathemas of their usurped authority? Their first false step, the assumption of the infallibility of the mere 'letter' of Scripture, compels them to take other false steps in the same direction, until they are landed in the frightful inconsistency of contradicting the very Scriptures for whose authority they contend.

How, then, may we avoid their sin and yet hold fast to the Bible as the truest and highest revelation of the will of God yet made to man? How may we at once reasonably account for the earthliness of the vessels which contain this Divine Treasure, and yet maintain that the Treasure itself is nevertheless divine? The old simple explanation is, I verily believe, as true as it is old. If God was to speak *through* men, He must take men as He found them. If He was to speak *to* men, He must speak a language they could understand. It was impossible to anticipate the effects of centuries of culture, except by a miracle which would have been useless, and even injurious. For had God miraculously moved the ancient Hebrew prophets to speak in the terms of modern science and philosophy, neither would they themselves have understood the words they were moved to utter, nor would the people to whom they were sent have understood them. And, moreover, had they been thus raised above themselves, that gradual training and growth in which lies the true hope of humanity would have been violently and fatally interrupted. To lift men suddenly to the high platform of accurate and complete scientific and moral conceptions would have been a miracle indeed. It would have been the creation of a new race rather than the education and development of the men who were then on the earth. And Science herself would have been the first to revolt from so sudden and fatal a break in the continuity of history, in the slow and therefore permanent process by which man is being raised to his ideal nature and conditions.

But even if we should grant such a miracle to be possible without a fatal strain to human powers; if we admit that holy men of old might have been moved to speak in the terms of modern thought; if we admit, still farther, that these modern terms are both accurate and adequate expressions of the facts of Nature and History—a very large assumption although it is so commonly made; if we admit that it would have been just and wise of God to write or inspire a book two or three thousand years before any man could read it, and to leave the world for all those years without the book it wanted: if we grant all this, have you ever considered what the Bible, formed on this model, would have been like? You know very well how many treatises are now required to set forth the ascertained results of any one province of human inquiry, and can faintly imagine how many would be necessary in order to cover the whole field of Science. Even now they are so many that no man attempts to read them all, or hopes to cover more than a modest corner of that wide field. Could these results, then, have been set forth adequately, and yet with brevity, from two to four thousand years ago? If not, to what must the Bible have grown? Who would have been able to read and to master it? Must not the moral and spiritual elements in it have been swamped in that immense mass of learning? In St. John's famous hyperbole, the whole world could not have contained the book that would have been written; or, at least, and without hyperbole, we may say that the whole world would not have contained a man to read it.

Do you object: 'But no one demands that the Bible should cover all knowledge and exhaust all discovery. It would have been enough if, when it touched on points of Science and History, it had employed terms *consistent* with the facts afterwards discovered. It need have been no bigger than it is, and yet more accurate.'

Are you advised of that? There are not many demonstrable errors in the Bible as it is when due allowance is made, as of course it ought to be made, for the Oriental and poetical forms in which so much of it is cast. But if, whenever it touched on points of Science, it had used terms which we should call accurate and complete to-day, surely it follows that it must either have explained these terms to a generation to which they were unknown, or have run the risk of being rejected for its divergence from the accepted conclusions of the time. Only one alternative was open: either the vessels must be earthen, with the natural flaws and defects of earth about them, in order that the heavenly treasure might not be refused; or the vessels must be as heavenly as the treasure, with this inevitable result, that the earthly eyes then bent on them would have seen no truth or beauty in them that they should desire them, and so would have rejected the treasure they contained.

So much you may admit, yet still be perplexed. You may say: 'I see well enough that, if God was to speak to men through men, it was inevitable that He should take them as He found them, and speak to them in the only language they could understand.

The vessels must be earthen if the heavenly treasure was to be effectually conveyed. But was not this necessity a very perilous one? Was there not, and especially *is* there not, grave danger lest the heavenly treasure should be refused because of the earthliness of the vessels which convey it? However precious, and even invaluable, the interior contents of a Revelation may be, if there be error and defect in its outward form, may not those who discover these errors and defects be honestly persuaded that the Revelation did not come from God? I see that for the sake of past generations, and perhaps for the sake of the great mass of men in all generations, the vessels must be of earth; but may not the very earthenness of the vessels present a difficulty to the men of this generation, or perhaps to the cultivated few of every generation? In fine, if I admit the Revelation contained in the Bible to be a perfect revelation, yet is there not grave peril lest even a perfect revelation should be rejected because of the imperfect media through which it reaches us?'

This, it must be confessed, is a serious difficulty, and a very prevalent difficulty. Thousands of the younger and more reflective members of every branch of the Church feel it keenly; and I myself have known men—and men whom I think Jesus Himself would have loved, and did love, and does love—who, because they were convinced that the physical theories of the book of Genesis were unscientific, or because they had detected errors in some of the historical books of Scripture, or because Criticism had rendered the date and authorship of some of the Sacred Writings dubious to them, or because they had found a defective morality taught or approved in some of the earlier books of the Bible, have felt that they could no longer accept it as the Word of God, and refused to believe in any written revelation of his Will. The difficulty which drives such men from the pale, with tears of sorrow and despair, must be a very grave one; it needs to be met fearlessly and kindly: and I would fain treat it as honestly and tenderly as I can.

To those who are troubled by it, or, untroubled themselves, have to deal with those who are repelled by it, I would suggest, first of all, that though earth is not so glorious as heaven, it nevertheless has a glory of its own, a beauty that lies nearer to us and touches us more pathetically than the greater glory above. And these earthen vessels of Scripture—these histories, psalms, prophecies, gospels, parables, letters: *are* they not very beautiful even though, in the eyes of the critical, they be not altogether perfect? Can you match them anywhere? Do you know any forms of literature more noble, more pure, more penetrating? or any book that can for a moment be set beside *the Book?* After having read most of the great religious books of the race, I am compelled to confess that for me, both in substance and in style, the Bible stands above all its rivals as high as the heavens above the earth. If it were more beautiful than it is, if it were of a heavenly beauty and perfection, might it not be too beautiful for our earthly appreciations,

> 'a thing too bright and good
> For human nature's daily food?'

If any one of you were the happy possessor of the most perfect vase in the world—I will say nothing just now of what might be *inside* it—would you be greatly concerned, so concerned as to break your vase or fling it away, if. the most delicate and refined Criticism convinced you that one or two out of the multitude of graceful figures carved upon it did not stand in quite the most noble pose imaginable, or that some sandal-string or brooch was not in the best historical keeping, or that in the legend inscribed beneath the beautiful procession this letter or that was not quite accurately cut, or had been tampered with by some later artist, or was a little defaced by time and use? When men speak of the defects of the Bible they are apt both to magnify them and to forget for the instant its innumerable, its unrivalled, excellences and beauties. I do not deny these defects, although many years' study of the Bible has convinced me that they are comparatively few; that when they are at all serious, the defects and errors of its earlier books are almost invariably corrected by its later books, and quite invariably corrected by its animating and ruling spirit: and that for the most part critics would never have discovered them but for the light they had drawn from the Bible itself. I do not deny, I frankly admit, all proved errors and defects. But I remember, and I ask you to remember, that even that in the Bible which may fairly be compared to earthen vessels is nevertheless of a peerless and incomparable beauty.

Suffer me still further to suggest that, practically, there is but little danger lest men should be really and finally repelled from the Divine Treasure by any earthliness or defect in its outward form. So long as they are ignorant and of a childlike heart, the very vessels are as heavenly to them as their contents. They see no flaw in them; they are troubled by no questions, no doubts. And when men grow wise enough and critical enough to detect an occasional error or defect in the media of Revelation, ought they not to be wise enough and sufficiently good critics to distinguish between the Treasure and the Vessels that contain it? Yes, and wise enough even to love the Vessels all the more because, like themselves, they are of the earth and have a touch of earthliness about them? If *you* are wise enough to detect some imperfections in the 'letter' of Holy Writ, ought you not to be wise enough also to discern the beauty and worth of the principles which underlie the letter of it, to admire the perfect and divine 'spirit' which breathes through every page?

'Ah, there,' you may say, '*there* you touch the very heart of the matter, and raise what to us is the most momentous and difficult question of all. If we must admit, as we can hardly help admitting, that much or little, but still something, in the outward form of the Biblical Revelation has become questionable, how can we possibly retain our old unquestioning faith in it? *How* are we to distinguish between the Treasure which is from heaven and the Vessels which are of earth, and to hold fast to that Treasure even if we should be compelled to yield the Vessels to the tender mercies of Criticism, which are so cruel?'

Well, that is the very question which I too hold to be most pressing and important, and to which indeed I have been leading up in all that I have yet said. And with a few brief hints on this momentous question I will conclude. Only be good enough to bear in mind that I am not now speaking to those who reject the very idea of Revelation; but to those of you who believe or hope that in the Bible we have a clear and sufficient revelation of the Will of God, but do not see how you are to distinguish between its substance and its form.

As I believe, then, the final appeal lies to that moral sense which in a thousand different ways you use and cultivate every day. Mark *how* you use it. Your little child, let me suppose, runs in from the nursery or runs home from school one day, to tell you that he has been sorely tempted to tell a lie, but adds triumphantly, 'I didn't tell it, Papa, because I knew that if I did God would blister my tongue!' What is your first feeling as you listen to his tale? Joy, that he did not tell the lie, or grief and vexation at the silly superstition which held him back from it? Surely your first emotion is one of gratitude and pleasure that he did not tell the lie, that he felt God would be angry with him if he did tell it. But, lest he should presently discover that lies do not always or commonly raise blisters on the tongue, and infer that there was therefore no harm in telling them; and, still more, because you want him to act on just motives, and to be free from silly superstitions, you proceed to teach him that the lie-and-blister theory is but a superstition of the nursery, and to give him better and higher motives for speaking the truth. That is to say, you see that the little fellow holds a heavenly treasure in an earthen vessel, a *very* earthen vessel; and in this case you have no difficulty in distinguishing the one from the other.

Take another case, then. Your boy grows up into a lad. You have to send him out into the world. With many fears and many prayers you place him in an office or warehouse, in which he has to associate with men who are older, harder, less pure-minded, than himself. You know only too well the kind of talk he will hear, the temptations to which he will be exposed, and in how many forms an evil influence will be brought to bear upon him. You therefore encourage him to make a friend of you, to talk to you quite freely of his work and comrades, and of how he gets on with them. One day, let me suppose, he tells you shyly that the talk is so bad, and the evil influence so strong, that he hardly knows how to bear it. But he has always been fond of flowers; they are so pure and lovely that they constantly suggest to him the pure divine Presence in which he stands. And so he has got into a way of taking a flower with him every morning, and placing it on his desk that it may speak pure sweet thoughts to him, remind him of the sacred and august Presence which compasses his path, and help him to bear the strain to which he is exposed. That is a true story; I once knew a lad who did just that, though he never found courage to tell his father of it.

Suppose *your* boy did it : what would you say to him? Would you tell him that it was very weak and silly of him; that God was no more present in the flower than in the desk on which it stood, and not half so divinely present as in the mind and heart of even the worst of his companions? Would you say *that*, and forbid him to pluck your flowers any more? Would you not rather take some pains to keep him supplied with them? Would you not rejoice in his endeavour to resist evil, and even in the innocent device which helped him to resist it? In this case, as in the last, you would have no difficulty in distinguishing between the heavenly treasure and the earthen vessel; but even the earthen vessel itself — that simple and natural faith in a special Divine Presence in flowers — would seem to you so fair and harmless that, in all probability, you would hardly care to criticise, much less to censure, it.

You *have* and use a moral sense, then, which enables you to recognise a heavenly treasure even in an earthen vessel, whether that vessel be as clumsy as the little fellow's lie-and-blister theory, or as delicate and graceful as the lad's trust in the suggestive purity of flowers. And what is to hinder you from applying that sense to the Bible? You may think the Biblical Vessels strangely imperfect if you fix your thoughts on some of the physical theories contained in the Word, for example, or on some of its historical contradictions, or on some of the imperfect precepts given to them of old time: or, on the other hand, you may think them strangely and divinely beautiful if you fix your thoughts on the noble and heroic figures to which it holds a glass, or on the solemn and pathetic music of its psalms, or on the compressed experience and sagacity of its proverbs, or on the exquisite simplicity and compelling charm of its parables. But, whatever you think of the vessels, ought you to forget the Treasure, the revelation of God's will and man's duty, which fills and overflows them?

Think for a moment *what* a Treasure the Bible contains for as many as will receive it.

Is there a God? Science cannot be sure. On the whole, and in its present mood, rather thinks not. But the Bible has no doubt, and will not suffer you to doubt, if only you will listen to it.

Is He good? Again Science cannot tell; but on the whole, and in its present mood, questions whether a perfect goodness would tolerate so many wrongs and miseries as are in the world. But again the Bible has no doubt, and will not let us doubt. Over against our tremulous question 'What is God?' it writes for answer, 'God is Love,' and shews that all the wrongs and miseries of time, since they are necessary to the training of man or of the race, are but proofs of his love and good will.

What is the duty and what the chief end of man? To live for self or for others? for the senses or for the spirit? for truth, righteousness, charity, or for gain, pleasure, self-advancement? Man's great duty, replies the Bible with one voice, in strange contrast to the divided and opposed voices of human wisdom, is to love God with all his heart and his neighbour as himself; and his chief end is to glorify God by becoming like Him and enjoying Him for ever.

Is this the end? or is there a life beyond the borders of the grave in which all the wrongs of time shall be redressed, and men shall rise to their true ideal and perfection? Men say 'Yes,' and men say 'No,' even the wisest of them and the best; but the Bible has only one answer to the question, and that the only answer which solves the mysteries of the human lot.

Is that life attainable by men who have sinned? nay, *Have men sinned?* or is this deep sense of sin by which the purest heart is haunted only the bastard fear cherished by tradition and superstitious fancies? 'Yes, men have sinned,' replies the Bible, 'and, falling short of their own proper glory, have also fallen short of the glory of God. But they have not fallen to rise no more. God Himself has wrought out redemption for them. And in history and parable, above all in the great history and parable of the life, death, and rising of Christ Jesus our Lord, the Bible shews us how we are to die in order that we may live, how we may find our life by losing it.

Now have not those who have found these truths, and such as these, in the Bible found a veritable and priceless treasure, even a heavenly? And does it greatly matter that this Treasure has come to us historically, as an inheritance from our fathers who enjoyed it before us, and therefore in forms adapted to their capacity and conditions as well as to ours? Need any sincere and reflective man fail to distinguish the Treasure from the Vessels that contain it, or to fling it away because he can discover in the Vessels that hold it, this slight flaw or that? Will any of *you* be so foolish as to reject this Divine Treasure because it is offered to you in Vessels which, after all that can be said against them, are the most perfect and lovely ever moulded of earth?

If you have got all *this* out of the Bible, does it very much matter even, at least so far as you are concerned, what becomes of the Bible itself? Not that you need have any fear even for that. Criticism is by no means likely to destroy the Bible, though it may teach, and is teaching, us to read it in a clearer light and to find in it a new and ampler sense. It may impress upon us a fact which we have too much forgotten, that even the Biblical vessels *are* of earth; but if it also, with its will or against its will, convince us that the Treasure is from heaven, who will not thank it as for a double service? Only let us keep the Treasure safe in our hearts, and what need we care for the Vessels save to get and keep them as perfect as we can, that they may serve the generations to come after us? When *they* are studying the Scriptures in which we have found eternal truth and eternal life, and are still drinking in from them the good wine of Divine Wisdom and Love, we, I trust, shall be reading a new and larger Bible in the kingdom in which only truth and righteousness can dwell, and in which the very vessels and media of Revelation may at last be as heavenly as the Treasure they contain.

IV.

GOD UNKNOWN YET KNOWN.

'Seek ye the Lord while he may be found, call ye upon him while he is near: Let the wicked forsake his way, and the unrighteous man his thoughts: and let him return unto the Lord, and he will have mercy upon him; and to our God, for he will abundantly pardon. For my thoughts are not your thoughts, neither are your ways my ways, saith the Lord. For as the heavens are higher than the earth, so are my ways higher than your ways, and my thoughts than your thoughts.'—Isaiah lv. 6–9.

I do not propose to give you an exposition of these most musical words this morning, nor to urge upon your acceptance the tender appeal they contain. I hope to do that next Lord's day. But to-day I wish rather to ask your attention to a paradox which can hardly fail to strike you when once it is pointed out, although you may have failed to find it in this familiar passage for yourselves, and that mainly because the passage is so familiar to you that you read it without reflecting on it. If, however, you mentally retire a few steps from it, and look at it reflectively and from a general point of view, you will find in the passage, I think, this notable paradox: that it invites you to seek a God who yet cannot be found, to know a God who yet cannot be known. For where should we seek God if not in his 'ways'; or how shall we know Him, except by coming to know his 'thoughts'? And yet, while we are urgently invited to seek Him, we are expressly told that there is the widest disparity between his thoughts and our thoughts, between his ways and our ways; that his thoughts and ways are as high above ours as the heavens are high above the earth.

Now this strange paradox, of a God unknowable and yet to be known, opens up to us what is, and is likely to remain, the great religious question of the time. There are many questions, no doubt, which still demand our attention, because they are still in debate within the borders of the Church,—questions of ecclesiastical form and polity, questions of Biblical criticism and interpretation, questions of theological dogma, and of how many of these dogmas must be held in order to secure Christian fellowship. But behind all these questions there rises the still higher and more momentous question, whether there is a religion at all, whether there is any revelation of the will of God, nay, whether there is any God to speak to us and to reveal his will; and, if there is, whether we know or can know anything about Him? And till this question is settled, at least for us, we shall do well to lay all other questions aside.

Is this question of questions settled for *you*, then? Do you believe that there is a God, and that you know Him or may know Him? and can you give a valid reason for the faith that is in you?

You do not need to be told that, in its higher modern form, Atheism does not so much deny the existence of God as declare that, if there be a God it is impossible to demonstrate his existence, impossible to have any true knowledge of Him and of his will, impossible, therefore, to have any real fellowship with Him. If the Atheism of to-day erect any altar at all—and some of its representatives are men of a profoundly religious temperament, and must have some form of worship, the only altar they will consent to erect is one which, like that at Athens, bears the inscription, ' To an *unknown* God.' Their researches yield them no proof that He exists. If He does exist, which some of them are not prepared to deny, they are sure that He cannot be what men have for the most part taken Him to be, nor like what even the best men are; sure that, being infinite and eternal, all virtues, all moral qualities and graces, must take a very different form in Him to that which they take in us.

No doubt this modern form of Atheism, which it seems almost cruel to call Atheism, since it does not so much deny, as doubt, the existence of God, and does not so much question his existence as question whether we can really know anything about Him:—this modern and qualified form of Atheism is doubtless in part a reaction, and even a wholesome reaction, from what has been called 'the devout impertinence of scholastic theology.' When we remember how the Church has refined upon, and how enormously it has added to, the simple revelation of God given in Holy Scripture; how it has babbled of the three Persons in the one substance of the Sacred Trinity, of the three Incomprehensibles which yet are one Incomprehensible, of the three Uncreated who yet are one Uncreated, of the three Almighties who yet are one Almighty: when we remember under what awful penalties it has bidden us 'worship one God in Trinity, and Trinity in Unity, neither confounding the Persons, nor dividing the Substance,' we cannot affect much surprise that men who want facts rather than words, have revolted from this terrible cloud of technicalities: we cannot even pronounce their revolt an altogether unreasonable or unhealthy one; we can see, we are bound to admit, that the Church is largely to blame for their unbelief; we can see and admit that it was very natural for them to assume that, instead of knowing all about the great unknowable God, as the Church affected to do, we really know nothing whatever about Him.

They *have* assumed that we know nothing about Him, that we *can* know nothing about Him. And their assumption, together with their calm and reasoned assertion that Science yields no proof of his existence, have bred some doubt even in the bosom of the Church itself—some doubt, and much fear. In the whole conflict with unbelief, indeed, nothing has been more amazing, nothing more saddening, than the readiness of the Church to 'doubt truth itself to be a liar,' and to fear lest, should the truth be spoken, it might land men in error. This most base and craven fear cannot be too heartily, or indignantly, denounced. To know *the truth* can do no man harm, must do him good. Truth cannot mislead us. If there be *no* God, it surely must be well that we should know it, and no longer believe and walk in a lie. And if there be a God—as there is—is it to be supposed that either other men's doubts or our own fears can possibly blot Him out of existence? What we think of the Sun does not much matter to the Sun, and cannot possibly alter its nature or put an end to its existence. And what men think of God does not and cannot change Him. He is what He is; He remains what He is, let men conceive, or misconceive, of Him as they will. Facts, realities, cannot be thought or talked out of being, or even out of shape. The clearer the light in which we see them, the more nearly do we see them as they are. Why, then, should we fear the light, from whatever quarter it may come? Our God is not like the teraphim of Laban; He cannot be stolen from us. We *are*, and He *is*; and, in ways which I will presently indicate, we have known and seen Him for ourselves. What have we to do with fear, then, whether for Him or for ourselves? Is the Sun going to be put out of the sky by the words and thoughts of men who cannot venture to look him straight in the face? And yet they might far more easily talk the sun out of the sky than banish God from the hearts into which He has shined, giving them the knowledge of his glory.

Science says, or some of her disciples say for her: 'In the whole range of visible and observed phenomena we find no proof of God.' What then? If men will go to the visible for the invisible, to phenomena for realities, how can they hope to find what they seek? They might as well go to the sand of the desert for water, or to the troubled sea for a solid foundation. Votaries of Philosophy say: 'In the whole range of human experience and knowledge we can find no proof that God is, or no means of coming to know Him as He is.' What then? So far as their affirmation is true, do they say anything the world has not heard, on still higher authority, before? anything which the Bible itself does not say again and again? The Bible claims to be the very Word of God. It is saturated with the sense and consciousness of God; to use the figure of Novalis, it is a 'God-intoxicated' book. And this Book professes to give a revelation of the will of God, professes to exist only for the purpose of revealing his Will. And yet does it not everywhere affirm, what Science and Philosophy are proclaiming as a discovery of their own, that God is past finding out; that He is unsearchable, neither to be discovered nor comprehended by man's feeble powers? When men tell us: 'Our investigations yield no proof that God is, and no hope that we shall ever know Him as He is,' they are but verifying and defending the Scripture which demands: 'Canst thou by searching find out God? Canst thou find out the Almighty to perfection?' They are but confirming the Scriptures which assert that, in this world, we see Him but as in a glass darkly, that we know Him but in part,—know only the mere edges and fringes of his ways; that not till we have escaped our bondage to sense and imperfection can we hope to know Him as He is, and as we are known by Him.

The Scriptures, then, do proclaim God to be unknowable, above our reach, in a great variety of forms; they declare that 'as the heavens are high above the earth, so high are his ways above our ways, and his thoughts above our thoughts.' So that modern Scepticism, original as it takes itself to be, is simply announcing, as its last discovery, what the Apostles and Prophets found out centuries on centuries ago. When, therefore, you hear it confidently affirmed that Modern Science and Thought find it impossible to demonstrate the being of God, and doubt whether He can ever be known as He really is, do not be disturbed. Remember that the Bible nowhere undertakes to demonstrate his existence, though it everywhere assumes and asserts it; and that God Himself has warned us that we must wait for a full and perfect knowledge of Him until this mortal put on immortality, and this corruption incorruption.

But you will naturally ask: 'Does not the Bible teach us something more than this? something more than that God cannot be found out by dint of intellectual research, that the finite mind of man cannot comprehend the Divine Infinitude?' And I reply: Yes, it teaches much more than this. Admitting God to be unknowable, it yet affirms that He may be known. We cannot find Him out to perfection, but He sufficiently, and most truly, reveals Himself to us in his works, in his Word, in his Son.

Take the illustration of my text to begin with. God's thoughts and ways, we are told, are as high above ours as the heavens above the earth. But the heavens, high as they are, are yet known to us;

and, though known, are yet unknown. We none of us know *all* that the heavens contain and reveal, nor all the laws which are at work upon and within them. There are probably myriads of worlds in the sky which we have not seen, with millions of inhabitants whose existence we cannot prove, whose modes of existence we cannot so much as conceive. And of the worlds we *have* seen, no man professes to comprehend all their movements, components, productions, influences, uses. The most accomplished astronomer will tell you that in the heaven above, as in the earth beneath us, there is very much more to be learned than he has acquired or hopes to acquire. But though 'heaven' be so imperfectly known to us, does any sane man doubt that there is a heaven, or that it holds within it the sun, moon, and stars? Does any sane man doubt that we know something of the mechanical and chemical structure of the heavenly bodies, of the laws by which their movements are governed and controlled, of the mode in which they affect us, and the world in which we live, and the other worlds related to them? Unknown to us, and even unknowable, not to be found out to perfection, we nevertheless know them—know, at least enough of the heavens to be sure that they exist, and to guide us in all the practical purposes of life. And it is precisely in the same sense that *God* is both known to us, and unknown. We have not learned, we cannot learn, all that He is, all that He does, or all the reasons which determine the several aspects and movements of his providence; but we may know, we do know and are sure, that He *is*, and that He rules over all.

No doubt we know Him, in part, by our reason. Many a man has felt, with one of the great thinkers of our own day, that the starry heavens and the inward law, the law of conscience, are a sufficient proof of the being and rule of God to the thoughtful and susceptible heart. And one of the leading expositors of Modern Science, a man who must I suppose be ranked as a Materialist, since he professes to 'find in matter the promise and the potency of all things,' has himself told me that, as he witnesses the annual arrival of Spring, as he sees life and song and beauty coming back to the dead world, he is aware of a Power at work around him which moves him to a wonder and a reverence too deep for words. That there is a God he can neither affirm nor deny; that we can discover and know Him he wholly doubts: and yet in his most open and best moods he is dimly aware of the Creative Power which we call God. And, for one, I am by no means sure that the logic and researches of Reason can carry us further than that. I doubt whether we shall ever *prove* the existence of God any more than we can prove our own.

What then? It is not to reason alone, nor to reason mainly, that the Bible appeals. The Bible nowhere deals with God as a problem to be demonstrated, nor professes to give a complete or a philosophical view of his Being and the qualities of his Being. It shews us a more excellent way of finding Him. It affirms that as we ourselves grow in righteousness we shall come to know Him who is righteous; that as we grow in purity we shall see Him who is pure; that as we grow in love we shall become one with Him who is love. Instead of appealing, on a moral and religious question, to the mere intellect alone, it also and mainly appeals, as is reasonable and just, to our moral and religious faculties. It says: 'The righteous God reveals Himself to righteousness, the pure God to purity, the kind God to kindness.' Our Lord Himself indicates the true path of investigation and research when He exclaims: 'Blessed are the pure in heart, for they shall see God.' When we are pure from the stains of sin and selfishness, when the moral nature is perfect, then we shall know God as He is; and in proportion as we approach to this moral purity and perfection we possess ourselves of the organ or instrument by which we may see Him. St. Paul, again, affirms that, though as yet we are mere babes, and know no more of God than little children know of the larger and deeper experiences of manhood, yet in proportion as we put away childish things, and nourish ourselves in faith, in hope, in charity, we shall come to know Him even as also we are known by Him. And St. John who, I suppose, knew more of God than any man who ever breathed, simply because he was the most perfect in love, expressly tells us that, though we are the sons of God, we do not yet know what we shall be, nor see God as He is, but that, if we purify ourselves, we shall hereafter see Him as He is, and be like Him.

And is not that the way in which we come to know all persons, and especially good persons? The child does not know his father perfectly: but need he doubt that he has a father? The child can never know the goodness of a good father until he becomes good himself and a father: but need he therefore doubt whether his father be a good man? And we, may not we in like manner know that God is, *do* we not know that He is, although we are but children in understanding? May we not know that our Father in heaven is good, although we cannot as yet comprehend the half of what his goodness means and includes? Nay, is not this Scriptural, this Divine, way of coming to know God the natural and reasonable way? Do we ever learn to recognize and appreciate purity except by becoming pure, or righteousness except by becoming righteous, or love except by cherishing love? O, it is not from arbitrary caprice that God often hides Himself from the wise who want to find Him out by logic, by quest of intellect, by force of reason and induction, and reveals Himself to the 'babes' who keep a simple, sincere, and loving heart! It is only because goodness and purity and kindness can only reveal themselves to kindness and purity and goodness.

If you would know God, then, be good, for He is good; be pure even as He is pure. Have you not already discovered, in your own happy experience, that this is the true way of finding Him? When you have been raised above your wonted level by some pure and sweet and strong emotion, when you have followed truth and righteousness and honour at some risk and cost, when you have refused the temptation to impurity to which your whole lower nature urged you to yield, when you have shewn kindness to those who had not deserved it and from whom you hoped for no return, have you not felt that God was near to you, that He was with you, that He was revealing Himself within you? And who are the men and women in whom you see most of God, or who go nearest to persuade you that God is, and that

He dwells in very deed with men upon the earth? Are they not the meek and pure and gentle souls who gladly sacrifice their own interests and comforts and pleasures in order that, moved by love, they may minister to the wants or the welfare of others? Are they not the brave and righteous souls who make a resolute stand for truth and righteousness, risking name and fame and use in the defence of a truth which the world, or the Church, has forgotten or despised, or for the furtherance of some noble cause ignobly surrendered by the Church or the world? Nay, who is He in whom of all the sons of men you see so much of God that you either call Him, or hardly know how to refrain from calling Him, God with us? Is it not He in whom alone you see purity without a stain, righteousness without a flaw, love without a bound?

You see, then, the true way to know God is by the heart, by the great moral qualities and emotions through which we are most closely akin to Him. Seek Him through these, live in that part of your nature which is unworldly and unselfish, which is pure and just and kind, and you will surely find Him. You will know Him with an intimacy and a certainty which no logic could convey, which no lapse of time and no change of view can disturb. If the Bible were proved unhistorical to-morrow, if criticism were to render the very Gospels themselves dubious to you, if you could be persuaded that Jesus Christ never wore flesh about Him nor walked the earth, yet how should even that incredible and impossible miracle disturb your faith? You would say: 'I know God for myself. In all my best and highest moods He has been with me. I find more of Him in the Bible, more that moves me to righteousness and purity and goodness, than in any other book: and, therefore, if I cannot read it as history, I must still read it and rejoice in it as parable and poem. I see more of God, a divine perfection of love and beauty, in Christ than in all other of the sons of men. And even if you should convince me that He never lived, and died, and rose again, I must nevertheless believe that the men who wrote the Gospels were moved by God to create a character so perfect, a life so divine, and to give it me as a Pattern of all excellence. He is still true to me, still a revelation of God, and the highest revelation I have found. All that is best in me leaps up to greet Him, to greet *the God* in Him; and this picture of Him, even if it were only a picture and not a sacred reality, must still be my most potent and unfailing incentive to all that is good.'

In short, if you have once come to know God for yourselves in this most natural yet divine way, you will cleave to Him, and to your faith in Him, though the heavens should fall and time should be no more. Your feet are on the rock, and the everlasting arms are about you for evermore. Let Science, let Scepticism, let Criticism say what they will, then. Do *you* say: 'At first we believed in God because we had heard of Him from the wisest and holiest lips we knew; but now we have seen Him for ourselves, and *know* that He is the great Lord and Lover and Saviour of men.'

V.

THE INCREDIBLE MERCY OF GOD.

'Seek ye the Lord while he may be found, call ye upon him while he is near: Let the wicked forsake his way, and the unrighteous man his thoughts: and let him return unto the Lord, and he will have mercy upon him; and to our God, for he will abundantly pardon. For my thoughts are not your thoughts, neither are your ways my ways, saith the Lord. For as the heavens are higher than the earth, so are my ways higher than your ways, and my thoughts than your thoughts.'—Isaiah lv. 6-9.

I spoke to you last Sunday of the strange paradox suggested by these words; viz., that while God is unknown, and even unknowable, He may nevertheless be known; that He is at once near and far off, findable and unfindable, within the scope and reach of our thoughts, and yet as high above our thoughts of Him as the heavens are high above the earth. In other words, we do not get hold of God by reason, by intellectual research, by logical demonstration. If we come to know Him at all, we come to know Him just as we come to know all other persons, and the moral qualities of persons, by experience, by sympathy, by fellowship and love. You can only learn what righteousness is *in a man*, *i.e.*, you can only learn what it means and includes and implies, as you yourself become righteous; you can only learn what purity is as you become pure; you can only learn what love is as you love. And, in like manner, in precisely the same way, on precisely the same terms, you come to know God. In proportion as you yourself become righteous, He who is righteous reveals Himself to you; in proportion as you grow pure in heart, you see Him who is pure: in proportion as you love, you comprehend the love of God, which yet passeth knowledge. A moral being *can* only disclose Himself to moral beings—can only disclose Himself even to them in proportion as they possess themselves of the moral qualities and affections which are in Him, and *are* Him. When, therefore, you hear ministers, in reply to the sceptical doubts and objections of the age, maintain that God cannot be found by mere intellectual research, that He can only be known by experience, sympathy, fellowship, you are not to suppose that this is a mere fetch or evasion on their part, or to suspect them of seeking to substitute authority for reason; they are simply declaring *the law* by which all moral perception is governed, and affirming that you can only know God in the very way in which you come to know men, and on precisely the same terms.

And the immense, the incalculable, advantage of coming to know God by experience and sympathy is this,—that, when once you have found God *so*, you can never lose Him; your feet are on the rock from which no stress of doubt and no storm of change can dislodge them. If the Church were to perish to-morrow, if the Bible were proved to be a mere collection of historical and ethical treatises, if the Lord Jesus Himself were to be refined into the hero of a fable, the most perfect poetical conception of the most creative of human minds, even in these incredible and impossible conditions you would not lose a God whom you had seen and known for yourself. You would say: 'When I have been most just, most pure, most kindly, I have had Him with me; I have felt Him at work within, upon, and around me: I could as soon believe that I myself am not, and that I have never sought Him, as believe that He is not, or that He does not reward them that diligently seek Him by revealing Himself to them.'

But if there be some who find it hard to believe that there is a God, there are others who find it equally hard to believe that He is good,—so good that He can forgive all sins, *even theirs*, and cleanse them from all their iniquities. And it is to these that, moved and guided by the Prophet's words, I am about to speak this morning. The *incredible mercy of God* was his theme, and will be mine.

Look at these Verses again, then, and mark their ruling intention.

The Prophet—whether Isaiah or another does not matter a jot from our point of view—had been commissioned to carry a message to the captive Jews who sat by the waters of Babylon and wept when they remembered Zion. The message was that, heinous as their iniquity had been, their iniquity was pardoned; and that to the merciful and relenting heart of Jehovah it seemed as if they had already endured 'double' for all their sins, *i.e.* twice as much as their sins had deserved.* Hence he was about to appear for them, to appear among them,—delivering them from their captivity, bringing them back with song and dance to their native land, making them the joy and praise of the whole earth.† In this word, this message, God was drawing near to them; finding *them*, that they might find *Him*. And the Prophet urges them to 'seek Him while He may be found,' to 'call upon Him while He is near:' that is to say, now that God is approaching them to deliver them, they are to fit themselves to receive, to recognize, and follow, Him, by putting away their unrighteous thoughts, by forsaking their wicked ways, and by turning in penitence, expectation, faith toward Him

---

* Chap. xl. 2.   † Chap. xl. 3–11; Chap. lv. 12, 13.

who was turning toward them in ruth and compassion.*

But sinful men, especially when they are suffering the bitter punishment of their sins, are apt to be hopeless men. When you speak to them of the Mercy that is more than all their sins, they are apt to think that Mercy incredible, or at least to doubt whether it is about to be shewn to them. As nothing is possible to doubt and despair, as above all the energy of active moral exertion is impossible, God sets Himself to remove the natural incredulity and hopelessness of the men He was about to save. That his mercy is incredible, He admits; but He affirms that it is only incredible in the sense of being incredibly larger and better than they imagine it to be. *They* might have found it impossible to forgive those who had sinned against them as they had sinned against Him. 'But,' pleads God, '*my* thoughts are not *your* thoughts, neither are your ways my ways. They are a whole heaven above them. And, therefore, *I* can forgive you the sins which *you* could not have forgiven had they been committed against you. Nay, your very unbelief cannot limit or defeat my mercy. The word I have sent you, this message of salvation and deliverance, *must* do the errand on

---

* Chap. lv. 6, 7.

which I sent it; and therefore you must and will go out of the house of your captivity with joy, and be led forth with peace, the mountains and the hills breaking forth into singing as you climb them, and all the trees of the field clapping their hands as you march through and under them.'* So that the main point of these Verses is not so much that God Himself is unknowable to us, as that his mercy is incredible to us,—incredibly higher, incredibly deeper and wider, incredibly more heavenly and inexhaustible, incredibly more affluent, and tender, and sweet: in fine, as high above our conceptions of it as the heavens above the earth, and so broad that it embraces the whole world of men as the heavens embrace the earth with all its mountains and woods and seas.

If, then, we would learn the lesson of these words, and take their comfort, what we have to do is to convince and persuade ourselves that the Mercy of God is immeasurably, incalculably, greater than we have conceived it to be, so much greater that it naturally appears to be altogether incredible to us. What we have to do is to believe, to get ourselves to believe, that the Divine Mercy transcends our utmost stretch of thought; that the more largely we think of it the more truly we think of it, if only we remember that it

---

* Chap. lv. 8-12.

is a Mercy which does not condone men's sins, but a Mercy which saves them from their sins, which calls upon them and compels them to abandon their 'wicked ways' and their 'unrighteous thoughts.' No mercy short of this would be true mercy. To make men happy *in their sins* is impossible, as impossible as to make them *good* in their sins. For sin *is* misery; sin is a bondage to an alien and malignant power which every free spirit must resent and abhor. And even if this ignoble miracle were possible, if a man could be made happy while violating the very law of his being, who that is capable of reflection, of virtue, of goodness, would care to have such a miracle wrought upon him? To be happy in sin he must cease to be himself, cease to be a man. What we really desire, if we are men and have discourse of reason, is to be freed from the chain of our sins; what we really desire when we ask for mercy is a mercy that will be at the pains to cleanse us from the soils of evil and strike its fetters from our souls. And so long as we cherish *this* desire, we may be sure that the Mercy of God stands waiting to meet it, to outrun all our thoughts and expectations, all our wishes and hopes. We are not to measure Him by ourselves, nor his mercy by our own. It is high above ours, so high that even the most merciful of men only apprehends it afar off; so great, so broad and deep, that the fidelity and tenderness, the inexhaustible love and pity of the very mother who bore us are lost in its unfathomable and unimaginable depth and volume. No man ever has, or ever can, explore it to its utmost verge; no man has or can, by searching, find it out to perfection.

The Mercy of God, viewed as saving men from evil thoughts and ways,—which is the only true mercy—*is simply incredible:* so the Prophet affirms, so we profess to think and to believe. But do we really believe it? Do we act as if we did? Millions will say to-day: 'I believe in the forgiveness of sins:' but how many of that vast multitude, do you suppose, will both understand and realize what they say? Many of them hardly believe that they *have* sins which need a great act of Divine forgiveness. Many more do not know that, in order to forgive, God must punish their sins. When the punishment comes, they take it as proving that He has *not* forgiven them, as proving the severity, the anger of God, not his mercy; and can hardly be persuaded that, if they seek God, they will find Him; that if they call upon Him, they will discover that He has drawn near to them in the very punishments which warn them that they have sinned, and that all sin is infinitely displeasing to Him because it is injurious to them.

In our turn, indeed, we all doubt the Mercy of God

when we most need to believe in it, distrust it when we most need to cast ourselves upon it. Any profound consciousness of sin is apt to make that Mercy incredible to us. And when, like the Jewish exiles by the waters of Babylon, we are suffering, and feel that we are suffering, the due reward of our iniquity, it grows too incredible, too airy and impalpable, for us to grasp. 'If God be merciful,' we say, 'why does He inflict this terrible agony upon me now that I see and repent my sin? If He were merciful, He would never have used me thus.' And so our anchor parts just when the storm is at its wildest and we are driving on the rocks.

In our cooler moments it may help us to remember that, as I have just hinted, the very punishments that wait on sin, since they wait on it by a constant and invariable law, are designed for our good. All natural and universal laws must subserve our welfare, if the world and human life be ruled by God; and, among others, the law which metes out to every man the due reward of his iniquities. In part we can even see *how* this law contributes to our welfare. It makes us terribly aware that we *have* sinned,—a fact we are very slow to realize. When the retribution comes upon us, we can no longer gloss over our transgressions, nor pretend even to ourselves that perhaps after all the wrong we have done was not so very wrong. All the plausible fetches by which we seek to hide our sin from ourselves are suddenly exposed, and we are left face to face with the sin which has become our torment.

We who preach the boundless mercy of God, and hope for the ultimate restitution of all things, do not therefore cease to believe in hell. We believe in hell because we ourselves have been in hell; for we have been in sin, and sin is the one unspeakable and eternal misery. But we also believe that the pains of hell get hold of men for their good; because when they have taken hold of us, when we have seen our sin in its naked deformity, when we have been overwhelmed with pain, shame, remorse, with an unutterable self-abhorrence and self-contempt, we have been constrained to cast ourselves on the Mercy of God, to pray and hope that He would cleanse us though we could not cleanse ourselves, that He would forgive us though we could not forgive ourselves: and thus, at least at times, we have passed through the very gates of hell to find ourselves in a heaven of pardon and deliverance. Those who have ever gone through such an experience as this—and some of us have gone through it more than once—have learned to see the Mercy of God in the pains that punish sin, as well as in the grace that forgives our sins. And even those of you who have not yet gone through it may perhaps gather from what I have said, you may understand even if you have not felt, that you ought to take the retributions which wait on sin, not as proofs that God has abandoned you and ceased to care for you, but as proofs that He is near you, so near that, if you seek, you will find Him, that, if you call on Him, He will answer you. By his merciful punishments God is at once convicting you of sin and calling on you to repent, that, repenting, you may be forgiven, purged, saved.

Finally, you remember what it was we agreed upon at the outset,—that it is not by arguments addressed to the understanding that we come to know God, or the mercy of God, but by experience and sympathy. A notable corollary from that conclusion is, that we must expect to be convinced of the pity and compassion of God, not so much by having the kindness of his laws demonstrated to us, as by listening to the men whom we believe to have had the largest experience of his ways and to enjoy the profoundest sympathy with his thoughts. Just as we come to know the righteous God by becoming righteous, so we may hope to learn more of Him from the men whose righteousness is far more eminent and conspicuous than our own. Just as we come to know the mercy of God by becoming merciful, so we may hope to acquaint ourselves more fully with Him by listening to men far more merciful and gracious than ourselves. Such a man, a teacher such as this, now stands before us in the Prophet who penned these words. If you are familiar with the critical controversies of the time, you may doubt whether Isaiah wrote the concluding Chapters of the Book that bears his name. You may even doubt whether the Prophet who did write them got every word he wrote straight from Heaven. But there is one thing which I do not see how you are to doubt if you have read these Chapters with attention. You cannot doubt that somehow, whether by inspiration or by reflection, he who wrote these words, whether Isaiah or another, knew far more of God than you do; that he had a far richer experience of God and a far deeper sympathy with Him.

This man, then, whoever he was, has a claim to speak of God with an authority which few can rival. And *this* is what he has to say to you of God,—that God's mercy is as much higher than your thoughts of it, as much broader, as much more pure and tender, as the heavens are higher and broader and sweeter than the earth; that it transcends all your conceptions of mercy, that it seems incredible to you only because it is so large and rich and free that you can very hardly bring yourselves to believe in it. He affirms that even here our great poet's description holds good, that we may lift a reverent eye to the very Throne of Heaven and say: 'Mercy is twice blessed,' blessing 'Him that gives,' as well as 'him that takes,' since God delights in mercy, and is—if I may speak of so great a mystery in words so homely—at least as pleased to forgive our sins as we are to have them forgiven.

My brethren, we are *all* sinners, all *great* sinners, for we have all offended against a great Love. And it may be—for who can tell what tumult of passionate emotion may be hidden under the smooth exterior you present to your neighbours?—that some of you are at this very moment feeling your sins very deeply. It may be that you are suffering from them, and for them, although you make no sign. It may be that in your pain and self-contempt and self-disgust, your hard thoughts of yourselves are breeding hard thoughts of God, and you are saying within yourselves: 'If He were merciful and meant to forgive, He would not treat me so.' If I do speak to any who are in this saddened and despairing mood, I bring you a great comfort. For I bring you the testimony of a man who knew God as but few have known Him: and his testimony is, that your widest thoughts of Mercy are not so wide as the mercy of God; that the highest hopes of Mercy you have ever indulged are as far beneath the mercy of God as the earth on which you stand is below the heaven in which He dwells. His testimony is, that in all those painful, restless, self-despairing moods bred in you by the sense of sin, God is drawing near to you, and calling on you to seek his face; and that, if you do seek Him, you shall find Him. Many of us have already listened to his words and put them to the proof for ourselves. And we attest, we cannot but attest, that his testimony is true. We too assure you that the Mercy of God is incredible, unfathomable, of an unimaginable sweetness and purity and depth. Be comforted, then; and seek, that you may find, your God, and in Him the Mercy that frees all faults, forgives all sins, and heals all the diseases of the soul.

VI.

ALL THINGS OURS.

'All things are yours; whether Paul, or Apollos, or Cephas, or the world, or life, or death, or things present, or things to come: all are yours, and ye are Christ's, and Christ God's.'—1 Cor. iii. 21-23.

'ALL things mine? O, how delightful that would be, if only it were true!'

But it *is* true.

'All things mine that I may make them Christ's? If that be true, it is hardly delightful, or hardly so delightful as having all things for my own.'

But it *is* delightful, and even far more delightful than having all things for your own. Nay, to give all to Christ is the only way to make all things yours.

So we might talk together on first reading this wonderful passage, finding much in it that is difficult, much even that seems incredible, but nothing so incredible as St. Paul's point blank and repeated assurance that all things are ours. Even this incredible assertion, however, may grow credible to you if only you approach it from the Apostle's point of view.

For the first thing he affirms, the very thesis which he has been arguing and elaborating throughout the Chapter, is that *all ministers* are yours. And that is true, is it not? Perhaps you are tempted to reply: 'O, yes, that is true enough; but what are we the richer for that?' Now there I differ from you. I am by no means sure that all ministers are yours. I am quite sure that, if they are, you are much the richer for it. Do you demand proof? You shall have proof.

St. Paul's general principle is that the teachers are for the Church, not the Church for the teachers. I admit that principle quite as frankly as you can do. I admit that, in the design and intention of God, the teachers exist for the sake of the Church, and not the Church for the sake of the teachers. But the intention of God is one thing, and the intention of the Church, as shewn by its conduct, is often another and a very different thing. God intended eloquent Apollos, learned Paul, and Peter with his practical sagacity and passionate enthusiasm,—God intended them all for the Church at Corinth: but did that Church possess itself of them all, and make them all their own? All these ministers were theirs in right; but did they make them all theirs in fact? On the contrary, some said, 'We are of Apollos,' mainly meaning thereby, 'We are *not* of Paul or Cephas.' They were charmed with the eloquence of the mighty expositor of Scripture, but they did not care for, they did not appropriate, the learned spirit of St. Paul or the plain sagacity of St. Peter. Others attached themselves to Paul, loved his logical disquisitions, his insight into all mysteries, but thought Apollos too rhetorical, and Peter too rustic and provincial for men of their culture. And still others gloried in St. Peter, boasting no doubt that he preached the simple Gospel; but distrusted the eloquence of Apollos as a too fascinating and worldly gift, and the learning and originality of St. Paul as likely to make him too broad or too sceptical. Thus this ancient Church flung away two thirds of its treasure. All these ministers were theirs, —Paul, Apollos, and Cephas; but they did not care to make them all theirs. Too many of them would only have *one* minister; and, not content with simply appropriating him, they spoke and set themselves against the other two.

Can we find no parallel to that in our modern Churches? Alas, where can we look without finding a parallel to it? All the ministers of the Church universal are *yours*, my brethren, yours in the design and intention of God : but do you make, do you permit them all to be yours? What, all the ministers of the Apostolic Church, all the ministers of the Patristic Church, all the ministers of the Mediæval

Church, all the ministers of the Roman, the Episcopal, the Presbyterian, the Independent, the Methodist, the Unitarian, and the Baptist branches of the one Catholic Church throughout the world? All are yours, and yet how few of them are yours! Every Christian man who has any truth to teach is a minister, is *your* minister if you will have him. And if you would learn from them all, from St. Paul down to Dr. Liddon or Mr. Spurgeon, would you not be rich indeed, at least, in teachers, and perhaps also in the highest wisdom?

But here you may fairly object: 'We have neither the means nor the opportunity of learning from many of Christ's ministers.' And that is true. But do you learn as much, and from as many of them, as you might? Might you not learn more at least from the best? Do you study the Apostolic preachers—St. Paul, St. John, St. Peter, St. James—with the devotion they deserve? When wise and holy men of other communions than your own—such men as Robertson, Lynch, Dykes, Dale, Maclaren, Martineau—publish a volume of choice discourses, do you take as much pains to get it as you take for the last new novel, and read it with even as much interest as you bestow on your daily newspaper? They are *all* yours; but do you *make* them all yours?

There are those in our Churches who so attach

themselves to *one* minister that they care to hear no one but him. There are those who so attach themselves to one that, like the Corinthians, they carp and detract, they set themselves against men of other and even of higher gifts, and refuse to see any power or wisdom save in the little god of their private idolatry. Now I do not say that, if you find a minister who can most effectually touch the springs of spiritual thought and emotion within you, you are not to love and to addict yourselves to his ministry. But I remind you that, in the purpose and design of God, *all* ministers are yours. I do say that, if you so addict yourselves to one that you can hear no other, or few others, with profit, you are flinging away the greater part of your spiritual heritage; and that, instead of paying a compliment to the minister you specially affect by declining to learn of others, or by speaking lightly of their work, you rather shew that he has laboured in vain so far as you are concerned, since the end and effect of the ministry of every true servant of Christ should be to open your minds to a thankful reception of truth in whatever form it may come to you, and by whatever voice it may be uttered. Remember, then, I beseech you, that *all* ministers are yours, from Paul, Apollos, and Cephas down to the sincere and devout teachers of every Christian Communion at the present day; and that you ought to rejoice in them all, and to thankfully learn from them all so far as you have opportunity.

But not only all ministers, *all things* are yours: the whole world, the whole ordered cosmos, with all that it includes,—life, death, things present and things to come, all are yours. And here perhaps your real difficulty begins. You can easily believe that all ministers are yours, that you have a clear right to appropriate any teaching or help they can give you; but you do not see how the whole contents of the world, and all the events and successions of time, are yours. They are yours in precisely the same sense in which ministers are yours: yours, not to do what you like with, but yours to do what you would like if you were wise; yours to use and to profit by. God has put them all at your disposal, in order that you may get the true use and good of them, in order that you may appropriate all that is best and most enduring in them, and compel them to minister to your welfare. If a deed of gift were placed in your hand which made over a whole county, or a whole country, or even a whole cosmos to you as your private estate, you might be none the better, none the richer, for that; you might be much the worse and poorer for it. So vast an estate would entail responsibilities under which any man, even the strongest and wisest, must stagger and faint. If you cared only to make a personal and selfish use of it, to enjoy all in it which most delicately ministered to sense and appetite; if you let it feed your sense of power till you grew proud, insolent, exacting; if your possession of it robbed you of all stimulus to labour, to mental effort and acquisition, to moral culture and improvement, you would simply sink into the most astounding sot and sinner under heaven; you would become at once the god and the devil of the world over which you ruled. And when the world perished, or you were ordered out of it, nay, and even while you held possession of it,—what the better would you be for it? nay, how much the poorer and the worse?

Property is what we can appropriate. We possess things in the proportion in which we can get the best out of them that they have to give, that which will minister to our own highest and most enduring interests. And what in the world is there of which, with due pains and trouble, you cannot get the best it has to give? The splendour and pomp of sunrise and sunset, the changeful glory of the seasons, the beauty of flower and herb and spreading tree, the starry canopy of heaven,—are not these, with all that they imply, open to every man, *given* to every man? Do they not become yours in proportion as you have power to discover and appropriate their beauty, their teaching, their value? If you love them, and study them, and suffer them to enter into and enlarge and beautify your soul, they are *yours*, yours for ever, yours in a far deeper sense than any house or piece of land that you have bought. *That* you may lose by a thousand accidents, and at the best you will soon have to leave it behind you: but the culture, the new and larger powers of thought and appreciation, the refinement, the beauty, the sweet and pure affections wrought into your very spirit by your love and admiration of the natural world, *this* will never leave you; you can never lose it; it is part of your very being; it is an everlasting inheritance.

The world *is* yours, then, if you care to make it yours; yours, as ministers are yours, that you may enjoy and appropriate and get the good of it, that you may be the richer and the better for it for ever.

And so are 'life' and 'death.' For what is there in all the forms and varieties of human life which you may not observe, and so observe as to learn its highest lessons, as to work the very essence of it into the very substance of your mind? What have men ever done, to what achievements have they risen, what great and noble thoughts have they uttered, of which you may not read, and so read as to make all that is permanently valuable in them your own? The noble thoughts and noble deeds of men are as an atmosphere in which you stand or walk: and who shall hinder you to breathe it if you will, till you feel that you too are akin to the wisest and bravest of the race, that their thoughts are your thoughts, and their influence a power framing you for noble enterprise? By awakening your spiritual manhood and perceptions, by teaching you that you and all men are children of the Highest, and that all the events of time are ordered with a view to your welfare, Christ has thrown open to you the whole domain of history and of human life; and it rests with you to determine how far you will go up into it and possess yourselves of it.

And He has made 'death' your friend and servant no less than 'life.' For if you believe in Him what is death to you, or to those whom you love, but a transition to more life and fuller? What have *you* to do with any fear of death now that Christ has not only conquered it for you as well as for Himself, but changed its very nature? Death teaches solemn lessons, indeed; for it teaches us that all which is temporal and corporeal in us, and in the world around us, must fade and pass away: but it also teaches most joyful lessons; for it teaches us that the temporal passes only to disclose the eternal, and the corporeal only that the spiritual part of us, released from its bondage to the flesh, may unfold itself in new vigour and beauty. If you have learned that, and believe it, *is* not death your minister and friend?

Two other possessions the Apostle confers upon us, or, rather, marks and denominates as ours. 'Things present,' with which we are so seldom content, and 'things to come,' which we are so apt to fear,—these, too, he pronounces to be 'ours': *i.e.* since God intended them for us, we may make them ours if we will. And, surely, you have all known men and women who were so certain that their present conditions, however narrow and straitened, were marked out for them by God and intended to nourish all that was best in them; so certain also that their future conditions were in the same wise and kindly Hands, that their life has been a sacred and tranquil possession to them; and they have gone on their way, vexed with no want, fearing no evil, although their lot and prospects would have filled you with discontent, anxiety, apprehension. 'Things present and things to come' *were* theirs, as they may be yours. All depends on the ruling aim and spirit of your life. If you are bent on getting the highest and most enduring good out of them, then 'all things' are yours, yours now, yours for ever: for what is there to prevent you from getting this kind of good out of them? and, when once you have got it, who, or what, is to take it away from you? But if you are only bent on getting a present and sensuous enjoyment out of them, then, though all things are yours in right, hardly anything is yours in fact; and what little you do possess will soon be taken away from you.

In short, the point to which the Apostle would bring us is this: that every province, every detail, every moment of our life is quick with a Divine intention, pregnant with spiritual good; and that when we recognize the ordinance and intention of God in them, and seek to learn the lesson and to appropriate the good with which they are fraught, all things in very deed become ours, ours now in this present life, and ours for evermore: we are no longer ruled and tyrannized over by our conditions; we make them our servants and friends. And if we could but reach this point, and maintain ourselves at it, who does not see with what a noble simplicity, what dignity and sacredness, we should invest our lives? Lords of ourselves, we should also be lords of lands, of all lands, of the whole world, and of all the successions of time.

All things are yours, then, whether Paul, or Apollos, or Cephas, or the world, or life, or death, or things present, or things to come: all are yours, but all are yours in proportion as you make them yours; and all are yours because *you* are Christ's, and that you may make *them* Christ's and God's. Nay, as I said at the outset, we can only make all things ours as we give them all to Christ and God.

That sounds like a paradox, I admit; but, nevertheless, it is demonstrably true. For, observe: all ministers are yours, from Paul, and Peter, and Apollos, down to the humblest teacher of the present day; all are yours in right, for God has sent them all for your good: but when do you make them all yours in fact? Only when you recognize the good and feel the power that is in them. Only when you learn what they have to teach, and take what they have to give. Only, that is, when you make the best use of the best that is in them, and suffer it to minister to your highest and most enduring welfare. And when you do that, do you not both take them as God's gift to you, and give them back to Him? You get from them stimulus and incentive to live a sober, godly, and righteous life; and in living that life you carry back to God what He has conferred on you through the ministers He has sent to teach you.

And in the same way you make 'life' yours. Here it lies all around you, taking innumerable and varied forms. And while it lies all around you and touches you on every side, human life also stretches back into the most remote ages. The past is full of noble forms which you reverence, crowded with heroic achievements, with great words and deeds, which command your love and admiration. Hands reach out of it and voices sound out of it which seize upon you, and guide your steps, and influence your character and thoughts and aims. And how does this vast and varied scene of life become truly yours? Only as you recognize and imitate that which is highest and best in it. Only as you yield to its nobler influences and suffer them to mould and reform you. That is to say, all life becomes yours as you give your personal life to God. The same great history lies behind every man. The same leading influences are at work upon every one of us. But while some seize upon what is best and noblest in them, others seize upon what is at least comparatively trivial and perishable in them. And only those make life truly theirs who follow its greater examples and yield to its finer influences,— the influences and examples which conduct to truth and righteousness and love, or, in one word, to God.

So, again, with death. Do all men own and possess death? What! those who fear it or shrink from it for themselves, or who hate it because it robs them of those whom they love best? No; *these* are not lords of death. Death is their lord, a tyrant whom they hate and dread. Only those who believe that Christ has overcome the sharpness and taken away the sting of death, only those who know that death is a minister of God for their good, and comes to give that which is spiritual in them the victory over the misleading powers of sense, and that which is eternal in them the victory over that which is temporary, can be said to have death for their servant and friend. And who are these but those for whom to live is Christ, and to die gain? Who but those for whom to depart is to be with the Lord? Death is ours only as we are Christ's and God's.

And only on the same terms are things present ours and things to come. For we do not own and rule our present conditions while we fret at them, and murmur against them, and would radically change them if we could. Nor is the future ours so long as we fear it and dread what it may bring. Present and future become ours only as we know and are sure that both are known to God, both ordered by Him, and ordered for our good. But let a man once be sure that his conditions are now, and always will be, just the most suitable and best that infinite Wisdom can contrive for his ultimate welfare: and will not *he* be content and fearless? will not things present and things to come be truly *his?* just what he would have them to be if he could bend and shape them to his mind?

You see, then, how true it is that *all* things—and not 'our wills' only are ours, and ours that we may make them God's, since only as we do make them God's can we make them truly our own. You see how vast an inheritance is conferred upon us in the purpose and intention of God,—the whole world with all that it inherits, the history of man, the successions of time, the events and conditions of life, the mysteries and splendours of death. And it only remains that we accept and enter on this inheritance, that we make it ours by appropriating all that is best, highest, and most enduring in it, by laying up its title deeds in the secret and inmost chamber of our souls, where neither moth nor time's effacing finger can reach them; and that we expend in the service of God the immense and growing wealth which He has bestowed upon us: for here, most of all, giving, we shall get, and, spending, thrive.

VII.

THE TOO GREAT PROMISE.

'All things are yours, whether Paul, or Apollos, or Cephas, or the world, or life, or death, or things present, or things to come: all are yours, and ye are Christ's, and Christ God's.'—1 COR. iii. 21-23.

I SPOKE to you from these words last Sunday, and tried to shew you that, incredible as it seems, all things are verily ours; ours in the truest, deepest, and most binding sense: and that all things become ours as we become Christ's and God's. In other words, my contention was that all things are ours *by right*, ours in the intention and purpose of God; and that we make all things ours *in fact* in proportion as we become of one mind, one will, one life with Christ Jesus the Lord.

In order to shew you that this great promise is as greatly fulfilled, I asked you to begin where the Apostle began. He had been arguing, he continues to argue, that all ministers of the truth belonged of right to the Corinthian Church,—Paul, Apollos, Cephas, with all their colleagues and successors, although, in point of fact, most of the members of that Church were refusing to make them all theirs: some saying, 'I am of Paul, and will have no other teacher;' and others, in the same exclusive spirit, saying, 'I am of Apollos,' or 'I am of Cephas.' All were theirs, if they cared *to make* them theirs, if they would only *let* all be theirs. And, in the same manner, all ministers of the Truth, from the Apostles downward, are ours,—not ours to do what we like with; nothing is ours in that sense: but ours to learn from, ours to profit by. We are entitled to make the best and highest use of whatever is best and highest in them all, whatever the Church or the section of the Church to which they belong. They are all the servants of Christ; and if we are Christ's they are all our servants, and helpers, and friends.

And in the same sense all other things are ours; the world, with all that it contains; human life, in all its forms; death with all its solemnities and splendours; 'things present,' *i.e.* all the conditions by which we are now surrounded; and 'things to come,' *i.e.* all the conditions into which we are to shift and rise when we pass from this present scene. *All* are ours in the same way, and for the same end, as the teachers and preachers of the Word are ours,—not to do what we like with, but that we may make the best use of them and get the greatest good from them that we can. And *that*, if you will think of it, is the only sense in which anything really belongs to us. If anything in the world belongs to you, it is, I suppose, your own body, or the money which you have earned by your own labour. And yet can you do what you like with either of them? Your body is yours; but is it yours to *sin* with, or to sin *against*? If you do sin with and against it, do you not instantly begin to damage it, to lose your property in it, your power over it? You cherish exorbitant appetites in it which you cannot control, or you so break down its health and vigour that you can no longer depend on it to do half its work. Abuse your body, and you begin to lose possession of it. It is only by using it according to God's intention, and for the ends designed by Him, that it becomes, and remains, really yours. So again, your hard-earned money is yours: but is it yours to do what you like with? By no means. If you make certain illegal uses of it, the law will step in and take it from you. Make certain other, legal but foolish, uses of it, and you will infallibly lose it. If you make a wise and lawful use of it, if, for example, you buy a loaf with it, that loaf is yours, but still not yours to do what you like with. You must not fling it out of the window; you must not eat too much of it; you must not even feed your dog with it if you know of some poor neighbour starving for want of it. Charity, good sense, conscience will not suffer you. You instinctively feel that you are responsible for the use you make of it; that only by making the best use of it do you, in the true and best sense, make it your own. In precisely the same sense, then, in which whatever you call your own belongs to you, do all ministers and all things—this world and the next, life and death, the past and the future—belong to you. They are not yours to do what you like with, but yours to turn to the best account you can—the best, the wisest, the most enduringly profitable.

This was my argument last Sunday, though I did not put it exactly in this form. And, after you had listened to it, I can well believe that, if some of you were convinced and instructed by it, others of you were disappointed with it and thought it by no means conclusive. It is almost inevitable, indeed, that those who are not of a spiritual turn, or whose minds are not informed by much thought and varied experience, should be dissatisfied with *any* interpretation of a promise which, as they read it, offers so much and yet confers so little. It may well be, therefore, that some of you, after you had listened to my explanation of it, thought that after all the promise meant very little; that all things are not really yours, nor even the things you most need and desire: and that, let ministers and expositors say what they will, they only evade the real point of such words as these, and take away with one hand what they seem to give with the other.

Now as I am very anxious to convince you that these words are literally and demonstrably true, I will ask you this morning to approach them from another side—from the side of your own thoughts and wishes. I will ask you to consider *what, and how much, you are willing and prepared to take* of the ' all ' here promised you; and then leave you to decide for yourselves whether it is God who is not ready to fulfil his promise, or you who do not care to let Him fulfil it, whether it is He who will not give or you who will not take. I warn and challenge you to keep a keen look-out, to see that I treat you fairly; for I fully believe that, struggle and object as you may, I can constrain even the youngest and least spiritual of you to acknowledge that the whole difficulty rests with you and not with God; and that He is even compelling you, against your will, to let Him be as good to you as his word.

If you feel at all as I imagine you to feel, and as I myself used to feel once, *this* is what you say to yourselves when you look at such a great promise as this. ' All things mine ? That is not true : I wish it were. Very few things are mine. If I only knew any good way, any sure way, of making all things mine, I would instantly and gladly take it. But when preachers talk about such a promise as this, they do not point out any such way; they don't explain the promise, but explain it away: they carry it up into the air, out of sight, out of reach, put some "spiritual" meaning as they call it, upon it—some forced, unreal, non-natural meaning *I* call it; and leave me as poor as I was before.'

Well, I will try not to do that. I will try to meet you fairly, on your own ground. And, therefore, I will not urge that this promise is made only to those who believe in Christ and love Him with all their hearts; for, though it is true that only those who have the Spirit of Christ in them *make* all things theirs, yet it is also true that God meant and wishes all things to be yours even though you have not consciously and fully given yourselves to Him. No, I will neither try, nor seem, to slip away from you and from what you naturally understand these words to mean. I admit, I affirm, that in the intention and purpose of God all things, without a single exception, are *yours*—yours in right, yours in fact even, if you care to have it so.

But *do* you care? Are you quite sure that you wish to have all things? If you do, I pledge you my word that you shall have them. But do you want them? What, *quite all?* All ministers and teachers of the Word, for instance; for these are the first things specified in the promise? Paul, Apollos, Cephas; St. Chrysostom, St. Augustine, St. Bernard; Luther, Calvin, Knox; Jeremy Taylor, Howe, Baxter; Channing, Lynch, Beecher, Robertson, Stopford Brooke; Newman, Martineau, Dale, Maclaren, Liddon, Spurgeon: all these, with a great company more, are yours. Do you very much care to have them? to have them *all*? Do you care to learn all that they can teach, and to appropriate every influence for good which they exert?

Look at the promise, look at the particulars of the promise, for yourselves, and tell me whether you are eager to possess yourselves of its whole contents, of all that it specifies and includes. What do you find? Besides ministers of the Word, you find 'life'; and perhaps you would be glad, though I doubt it, to have all that Life can give you. But read on, and you find 'death.' Now, honestly, do you want to make *death* yours? to enter into its secrets and mysteries, learn all that it can teach, possess yourselves of all that it has to confer? Some of you, at least, do not want to die, or even to think of death and to prepare yourselves for it now while you are in the full vigour and glow of life.

What else, then, do you find in the promise? 'Things present.' Well, you would like, perhaps, to have *things present*, *i.e.*, to have all the conditions amid which you live at your command, so that you could turn them this way or that at your pleasure. But again read on, and you find *things to come, i.e.*, all the conditions of your future existence, your existence when you shall have passed away from earth. Do you want *these* to be yours, or even to think about them and to make ready for them?

And yet it is but reasonable that as rational creatures, as mortal and yet immortal, you should think of death as well as of life, of the future as well as of the present, and of how what you do here and now may affect your character and state hereafter. The promise is not too big for reasonable men, looking before and after: but is it not a little too big for *you?* It would almost seem that you would like it better if it were not so large, if it did not cover so much. It would almost seem as if it offered more than you care to take. You could do with 'life,' but you don't want 'death'; you would be glad to have 'things present,' but, for the present at least, you don't want to be pestered about 'things to come.' And as for all the ministers of the Universal Church, from the Apostles downward, you could very cheerfully dispense with them all, or, at best, you would far rather dispense with them all than be condemned to listen to them all.

See, then, how the tables are turned upon you. At first the promise was not large enough and real enough for you; but now it is *too* real, *too* large! If it puts at your disposal much that you would like to possess, it also presses on your acceptance much that you would rather not take, although you cannot but admit that it offers nothing with which any reasonable man would willingly dispense. Did I not forewarn you that the difficulty was with *you*, and not with God? He gives all; but you want only a part, and that the part which, as I will try to shew you, is the least and the worst.

But here, perchance, some of you who have taken my advice, and have looked at the promise for yourselves, may object: 'Sir, you are not dealing quite fairly with us after all. For among the "all things" the Apostle expressly specifies "the world"; and you have said nothing about that, though *that* is what we should like best of all.' My friends, I did but leave it to the last, because I thought some of you would like it best, and because it answers my turn best to take it up here.

You would like the world, then, would you? Will you be good enough to tell me how much of it you would like? Do you want what St. Paul here means by the world: *i.e.* the whole ordered cosmos,—the starry heavens, with all their train, the broad fertile earth, with all its continents and seas? Many a baby cries for the moon who would be not a little incommoded if the moon, with its icebergs and volcanoes, were cast into its lap. You do not surely want the whole cosmos for your own! And yet it *is* your own, so far as you care and are able to make it so. God has given you a right to it all. He has made you free of it all. So far as you can apprehend it by science, or be charmed by a perception of its beauty, or turn it to any good practical account, it is yours: God Himself has placed it at your service and disposal. Again, therefore, I must ask: Is the promise, is the gift, too big for you? Do you want something less, and more manageable? Must God be *worse* than his word if He is to please and satisfy you?

Well, then, if you do not want the whole cosmos, how much of it *do* you want or think you want? and are you ready to take it, as you must take all property, with its natural, its inevitable, conditions and consequences? Tell me frankly what is your idea of a comfortable, a desirable, estate. You don't want the cosmos; you don't want the whole earth; you don't want a whole continent, or a whole country, or a whole county even. But perhaps you would like—many men assume that they would like—so much of the world, and of life, and of things present, as would enable you to live without labour or trouble—which means, remember, that you would like to live on the labour and trouble of other men. You would like to have plenty of leisure for study, for travel, for amusement. You would like not to be obliged to take thought for what you should eat and drink and wear, but always to have, and to be sure that you always would have, the best of everything at your command. And you would also like to surpass and excel your equals, to be eminent and conspicuous in various ways, an heroic, or, at least a commanding, figure likely to live in the thoughts and praise of men. Let me suppose that this is the sort of portion you would choose for yourselves, if you were free to pick and choose; it is a sufficiently common ideal, and, let me add, a sufficiently low and selfish ideal. Still, I may assume perhaps that if you had so much as this at your command, you would feel that in a very real and practical sense 'all things were yours,' since you had pretty nearly all that you cared to possess at your disposal.

But now, if you had it—which God forbid, if you can frame no higher ideal of life and happiness than this!—would it after all prove to be enough? You would have to spend a few hundreds or a few thousands a year. *Could* you, with a quiet conscience, spend all that *on yourself*, on your own appetites and pleasures?

'O, no,' you say; 'that would be too selfish. If I want to enjoy myself, I also want to be good and kind to others. I should like to give away quite as much as I spend.' *Should* you? But is it so easy to give away without doing more harm than good? To *give* wisely involves as much thought as to spend wisely, or even to earn wisely. And, again, have you considered that, if you lived as you like, on the best dishes and the choicest wines and in what is called 'the best style,' you might soon grow very intimate with your doctor, easily fall into habits of excess, and either lose all power of enjoyment or end your days in an asylum or a madhouse? Have you considered that, if you had wealth, you would also want health miraculously preserved, or a sobriety and temperance such as few attain to whom the luxuries of life are suddenly laid open? Have you considered what sort of a figure you would make if, having wealth and the means of enjoyment, you lacked manners, culture, refinement, if your vulgarity, or your ostentation, or your grammar, or your very intonations made you a laughing-stock to those with whom you wished to associate? And must God, besides giving you wealth and the means of enjoyment, miraculously confer on you health, refinement, culture, and all else that your new station would require?

But think what *that* comes to. God offers you 'the world.' You don't want the world, you say; but you would like a little of it. And this little, it turns out, if you are to be content with it, must be cut out of a quite different world from this, with other ethics, other laws, a world in which men are wise without reflection or experience, cultivated without study, refined without training or effort, always young though the years move as swiftly as with us, in good health though they eat and drink too much, valued and esteemed although they do not possess the qualities which here command esteem and respect! It sounds modest in a man to say, when all the world is offered him, 'I don't want all that; a very little will do:' but if it should prove that this little must be specially created for him, and then sustained by a series of grotesque miracles, is there anything so very modest in his demand? If a man is not content with the world and the laws of the world into which he is born; if he wants wealth without responsibility, wisdom and culture without labour, enjoyment without peril to health, experience without lapse of years, or a lapse of years that will leave him neither older nor feebler, or distinction without achievement, or goodness without effort and self-denial,—I think we must admit, that, whatever other excellent qualities he may have, he is not precisely what we should call a modest man.

How shall we treat such an one as this? It is easy to see how a wise Stoic, Epictetus for instance, would have treated him. He would have said to him: 'God has set before you this great and solemn spectacle of human life and destiny. You do not care to witness it? It is not precisely what you wish? Very well, then; give up your seat—nobody will miss *you* much—and make room for another who *will* care to witness it, and who will praise the Giver with a thankful heart.' But Christ and his servants are more gentle and considerate than the wise Stoic; they make a wider allowance for ignorance and inexperience. And, therefore, they say to you: 'You ask for too little, for far less than you will want by and bye, when you know how much man really needs if he is to be at peace. You *must* meet death as well as life; and therefore you ought to think of it, and prepare for it. The 'things to come' *will* come, and therefore you should not wrap yourselves up in the present, and still less in mere present enjoyment, but should prepare to meet the future which, ready or unready, you must surely meet. The whole cosmos is not too great an inheritance for those who must live for ever, and will for ever need new fountains of wisdom and new fields of action. God, who made all things, made you for Himself; and you can only rest as you find rest in Him, as you make *Him* yours.

And, therefore, he has made all things yours, and so yours that they may all lead you to Him, and make you his. You would be content with 'life' if you might choose only what you like in life; and hence He both lets you taste the sorrow as well as the joy of life that you may not be content with it, and sends 'death' to you that it may raise you to a higher life. You would be content with 'things present' if you might select only that in them which answers to your wishes and desires; and therefore He mixes the bitter with the sweet in your present conditions, that you may be willing to leave them, and then shifts the scene that, in 'things to come,' you may find a nobler discipline and a higher good. You would be content with that which is poorest and most transient in 'the world,' with that in it which will perish when the world is burned up; and so He draws your thoughts away from that which is merely visible and temporal in it, fixes them on its imperishable beauty, its spiritual and eternal laws, and makes the whole cosmos yours, with all its worlds, even the new heaven and the new earth in which these laws will be revealed in nobler forms and work out to larger and happier results.

This is the real reading of this great promise: and, if you will receive it, you must admit, I think, that it is no slight or dubious good which it confers upon you, but a good, a vast inheritance of good, far greater than you had supposed it could include. You must no longer say that it is not true, or that it gives you little while seeming to bestow much. You must rather gratefully confess that, whereas you had been craving only a part, only a small and poor and transient part, it throws open to you all that the reasonable soul of man can need or desire whether for life or for death, whether for this world or for that which is to come.

VIII.

LED BY A CHILD.

FIRST PART.

'The wolf also shall dwell with the lamb, and the leopard shall lie down with the kid; and the calf and the young lion and the fatling together: *and a little child shall lead them.*'—ISAIAH xi. 6.

THE prophet Isaiah positively revels in these pastoral and picturesque descriptions of the Kingdom of God. Whether or not, when these fair ideals floated through his mind, they were set in any framework of time and circumstance; whether or not he knew *when* those things should be which he foresaw, we cannot be certain, though, on the whole, it seems more probable that he did not know. There are those, indeed, who have no doubt that he *did* know, who have no doubt even that *they* know. They confidently apply all these descriptions to what they call 'the millennial reign of Christ;' they hold that only in the Millennium will the discords of nature and of human nature be stilled, but that then they will melt into a harmony so pure and sweet that an innocent and fearless child, leading wolf and lamb, leopard and kid, lion and calf, by rosy ribands gathered into its rosy fist, is but a true and fair symbol of that fair and happy time. To many of us, however, and that mainly because we so strongly believe in *the present and eternal reign* of Christ, it is not easy to believe in that millennial reign of which in our earlier years we heard so much. We doubt whether the prophetic symbols and apocalyptic types admit of so literal an interpretation. We hope that the work which Christ began when He came and dwelt among us in great humility has ever since then been growing toward perfection and will never cease; that He will reign over an enlarging empire in heaven and on earth, not simply for a thousand years, but for all the ages of time, and even through that eternal age on the surface of which all the years of time rise like passing bubbles, and into which they burst and lapse.

And we are confirmed in this view by the New Testament writers. For they interpret these ancient prophecies as we interpret them, and apply them, not to some far-distant millennial æon, but to the reign which Christ commenced when *He* became 'a little child,' and dwelt among us. According to them, *He*, in the days of his humiliation, was the Branch, or Sprout rather, that shot from the decaying stem of Jesse; the Spirit of the Lord came upon Him, with-

out measure, to make Him of quick understanding : *
and we have no right to sink an interval of many
centuries between the Verses of this brief prophecy,
and to say that while one part of it was fulfilled at
the Advent, the other will only be fulfilled in the still
distant Millennium. We are rather bound to say : 'If
the Lord Jesus was the Branch that shot forth from
Jesse's root, and the Spirit of the Lord did really
come upon Him that He might rule and reprove the
people, then, from that moment, the wolf began to
dwell with the lamb, the leopard to lie down with the
kid, the lion with the calf; and the little Child went
before them, leading them to the holy mountain in
which they neither hurt nor destroy.' We need fix
no date to these words. We have no right to date
them, and thus to limit them to any single era. They
are not for an age, but for all time, and for eternity
too. They describe the *universal* reign of Christ.
They tell us what the spirit, what the distinguishing
characteristics, of that reign always have been and
always will be.

2. *A little Child shall lead them*. But how should
a little child lead the savage wolf, the fierce leopard,
the powerful and majestic lion ? Even a man can
hardly do that. Before he can tame them to his will,

---

* Isaiah xi. 1-5.

he must show himself strong as the lion, fierce as the leopard, cunning as the wolf. The beast-tamer is distinguished by a quick eye, a prompt punishing hand, a courage and self-possession that never falter: and how should we look for these features and qualities in a child? We cannot expect them; we should be sorry to see them in any child we loved. But may not a child have other qualities quite as potent, and even more potent? Is brute force the only force by which even brutes are ruled? Surely not. Baby lies on the rug with dog and cat. He is not so strong or lithe or quick as they are, or even as you are. Yet he takes liberties with them which you cannot take,— and remember, the cat is of one blood with the leopard and the dog with the wolf. He lies upon them, rolls over them, treads on their sensitive feet, lugs them about by fur or hair; and yet by some wonderful instinct they recognize his innocence of ill-intention and respect it. Were *you* to inflict half the pain on them which he inflicts, they would soon let you know that they had teeth and claws; but they hardly ever turn on him. The little Child leads them where he will, and pretty much *as* he will.

Nor are even wild beasts insensible to his claim and charm. Else what mean all those stories of helpless and abandoned children suckled, fed, guarded by wolves and bears and lions; or of children chosen by caged wild beasts, the more savage for their captivity, to be their playmates and companions? Many of these stories are quite true, and shew what power a little child may have, a power beyond that of man. They shew too, I think, that there is a certain *humanity* in the very brutes, a spirit which responds to the claims of innocence and gentleness and love. It is because they exhibit such gleams of a moral and humane nature that some of us find it quite impossible to believe that 'the spirit of the beast goeth down to the earth' and becomes extinct; or, rather, we can only believe that, if their spirits do go down to the earth, they go by *that* road to God, while ours reach Him by another way.

3. But when the Prophet tells us that in the Kingdom of Christ, a little Child leads the wolf and the leopard and the lion, as well as the lamb and the kid and the calf, he cannot simply mean that an innocent babe may have more power over the brutes than a grown man. He also meant, no doubt, that in proportion as Christ reigns on the earth the primal order will be restored; that men, reconciled to God and to each other, will also be at peace with all the forces of Nature, will rule over them, and bend to their service even those of them which are the most fierce, lawless, hostile, and untameable, and thus regain all, and more than all, that Adam lost. The

earth, which was only a paradise to innocent man, is a heaven to redeemed and righteous men. For what is heaven save the place, or state, where God is, and where the sense of his Presence gives an unbroken peace? And men, wholly redeemed from evil and the fear which evil breeds, find God everywhere, find Him *here*. Hence the kingdom of Christ is called 'the kingdom of heaven.' And in proportion as we are in that kingdom we are even now already in heaven, and taste a heavenly peace.

But some man will say: 'Now how can that be true? How can we be in heaven so long as we are under a sky often darkened by storms, and on an earth often bleak and cold and unfruitful? How can we be in heaven while we are still the sport of adverse accidents, and our hearts are torn with the pangs of sorrow and bereavement?' Thou foolish man! *If God be with you, and for you, how can you be anywhere else than in heaven?* If the stormy winds fulfil his word, and adverse accidents express his will, why should they disturb your peace? *Is* there no change, no sorrow, in heaven? If there be not, how did certain spirits 'fall away from their first estate'? If there be not, how should God Himself be afflicted in all our afflictions, and feel them even more keenly than we do because his heart is so much more tender and gracious than ours? My brethren, the laws of

Nature need not be relaxed, nor the wild winds tempered, nor the wild beasts tamed, in order that we may be in heaven. Let us only know and heartily believe that God is in very deed with us, that all changes and losses are but expressions of his gracious will whose will is our salvation, and even though the wild beasts tear us limb from limb, or the storm of change sweep away all that we possess, we shall nevertheless abide in the heaven of his peace. The storm which robs us of all we had acquired only makes us a little more obviously dependent on the Divine Bounty on which we always depend whatever we possess; and the wild beast, by rending the body, only brings us a little nearer to Him in whom alone we always live. Heaven lies all about us, did we but know it, even as we walk the earth. Lord, open Thou our eyes, that we may see Thee, and our heaven in Thee.

4. *A little Child shall lead them.* Lead whom? The leopard, the lion, and the wolf? Surely not these alone. The familiar interpretation which takes these fierce wild beasts as symbols of the savage and ravening passions of men is at least a permissible interpretation, if not a true one. If the Prophet had not these passions in his mind when he wrote, we may have them in our minds as we read; for the Spirit which moved him gives us understanding also.

Man is king of the world in many senses. As in his body all the forces of the physical universe meet, so in his soul are gathered up the qualities, energies, passions, cravings, of the animal creation. If the simplicity, tenderness, and playfulness of the kid and the lamb rise to their highest expression in him, so also do the cunning and fierceness of the wolf and the leopard. Naturally enough, therefore, the Hebrew prophets often use the wild beasts of the forest and the desert to symbolize the lower and fiercer passions of man. Take them thus here, and the prediction is that, under the rule of Christ, even the most savage and unruly appetites, even the fiercest and most cruel passions of humanity, shall be chastened into harmony with its gentler attributes; and that, with their nature thus balanced and harmonized, men shall be led in peace as by the hand of an innocent child.

Has not the prediction been verified again and again, and that even on the lower levels of our life? Here, say, is a bad man,—brutal, fierce, ungoverned and ungovernable. God sends him a little child— conceived in sin perhaps, and born in iniquity. But the child, coming from God, takes no stain from its evil earthly origin. And the rough man and the abandoned woman, as they lean over it, are touched, softened, purified. In its innocence and helplessness and loveliness there is that which appeals to all that is best in them, reviving memories of their own early days, and quickening in them at least a vague desire to amend and live a better life. But what is all that but just God leading them by a little child toward his holy mountain? The emotion may soon pass, stifled by force of habit or the pressure of want. Still, at least for a moment it was *there*, and spoke for God, and shewed that even yet they might be redeemed—redeemed by a little child.

God leads almost all men by their children, leads them to the 'holy mountain,' *i.e.* to higher levels of life where they breathe a purer air and gain a wider outlook. He sends the 'little child,' and forthwith even the hard and selfish grow tender and unselfish, at least in some of their aims. They no longer live to and for themselves alone. They unbend in childish sports to please their child, and find in innocent homely amusements and intercourse a pleasure sweeter and more satisfying than that of base and animal delights. Sacrificing their own comfort to promote the comfort of their children, they acquaint themselves with the joy of self-sacrifice. They labour to support their children, to educate them, to give them a good start in life; and all the while, though they may not know it, God is educating *them* through their children, enriching them through their expenditure and sacrifices, and conducting them to a higher life. A little child leads them, and they follow his guidance when they would follow no other, his tender fingers clasping not their hands only but their very hearts. They will follow him even to the house and worship of God—for many a man repairs to the house of God for his children's sake who would not come for his own—and find themselves in 'the holy mountain' or ever they are aware.

5. So that, when God sent the Holy Child Jesus to lead men into the Kingdom of Heaven, He took no new and untried way with us, but a way long tried and approved. Which of us, even though he have no child of his own, is happier than when with unspoiled and childlike children? Their very presence is a redemption—a redemption from the fretting cares of life, from its impure cravings, from self-pleasing and self-indulgence. And if little children, any of them, can do so much for us, what wonders may not the perfect and holy Child do? nay, what wonders does He not do? Think what He does for us at this hallowed time. Christmas after Christmas we gather round his cradle, led by his star, or by the song of his nativity; and our hearts grow tender and humble and childlike within us as we worship the Child. What would the year be without Christmas? and what Christmas without the Child who, born of woman, was yet the Son of the Highest? Now, if

never else, the little Child leads us; and, following Him, we tread the holy mountain seen from which all the lower world of our common life takes new and brighter forms.

But, for us, the Lord Jesus is not the Holy Child only at Christmas, or only because He was once a babe in Mary's arms. When He grew to be a man, He Himself took a child in his arms, and taught his disciples that to enter his kingdom they must become as little children, and that whosoever most fully possessed himself of the Childlike spirit would be greatest in that kingdom. But to enter his kingdom is to begin to grow like Christ; and to become great in it is to grow as like Him as we can. To grow childlike is, therefore, to grow Christlike. But how can that be unless Christ Himself is like a little Child? And *that*, no doubt, is the very lesson He would have us learn from his words. We are to believe that his heart is as the heart of a child,—pure, friendly, unworldly, loving, pitiful; and that therefore we need not fear to come to Him. We are to learn that as we reverence little children, and would not willingly bring anything evil into their presence, so we are to reverence Jesus Christ the Righteous and to put away evil from our hearts. *Thus* the Holy Child makes us holy, leading us to the mountain where there is nothing to hurt or destroy.

The Child makes us Children. *That*, indeed, is the only condition which children exact of us if we would be with them. *Be* a child, and you are welcome to them, but not otherwise. Affect to be a child, put on a simple merry air foreign to your nature, pretend to like them and to be like them, and they soon find you out and will have nothing more to do with you. And, in like manner, the Lord Jesus exacts of us that, if we would be with Him and abide with Him, we become as little children. He has the simple, kindly, tender heart of a child, and to be welcome to Him and to abide in fellowship with Him, we must get a heart like his, we must become of one spirit with Him. And, O, how clumsy we are at first, and for long! how we misapprehend his simplicity and limit his tenderness! how we think to please Him by shewing a spirit alien to his,—by trying to keep other children from Him, as the disciples did once, or by judging them instead of leaving them to his judgment, or, rather, to his forgiveness! It is well for us that, to the grace of a child, Christ adds the wisdom and patience of a man, nay, of a God. If only we love Him, and are trying to learn and do his will, He leads us, and bears with us, teaching us through our very mistakes, raising us by our very falls, until at last He brings us safe to the top of that holy mountain all whose slopes are in the kingdom of heaven, but whose summit is the very heaven of heavens,— brings us to the eternal city on the shining tablelands which needs no light of the sun, neither of the moon, because the glory of God shines in it, and the Lamb is the light thereof. To which city and home of the soul may He finally bring us all; and, with us, all men : Amen.

IX.

LED BY A CHILD.

SECOND PART.

'The wolf also shall dwell with the lamb, and the leopard shall lie down with the kid; and the calf and the young lion and the fatling together: *and a little child shall lead them.*'—ISAIAH xi. 6.

WITH these words we opened our Christmas week. Let us close and seal it with the same words.

6. A little child *shall* lead them. But does he not lead them already? A man takes his little girl out for a walk:—and I saw the very scene I am about to describe last Sunday morning as I went home after speaking to you from these words, and felt, as I looked at it, as if my homily had suddenly grown incarnate. He holds her by the hand, bends over her with an air of protection and concern, abates his manly strides into short slow steps that harmonize with hers, feigns—feigns? nay, takes—an intense interest in this or that that he may interest and amuse her, guiding her lest she should stray, supporting her lest she should trip. He seems to be leading her: but is

it not she who is leading him? Very probably they are out at all for her sake rather than for his. Quite certainly it is she who determines the pace at which they walk, the distance they will cover, and, most likely, the direction in which they will go. That is to say, he leads the little child, and yet, all the while, it is the little child who is really leading him, and bending the tall strong man to her will.

Is that an illustration of my text merely, or of the whole round of human life? Are not all men led, and in some measure *saved*—saved from selfishness, the root of all sin—by their children? When the little ones come to them, who is it for whom they think, and work, and plan? Who is it that determines the amount of their toil, and even the kind of amusements in which they indulge, and often determines also the very aims and methods of their lives? Go into almost any household you will, and you will find that the children are the real centre of it, the determining influence. A man commonly lives, if possible, nearer to the school to which he sends his children than to his own place of business. It is the children who commonly fix the hour at which he shall dine, and often even what he shall have for his dinner, their health and convenience being consulted before his own. He often goes shabby that they may be well clothed, and sometimes hungry that they may be well fed. His very home is furnished with an eye to them; and the new carpets or the costly furniture which he would like to have are postponed till the children are grown up, or the good piano which his wife would like till the children have got through their practising. Where shall the summer holiday be spent? is a question in which the children have a potent voice, the casting vote. He would like to go abroad perhaps, and see strange men and strange cities. But he can't afford to take his children with him, and can't bear to leave them at home; and so summer after summer finds him in the old crowded seaside lodging of which he, poor fellow, has grown weary, or would have grown weary if they were not so delighted to get back to it. How many a man, too, long after he has laid by enough for himself and his wife, and craves retirement and rest, goes labouring on, either that he may provide for children who cannot provide for themselves, or that he may leave them a little more money when he dies! How many a man who cannot afford to retire works beyond his strength, instead of reducing his labour as age creeps on, in order that his children may be better educated than he was or get a better start than he had! In short, no sooner do we consider the point than we find that even those who seem to be living the most free and independent life, and to have their children in the most perfect control, are really guided and controlled by them,—the whole mode of their life and its ruling aims being determined by the little children whom they seem to lead at their will. The children's health, the children's education, the children's pleasure and amusements, the children's welfare and advance, these are really the shaping and dominant elements in almost every Christian household.

And when the children grow up into young men and women, is it not they who lead the world as once they led their several households? The ruling and shaping spirit of the world changes with every generation. Without much ado, without spending more thought and trouble on it than it is worth, we cannot even get clothes of the same cut,—the same collars and cuffs and coats and hats—we wore twenty or thirty years ago, nor get our hair, if we have any left, cut in the same fashion. Much less can we think the same thoughts, and cherish the same purposes. Our conceptions of art, of science, of theology, our very modes of speech and action, are all changed. And at whose bidding, pray, if not that of the young? It is they who are our masters, our tyrants; they who say to us 'Do this' and we do it, or 'Do that no more' and we no longer do it. The fact is that we are all in bondage to our children;

they rise up and push us from our wonted seats: we must think as they think, and live as they live; we must move with the moving spirit of Time or we are left stranded and useless, if we are not also openly condemned as behind our time, lagging in the rear and hanging on the skirts, a hindrance to all progress and advance. It is the young who give the tone to the age, who fix the direction in which we travel, and who, to do them justice, achieve the discoveries and reforms which characterize the time. Only as we retain a childlike heart, a heart of youth within us, will they admit us to their fellowship, or suffer old experience with its prophetic strain to blend with and modify their ardent song.

And it is well that it should be so. Their rule, if it be a despotism, is at least a benevolent despotism. It is God who is ruling the world through them, *leading* the world onward and upward, widening its thoughts, redeeming it from ignorance and selfishness, shattering even good customs so soon as they stiffen into bonds and threaten to enslave and corrupt the world, in order that better customs may come in and a freer larger life. One often hears elderly men say of the young, and say kindly enough: 'Well, well, we have had our day; let them have theirs.' But that is not sufficient. Like a wise Master-Scribe, God is for ever bringing things new, as well as old, out of his store; and naturally the new things, if they come from God, are the best, or at least the best for the time. Naturally, too, He puts the new things into the minds and hearts of the new men,—the young. And, surely, it is strange that we are so slow to recognize the fact that it is *God* who is speaking to us through them. Can anything, indeed, be stranger or more unreasonable than this?—that a man who believes God to be gradually educating the world to a larger purer wisdom should hold on to his *first* thoughts and refuse to believe that God can have better thoughts to give him! *Or this:* a man, proud of the ability and promise of his son, endures toil and sacrifice to give him a better education than he had himself, and bids him start where he began; but no sooner does the young fellow start, and make a little way, and turn round to tell his father what new things he has seen, than his father frowns upon him and wholly declines to admit that *he* can have seen anything but what had been seen a thousand times before! How is the world to grow wiser, to become of quicker understanding in the fear of the Lord, if the most ardent and forward-looking spirits of the race are to be no wiser than their fathers were, to discover nothing but what has long been known, and never on any account to see a single inch beyond the paternal nose?

Are we, then, to discrown Age, Experience, Authority, and enthrone Youth, Inexperience and Insolence? Are we to listen to *whatever* our children may say, and let them lead us where they will? By no means. That would be as injurious to them as to us. But we are to realize the fact that God is educating the race; we are to understand that He is guiding every generation, and conducting it to a point beyond that of the generation which preceded it. We are to believe that it is his method to lead us by our children, while yet we lead them. And, therefore, we are to be sure that in whatever is commonly believed by the cultivated younger men of the day there is at least an element of truth which it will be wise of us to study, whatever the errors and caprices that may be blended with it.

This reverence for youth as the new element, the progressive and advancing element, of the world is, I believe, peculiar to Christianity, and even in some measure to the Christianity of the present day. There never was a time, we may be sure, in which parents did not love their children, and were not to a large extent led by them. And yet in that great Roman Empire into which our Lord was born, the father had power over his grown-up son, power even of life and death. And even among the Jewish race, from which He sprang, the son was at his father's commandment in only a lesser degree. The authority of the man over the woman, and of the old man over the young, was carried to a frightful and debasing pitch even in those dark middle ages which some, who would be very sorry to have lived in them, still call 'the ages of faith.' And even those of us who can look back forty or fifty years must have heard of, if they cannot remember, a time when a son, even though he were himself the father of a family, did not venture to sit down in his father's presence until he was bid. It is only of late years that 'the rights of children' have been recognized. It may be doubted whether, though in some respects the cultus of children is carried too far, the right of the young to think their own thoughts is fully recognized even yet; whether even in this day we hope and expect that God will reveal Himself in new and larger forms to them, and cause a light to break forth upon them from his Holy Word which was denied to us. And yet only as they see more, and see more clearly, can the world grow in wisdom; only as they receive a finer and ampler inspiration from above can we hope that the world will grow better.

7. 'A little child *shall* lead them.' These words, as we have seen, refer not simply to the future, but also to the present and the past; they describe a great and common feature of the Kingdom of Christ in every age. But, of course, they do refer to the

future, as well as to the past and the present. There is a promise in them even for us who are in the Kingdom of the Holy Child. And the promise is that as the Kingdom of God *comes*, in proportion as his will is done on earth as it is done in heaven, we shall be more and more conspicuously led by a little Child; *i.e.* we shall be more and more animated by the Child-Spirit, which was, and is, the Spirit of Christ Himself. In proportion as the Kingdom of God comes *in us*, this great blessing will be *ours:* in proportion as it comes *in the world*, this great blessing will be *the world's*.

But what is this blessing, and why is it so great?

Well, consider. Consider how *fearless* a child is, so that it can play and take liberties with many a fierce creature whose talons or teeth keep you at a respectful distance. Consider how *innocent* a child is as compared with you, and what you would give to be equally clear of stinging memories and impure desires. Consider how *friendly* a little child is, responding with smiles and caresses, to every genuine and tender advance. Consider how *cheerful* it is, with how little it is pleased; how *unworldly*, making no distinction between beggar and prince, loving its poor nurse better than the fine lady in all her bravery. Consider how *free from care* a child is, because it trusts in a wisdom, an ability, a goodness beyond its own—taking no thought for what it shall eat or drink or wherewithal it shall be clothed. Consider, too, how *lordly* a child is. Hardly anything strikes one in little children so much as their calm assumption that all the world was made for them, and that all the men and women in it have nothing else, or nothing else so important, to do as to wait on their will and minister to their whims. 'Cry for the moon'! Of course they do. What was the moon made for save to comply with their wish and come at their call?

I might cite many more characteristics of the little Child; but it will be enough if you will only consider these, and compare them with the characteristics of which you are conscious in yourselves, of which you are at least aware in the men and women about you. You have only to run this contrast in order to see how immense is the blessing promised by the words, 'A little child shall lead them.' Ah, think; think of the fears by which *you* are oppressed, fears for to-day and for to-morrow, fears of the night and of the day, fears for the body and for the soul, fears for yourselves and for those dear to you,—you who were once a fearless child. Think of the sins by which your memory is defiled, of the impure cravings by which you are urged and stung, of the amazing difficulty with which you bring your guilt home to yourself and repent of it,—you who were once an innocent child, to whom a fault was terrible, and yet was so easily swept away by a shower of tears and a mother's forgiving kiss. Think how unfriendly you have grown, insomuch that you suspect almost every strange face and dislike many of the faces you know, not trusting your neighbour because you can so little trust yourself,—you who were once a frank warmhearted child to whom every advance of love was welcome. Think how sad you are, how easily irritated and depressed, how commonly even the brightest day is darkened for you by some foreboding of evil to come,—you who were once so bright and cheerful that all the year seemed summer to you, and all the world was full of hope and joy. Think how worldly you have grown, how selfish, how apt to defer to opulence or position, and to be afraid of being much with the poor, how you long for riches or cleave to them, how you crave distinction or pride yourself on it,—you to whom, when a child, all differences were inward, not outward, natural, not conventional, differences of kindness or unkindness, cleverness or dulness, not differences of wealth or poverty, of high or low degree. Think how careful you are, what burdens you impose on yourself, as if there were none to care for you, or as if God could not provide for to-morrow as well as for to-day, or as if He could not make you rich by poverty, and glad through sorrow, and holy by discipline, and wise by hard and painful experience,— you who, when a little child, had so absolute a trust in the love and providence of a man or a woman, father or mother, that care was unknown to you. And, finally, bethink you that, though all things are yours and work together for your good, you often feel as if you could count on nothing, and long for what you *have* if you did but know it, and fear and tremble as if neither life were yours nor death, neither things present nor things to come,—you who, when you were a child, claimed the whole universe and dreamed, with Joseph, that sun, moon, and stars did obeisance to you. Think of all this, and then say would it be nothing to you, would it not be *all*, if you could but get back the simplicity, the fearlessness, the innocence, the friendliness and cheerfulness, the freedom from worldliness and care, the lordship over all things which you once knew; and get them back in even higher forms than those with which you were then familiar? Alas, we may well cry : 'And, O, for a man to arise in me,'—the new man, the childlike man, the man formed after the image of Christ,—'that the man I am may cease to be!' For it is to this man, it is to men of this Divine stamp, that the promise is given: 'A little child shall lead them,' since they too have become 'as a little child.'

And who that believes that this promise is to be fulfilled in the world at large; that, through the grace of God, all men are at last to carry in a manly mind and heart the spirit of a little child:—who can wonder at the raptures which that divine prospect kindled in the Prophet's breast? If we compare with the world as it is a world full of little children led by a little Child, a world, that is, full of spiritual men animated by the spirit of Christ, we shall no longer marvel at the songs and fairy tales of prophecy. It will only seem natural to us that in such a world as that the wolf should lie down with the lamb, and the leopard with the kid, and the lion eat straw like the ox. To such a race it is but reasonable that God should say: 'For brass I will bring gold, and for iron I will bring silver, and for wood brass, and for stones iron. I will also make thine officers Peace, and thy governors Righteousness. Violence shall no more be heard in the land, nor Destruction within thy borders; but thou shalt call thy walls Salvation and thy gates Praise. The sun shall no more be thy light by day, neither for brightness shall the moon give light unto thee; but the Lord shall be unto thee an everlasting light, and thy God thy glory. Thy sun shall no more go down, neither shall the moon withdraw itself; for the Lord shall be thine everlasting light, and the days of thy mourning shall be ended.'

X.

THE LIVING GOD OF LIVING MEN.

'But that the dead rise even Moses implied at the evergreen thorn-bush, when he calleth the Lord the God of Abraham, and God of Isaac, and God of Jacob. But he is not the God of dead men, but of living men; for all live unto him.'—St. Luke xx. 37, 38.

It would be difficult, if not impossible, to name three men so closely related to each other, and yet so conspicuously different from each other, as were Abraham, Isaac, and Jacob. Abraham is of the grandest heroic type—heroic in thought, in action, and, above all, in that faith which is the inspiration both of the highest thinking and of the noblest forms of conduct. More than any man of his time, more than most men of subsequent times, he believed in the sacred and august realities of the spiritual world, longed to possess himself of them, and was capable of making any sacrifice, facing any peril, in order that he might live in and by them. On all sides, by all the leading races of mankind, he is held to have been one of the grandest of men; his heroic stature is admitted; it is confessed that one of the most noble and momentous rôles in the human drama was committed to him.

But what a falling off is there in Isaac! He hardly seems his father's son. Quiet, thoughtful, a lover of ease and good fare, with no genius for action, his very wife chosen for him as if he were incompetent even to marry himself, unable to rule his own household, unable even to die, it would almost seem, when his time was come, he fades out of history years before he slips his mortal coil. His light, such as it was, is lost in his father's greater light; his story in the more stirring and eventful story of his sons. And yet, unlike to Abraham as he appears, he probably derived at least his thoughtfulness from him. Abraham is so great in action that we too much forget the originality and daring and power of his mind. Yet he who raised himself from the service of the multitudinous and cruel Gods of the ancient East to the worship of the one only and righteous Lord must have been gifted with rare mental powers; he must have known hours and days of patient and strenuous thought, and must have passed through a long and terrible conflict with doubt. The familiar tradition which represents him as successively worshipping the stars, the moon, the sun, and as saying when the stars vanished, the moon waned, the sun set, 'O my people! I like not gods that change and pass; henceforth I turn from these to Him who made the heavens and the earth,' sums up in a striking and memorable form the habit of bold and patient meditation which made Abraham so wise and great in action. And this habit of meditation Isaac seems to have derived from him, though in the son it took a more subdued and placid cast, answering to his less original and less enterprising nature.

Jacob, again, strikes one as unlike both his father and his grandfather. We think of him as timid, selfish, crafty, unscrupulous, with none of the innocence of Isaac, little or none of the splendid courage and generosity of Abraham. And yet, obviously, he derives his love of ease and quiet from his father; and, though less obviously yet quite as certainly, he derives his faith in spiritual realities, his craving to possess himself of them at any cost, from his grandfather. He is not free from great faults, like Isaac; he is not conspicuous for great and rare virtues, like Abraham: and yet both his father and his grandfather live again in him. Even his craft and duplicity, or at least the germs of them, were in Abraham, though in *him* we almost overlook them. Twice in his life 'the father of the faithful' exposed his wife to the gravest peril, and bade her lie in order to save himself from the danger involved in fidelity to truth. And if the sacrifice of Isaac was prompted, as many conclude that it was, by Abraham's desire to prove to himself that he loved the Creator more than the creature, and so to save his own soul alive, we may even see in him the very kind of subtlety, that selfish and sinful pursuit of *spiritual* gains and ends, which we reprobate in Jacob.

Still though, if we look for them, we can trace points of resemblance in the three men, we *have* to look for them before we discover them; though we can see the characteristics of Abraham reappearing in his descendants, our first, and perhaps also our last, thought about them is, that they greatly differ from each other, differ so greatly that Isaac hardly seems the son of Abraham, and Jacob hardly the son of Isaac. And what I want you to mark is the grace of God in calling Himself, as He did for more than a thousands years by the mouth of his servants the prophets, the God of each and all of these three men. Different as they were from each other, they are all dear to Him. He has room enough in his heart for them all.

That He should call Himself, the God of a man so pure and strong in will as Abraham, a man whose heart was set on aims so noble and lofty, may not surprise us. But that, with equal emphasis, He should call Himself the God of a man like Isaac, who seems hardly to have had any will of his own, and, still more, of a man like Jacob, whose will was crooked and perverse,—this surely is a grace which should both surprise and touch our hearts. For, though we may be less innocent, yet which of us is weaker than Isaac was, or more apt to drift on the tide of circumstance? though we may be less intensely set on spiritual aims than Jacob was, yet which of us is more selfish, more crafty and ungenerous, more apt to complicate spiritual with temporal aims, or to pursue them in a more crooked disingenuous way? If God is not ashamed to call Himself their God, may He not, will He not, be our God too, and train us as He trained them, till all that is weak and selfish and subtle in us is chastened out of us, and we recover the image in which He created us?

Rightly viewed, then, there is a great hope for us and for all men, and a most touching appeal, in the familiar phrase: 'I am the God of Abraham, the God of Isaac, and the God of Jacob.' No man, not even Abraham, is so great as to be beyond the need of God's love and care; and no man is too weak or too mean, not even Isaac or Jacob, to be beyond the reach of his care and love.

2. This is the first thought suggested to us by the passage before us. But there is another lesson in it, —the lesson evolved from this familiar phrase by our Lord Himself. The Pharisees of his time were not

content to accept any new truth unless they could find authority for it in the law that came by Moses. Many truths were floating in the air of their time which were not known by Moses, or were not distinctly taught by him,—such truths, for example, as the immortality of the soul, the resurrection of the body, and the retribution which follows on the deeds of men in the world to come. The Pharisees would not admit that such truths as these had been hidden from Moses, or hidden by him; and hence they found them in his teaching by the common and easy expedient of first putting them there: and that in two ways. First of all, they exposed his writings to what is called a spiritual and figurative interpretation, so bringing out of them what they would. And, then, they supplemented his writings by a vast oral tradition, the growth of many centuries, which they affirmed to be an accurate report of what he had said, though he had not taken the trouble of writing it down. Thus, by a double process, they made void the law, substituting the traditions of men for the commandments of God.

In a natural reaction against this double method of wresting the plain meaning of the Law, the Sadducees refused both the oral tradition of the Pharisees and their too subtle and ingenious methods of interpretation. They themselves held, indeed, that all truth was contained in the law of Moses; they too were unwilling to believe any truths uncertified by him: but they insisted on taking his words in their plain honest sense. And as, taken thus, they found no disclosure in them of the resurrection of the body, or of the life to come, they rejected these doctrines as the inventions of men, as a late and incredible addition to the teaching of Moses. They said to their rivals: 'Find us a plain text in Moses which, when honestly read, affirms a life to come, and we will discuss the doctrine with you; but till then you have not a foot to stand upon.' And the Pharisees had been unable to meet this challenge. They had searched the writings of Moses for some such text as the Sadducees demanded; but, so far as I can learn, they had discovered none. It is easy, therefore, to imagine their delight when our Lord confounded the Sadducees by adducing such a text. If the text does not seem very plain or conclusive to us, let us remember that it appeared quite conclusive both to the Sadducees and to the Pharisees; and that even to us it may suggest the very grounds on which the natural hope of immortality rests in our hearts.

The text our Lord quoted was this:—To Moses *at the Bush*,—between four and five hundred years, that is, after Abraham, Isaac, and Jacob were dead—Jehovah had said, 'I *am*'—not, I was—'the God of

Abraham, and of Isaac, and of Jacob.' But how could He still be the God of these men if they had long been extinct? He is not the God of dead men, but of living men. The three Patriarchs were very certainly not living in this world when God spoke to Moses. They must, therefore have been living in some other world. Dead to men, they must have been alive unto God. Obviously, then, men do not all die when they die. After death their souls live on. And as for the resurrection of the body, what does that mean but that, as man is compact of body and spirit, if the whole man is to survive the dissolution of death, then to his living soul there must at some time be added a living body?

To us, as I have admitted, this text and the argument founded on it may not seem conclusive. It may sound like a mere verbal quibble; it may only remind us how little there was in the Old Testament to suggest the life to come when even our Lord Himself could find in it no better proof-text than this. I am by no means sure that we do this text justice if we regard it thus. But, however we regard it, we must, I think, admit that it was admirably suited to the purpose for which our Lord adduced it. The Sadducees were as rigid and literal in their interpretations of Scripture as the Pharisees, though they were much more honest. They demanded a text which, read and interpreted by their own method, affirmed or implied a future life. Christ found them such a text. And the Sadducees have nothing to allege against it, or against his interpretation of it; while the Pharisees are charmed with it, so charmed that they press round Him to compliment Him on his profound knowledge of the Law and his singular dialectical skill: 'Thou hast *well* said.' And from their point of view, as from that of the Sadducees, He *had* said well. He had convinced them out of their own Scriptures, found the text they had sought for in vain, and produced the very kind of argument that would bite into their minds most deeply since it fell in with their canons and modes of interpretation.

3. Possibly if Christ had been arguing *with us*, meeting our doubts and objections, He would also have said well, though He might have uttered very different words and adopted a very different method. But even from these words I believe we may gather real and sure grounds for hope: and that in two ways.

(1.) Because our Lord saw in God the God of Abraham, and Isaac, and Jacob, He inferred that these men could not die; that even when they did die, they must have lived on unto God. And that after all is, I suppose, the argument or conviction on which we all really base our hope of immortality. Some good and able men doubt, indeed, whether *all* men are to live for ever. They can find no clear revelation of the natural and inherent immortality of the human soul, either in the structure of the soul itself or in the teaching of the New Testament. But the unsophisticated common sense of the vast majority of men responds to the courage with which the prophet Habakkuk leaps to the conclusion: 'Art *Thou* not from everlasting, O Lord my God, mine Holy One? *We* shall not die.' The eternity of God implies the immortality of man. We cannot, or cannot easily, believe that the Great Father of our spirits has called us into being only that we may cease to be when this saddened and imperfect life is over. It is as repugnant to reason as it is fatal to trust and hope to believe that our Father will leave Himself childless when time shall be no more, or even destitute of human children, or even permit vast multitudes of his children to fade away into nothingness and extinction. We were not made to die, but to live. We have capacities which are not developed, or are only partially developed, when we pass out of this world; and in these latent capacities we find a proof that another and a higher sphere of life and training lies before us. If God be our God, He will not suffer us to perish before our character is formed, while we are still capable of becoming what He would have us be, and of meeting his love with ours: and still less will He suffer us to perish when our character is formed, and we stand before Him complete in righteousness and charity, bearing his image, reflecting his glory. What father *would* let his children perish if he could help it, and be left solitary and alone? And why should the Father of us all suffer any one of us to be 'cast as rubbish to the void' if at least He can make anything better than 'rubbish' of us? Because He lives, we shall live also.

This is our main ground for hope, for faith, in the life to come; and this is the ground on which Christ here plants this hope. God is still the God of Abraham and of Isaac and of Jacob; and therefore they cannot be dead; they must still be alive.

(2.) But our Lord at least reminds us by his words of another ground for hope. Nature has many symbols which speak of a life capable of passing through death, a life which grows in volume, in power, in beauty, by its submission to death. Every spring we behold the annual miracle by which the natural world is renewed into a richer lovelier life. Year by year it emerges from its wintry tomb into the fuller and more fruitful life of summer. And I have often thought it a very kindly providence—at least to us on this side the world—which placed the resurrection of Christ, his triumph over death, in the genial spring time that speaks to us by so many voices of a life over which death has no power, save to beautify and enrich it. We may not care to base any very weighty arguments on these delicate and evanescent yet continually-recurring symbols; but, nevertheless, they speak to our imagination and our hearts with a force and a winning persuasiveness beyond that of logic. The hope of immortality, and even of a resurrection from the dead, has been fed and sustained in myriads of hearts by the symbolism of the gracious springtide. And of one of these gracious natural symbols our Lord puts us in remembrance, when He speaks of God appearing to Moses *in the Bush*. For this bush was a kind of acacia shrub resembling our bramble or our blackberry bush; but with this notable difference, that it was *an evergreen*, that its leaves did not wither and fade. And the evergreen, untouched by death and decay, has been regarded by many races as a symbol of the continuous and unbroken life of man, of his proper immortality.

So that, in this passage, we have our main argument for immortality, viz., the pledge implied in God's eternity, the reasoned and reasonable conviction that so long as our Father lives He will not let his children die; and are also reminded of those natural symbols which whisper the hope of immortality to us with most eloquent and persuasive voices.

4. Finally. Besides the lessons we have already learned from these words—the first, that God is the God of all men, however different from each other they may be; and the second, that God our Father will never let his children die—there is still a third lesson to be gathered from this passage. For surely we may adopt our Saviour's *method* of argument, and by varying the application of it reach with entire safety a still more recondite conclusion than his. He argues, as we have seen, that since God was still the God of Abraham, Isaac, and Jacob long years after they were dead, they cannot be dead, but must be still alive. And what is to hinder us from arguing that, if God is still their God, and they still live unto Him, then God must even now be carrying on the discipline and training which He commenced upon them here, and carrying it on to still larger and happier issues? If they live, and live unto God, must they not be moving into a closer fellowship with Him, rising to a more hearty adoption of his will, a fuller participation of his righteousness and love?

No one of you will question the validity of such an argument as that, I think. You will all gladly admit that, since *he* still lives, Abraham must by this time be a far greater and nobler man than he was when he left the earth, and must be engaged in far nobler discoveries and enterprises. You will all admit that, since he still lives, and lives unto God, Isaac has grown more like his father,—less weak, less timid, more capable of action, of authority, of service. You will all be glad to think that, since he also still lives and lives unto God, Jacob has purged himself of his old sins, has lost every trace of mean and selfish craft, has grown honest, and frank, and bold. And you will all, I trust, gather from this conviction a firmer and more animating hope for yourselves and for one another. For if God be your God, and if when you die to men you will still live unto Him, then *your* training and discipline will be carried on and completed in the world to come. Your virtues and graces, now so weak and ill-balanced and insecure, will gather strength, proportion, certainty; your faults now, as you sorrowfully admit, so many and so heinous and so inconquerable, will gradually fall off from you, until your Father can look into your faces and see in every one of them some fair and perfect, if miniature, reflection of his image.

O, it is a great hope! a most animating and sustaining hope! And if we indulge in it for ourselves, shall we not also cherish it for the world at large?

'Willingly, gladly would we cherish it if we might: but may we?'

May we not? I reply. All *our* hopes of immortality, or all at which we have glanced this morning, are grounded on the fact that we are God's children, and that therefore He will not let us die, and on the sweet and tender symbolisms of Nature which speak of life through death and beyond it. And are not *all* men God's children as well as we, with capacities not half developed when they pass out of our view? Does not Nature speak to *them* with a voice as authentic and tender as that in which she appeals to us? And what says Christ Himself in the very passage before us? He says: 'God is not the God of dead men, but of living men; for *all* (that is, both the dead and the living) *live unto Him.*' None of us know so much, whether of the will of God, or of the world to come, as Christ knew. You hear what He says,—that *all* men, even after death, live, live and are trained by the Father of their spirits. Let others limit the scope of his words, if they will; but as for us, let us wholly and gladly commit ourselves to them, and heartily believe that in ways we know not, by a discipline ' beyond the reaches of our thoughts,' God will not only keep all men in being, but will also quicken and train them unto life everlasting.

XI.

DEATH AN EXODUS.

'And, behold, there were talking with him two men, who were none other than Moses and Elijah; who appeared in glory, and talked of his exodus which he should accomplish at Jerusalem.'—St. Luke ix. 30, 31.

It is difficult to say whether the transfiguration of our Lord is, or is not, to be reckoned among the miracles of the New Testament. If He was what He claimed to be, what those who knew Him best acknowledged Him to be, 'the Son of the Living God,' while we confess his transfiguration to be 'a sign,' we need hardly account it 'a wonder.' For who has not seen even a homely face transfigured under the stress of some intense and sublime emotion? Who has not seen the inner beauty of the nature lend a strange exaltation and loveliness even to those whose powers, originally very limited, had been trained and refined by but little culture and a narrow experience? Where is the wonder, then, if the inner glory of the Perfect Man, who was also 'very God,' should so shine forth at a moment when He was wrapt in a Divine Communion, when He was deliberately bracing Himself to give his life a ransom for the world, when, stedfastly contemplating the end which was to crown his work, his spirit was stirred within Him to its utmost depths? Where is the wonder, I say, if, under the stress of emotions so profound, 'the fashion of his countenance was altered,' and the inner glory of a nature immeasurably superior to ours shone out, rendering his whole person luminous, irradiating it with a glory so intense that it penetrated the very garments He wore, and made them 'white and glistening'? The wonder is, rather, that his glory, 'the glory as of the only begotten of the Father,' could so often, and so long, be suppressed.

The Transfiguration, as reported by St. Luke, presents three phases or features. There is, first, the personal glorification of the Man Christ Jesus; and, second, the apparition of Moses and Elijah; and, third, the utterance of the Divine voice, the testimony borne by the Eternal Father to the character and claims of his beloved Son. It is to the second of these phases, or, rather, it is to a single point in this strange and significant event, that I am about to direct your thoughts.

St. Luke's report of it is contained in my text. It is very graphic, very picturesque, though so brief.

He opens it with the exclamation, 'Behold!' to express the suddenness of the Apparition: to express also the surprise with which the Apostles, suddenly wakened from sleep by the glory that shone round about them, became aware that the Man whom they knew and loved was no longer, as they had left Him, alone, but was conferring with Visitants from another and a higher sphere. As if sharing and reflecting the experience of the eye-witnesses of the scene, the Evangelist does not at once name Moses and Elijah. He says only that '*two men*' were talking with Him, —the very form of his phrase implying that they had been talking with Him before the Disciples awoke; that they awoke only in the middle of a long earnest conference, and were naturally, therefore, dazed and perplexed by what they saw and heard. Then, with a strong accent of surprise, he adds, '*who were*,' who proved to be as the talk went on, '*none other than Moses and Elijah!*' Then, as if to account for the difficulty the Apostles experienced in recognizing men so familiar to their thoughts, he subjoins: 'they appeared *in glory*.' And, finally, he gives us the theme of their conversation: 'they talked of *the decease*' literally, of *the exodus*—'which he was about to accomplish at Jerusalem.'

In short, if we read it carefully, with a quickened imagination, St. Luke transports us to the very scene, and enables us to share in the awe and perplexity and surprise of those who witnessed it.

But here, again, I must limit myself. There is much even in this section of St. Luke's report which we must lay aside and pass by if a manageable topic and an effective impression on our thoughts is to be secured. But there is nothing, I think, in that which we must leave untouched more striking, more suggestive, or more consolatory than the new and distinctively Christian idea of death presented to us in the conversation of Moses and Elijah with their Lord and ours. For what it comes to is this: that all three of these august speakers,—that is to say, even if we put it at the lowest, three of the very greatest men in whom our race has flowered, the greatest Lawgiver, the greatest Prophet, the greatest Teacher and Saviour—regard death *as an exodus;* and talk familiarly of it under this figure, as if *that* were the spiritual and heavenly mode of regarding it. Seen from beneath, seen from earth and time, death may be an appalling darkness haunted by terrors of which the loathsome accidents of the tomb are but the faintest type; but seen from above, seen from heaven and eternity, death is a boon, a joy, an emancipation from the house of our bondage, an exodus or going out, a journey to a large land and a good, a land flowing with milk and honey.

This is the conception to which I shall ask you to confine your attention; for surely, though it be so small a part of the story of the Transfiguration, it is sufficient to engage your thoughts and to illuminate them with the hues of wonder, joy, and praise,—sufficient even to uphold you in the prospect of death, and to comfort you under the pangs of bereavement.

1. And it is strange how much, when we reflect on it, we can find in that great scene 'on the holy Mount' to illustrate this conception, and to impress it on our minds. Look, first, at the speakers—Moses, Elijah, Christ. Was not the death of Moses an exodus? A sacred mystery hangs over the decease of 'the Man of God.' All we are told of it in Holy Writ is that, while his 'eye was not dim nor his natural force abated,' the Lord took him up into a mountain to die, and buried him in the untrodden recesses of a lofty mountain-valley undiscovered, undiscoverable even to the searching and inquisitive eye of love, so that 'no man knoweth of his sepulchre unto this day.' The whole world has felt that his death is wrapt in impenetrable mystery, that he did not die as others die. And the Jewish rabbis, striving to penetrate that mystery, fondly fable that, when Moses saw the grave which the Lord had prepared for him, he trembled to enter it; and that in his com-

passion Jehovah promised that, if he would stretch himself in it, He, Jehovah, would kiss him on the mouth and draw his soul out of him in that supreme embrace. 'He who died by the kiss of the Eternal' is a not infrequent synonym for Moses in the Rabbinical schools. But, whatever the mode of his death, the Church has always and naturally believed that Moses, or the spirit of Moses, was instantly translated to the very presence of the Almighty; that, like Enoch, 'he was not, because God took him' to Himself.

Elijah, again, was rapt, we are told, and carried up into heaven, as by a whirling cloud of fiery chariots,—the fire symbolizing, I suppose, the purification which even his great and burning spirit required before it could be admitted to the Divine Presence; and the swift chariots and still swifter whirlwind the immediateness, the instantaneousness, of the process by which he was purified, transfigured, made meet to take his place among the saints in light.

If, therefore, any of the sons of men should be permitted to pass from the spiritual world to hold converse with Christ in the moment of his glory, these were the 'two men' whom we should expect to hear talking with Him on the Mount; and that not only because they were the most illustrious of his predecessors in the great work of teaching and saving the world, but also because they had already and fully achieved the exodus or journey of death, and had passed into the large fair land beyond.

'They talked with him of the exodus he should accomplish at Jerusalem.' Did they talk with Him for our learning alone, or also for their own, and even for his? It would be to rob the scene of all force and naturalness and dignity were we to conceive of it as an histrionic performance, a spectacle arranged simply for our instruction. Let us be sure, therefore, that Moses and Elijah gained much from their communion with Him, and that even He gained much from his communion with them. It is not well or wise to draw sharp lines of distinction between Heaven and earth, or even between God and the men who are made in his image and likeness, as though they were far off from each other, divided by impassable gulfs, or even by gulfs so wide and deep that they are rarely passed. Heaven lies all about us, and may be within us. God is not far from any one of us; in many of us, I trust, He has taken up a constant and eternal abode. If the Man Christ Jesus could be strengthened by an angel out of heaven, why should He not be both strengthened and comforted by 'the spirits of just men made perfect,' of men gifted and honoured as Moses and Elijah had been and were? They must have had much to tell Him of their experience of death, of how they had found it but a brief fiery passage to the Eternal Love and Home. And why should not they, while strengthening and comforting Him by recounting their own strange and glorious experience, have also learned much from his larger wisdom, his diviner and more glorious doom? He was to pass into the upper world by the way of the Cross, not in state and splendour, but in humiliation and pain; not in a whirlwind and chariots of fire as one whom God delighted to honour, but on the accursed tree, as one abandoned by God, as one whom even men rejected and despised. He was not to die 'by the kiss of the Eternal,' nor was He to be buried by the hands of Jehovah, but to be killed by 'his own' who would not let Him save them, and to be laid in a grave He owed to the kindness of a friend who was so little of a friend that he would not confess Him before men, by the hands of men and women who were even less to the world than He Himself. And as they talked together of this strange, agonizing, shameful 'decease,' might not Elijah well learn that there was a still more excellent glory than that of being carried up into heaven by the chariots of God; that to renounce such a triumphant exodus from this world of sin and strife, to condemn oneself to die in ignominy, amid the execrations of men and the hiding of the Father's face, in order that the strife of the world might be composed and its sin taken away, was still nobler, far more heavenly and divine, than to be taken up to God and leave the world to its fate? Might not Moses learn that to be made sin for sinful men, to pass out of the world with every sign of being forsaken of God and hated by man, was an end, an exodus, still more sublime than to die 'by the kiss of the Eternal' and to be mourned for 'for thirty days' by a bereaved and inconsolable world?

And what shall *we* learn from the exodus accomplished at Jerusalem? We may learn from it all that Moses and Elijah learned, and more. For if we possessed only the record of their last end, though we might see that to them death was but a joyful exodus from bondage, from the hampering conditions of time and sense, into the large freedom and abiding peace of the better country, even the heavenly; yet how could we hope that *we* should be called to take the path they trod and share the honour conferred on them? We could not expect it; nor, enormous and all-pervading as is our conceit of ourselves, could we account ourselves worthy either to die by the kiss of God and be buried by his hands, or to have his chariots sent down to convey us to his high abode. But when we consider the exodus of Christ—his death of shame, desertion, reproach—then we may surely take heart for ourselves. For in Him we are taught that no conditions can be so mean and painful, no death so lonely and clouded, but that it may be, if we will and if God will, a glorious emancipation from all evil, a sublime and triumphant journey to the peaceful and fruitful land of which God Himself is the Sun and the Shield. It was not in state, but in great humility, not in honour but in shame, not in the embrace of God but 'forsaken' by God, not wept and bewailed by men but reviled and cursed by men, that the Lord Jesus set out on the great pilgrimage which we too must soon take; and yet He was, and is, the one true Victor over death and the grave. His death was the most noble, the most heroic, the most far-reaching and blessed in its influences that the world has ever seen or will see; for He died from pure love to men, died to take away the sin of the world, died that we and all men might live. And if we love and follow Him we need not doubt that we shall be 'made partakers of his death' in this high sense,—that for us, as for Him, death will be an exodus, a journey home. If those whom we loved, and love, but have lost for a while, were humble followers of Him, we need not doubt that, as they shared in his humiliation, so also they will, and do, share in his glory; that for them the journey is over, that they have arrived in that great home in which a place is being prepared for us, and in which, therefore, we shall be reunited to them for ever.

Let no man fear death, then. Let no man weep for the dead. It is life, rather, that we ought to fear. It is for ourselves that we need to weep, and for what we have lost in losing them.

2. The more we study this conception of death the more instructive and suggestive we shall find it to be. As I have already said, we cannot but assume that if, on an occasion so sacred and by personages so illustrious, death was spoken of as an exodus, this figure must be taken as indicating one of the most spiritual and adequate conceptions of death our thoughts can grasp. And I suppose that the event, the illustration which this figure first suggests to all our minds, and which it was intended to suggest, is the exodus of Israel from Egypt. But if we consider what that exodus was and implies, if we then proceed to infer that death will be to us very much what their exodus was to the captive Hebrew race, we shall reach some thoughts of death, and of the life that follows death, which can hardly fail to be new and helpful to us.

The exodus from Egypt was a transition from bondage to freedom, from grinding and unrequited toil to comparative rest, from ignorance to knowledge, from shame to honour, from a life distracted by care and pain and fear to a life in which men were fed by the immediate bounty of God, guided by his wisdom, guarded by his omnipotence, consecrated to his service. And if *death* be an exodus, if that is the truest and highest conception of it we can frame, then we may say that, by the gate and avenue of death, *we* shall pass from bondage to freedom, from toil to rest, from shame to honour, from ignorance to knowledge, from a life too often conditioned by care and pain and fear to a life which God Himself will guide and cherish and protect; and, in fine, to a life in which we shall be drawn into immediate and habitual fellowship with Him. Then, too, we may and must believe that the friends who have left us, dying in the faith of Christ, have already passed into the ampler happier conditions which death will bring to us when we follow them from this world to the next. The very word *exodus*, therefore, as applied to death, when used as a synonym of death, throws what to many minds is a new, what to all our minds is a most welcome and auspicious, light into the darkness whether of dissolution or of bereavement. It is impossible for us to stedfastly regard death in this light without feeling how blessed are the dead who have died in the Lord; without feeling also that, though life must be good for us so long as God bids us live, death will be better still because it will conduct us to a better life. It ought to make new men of us that, being delivered from that fear of death which hath torment, we can press resolutely on to the end of our course, knowing that what we call our 'last end,' will really be the beginning of a new and happier course.

And it is with no desire to limit and restrain the strength and joy which such a conception of death must naturally kindle in your hearts, it is rather with a desire to enhance and complete your joy in it, that I ask you to bear in mind that, after the exodus, nay, even after they were at home in the goodly land, the men of Israel did not cease to learn, nor cease from labour, nor sink into any mere easy and slothful delight. Even when they were in the land that flowed with milk and honey, to eat honey and drink milk was not their sole, nor even their main, employ. On the contrary, they had never learned so much, never laboured so hard, never grown so fast in the knowledge and obedience of the Divine Will. And, in like manner, we may be sure that the journey of death will land us in no easy ignoble Paradise, in which all real advance will have come to a close, where we may lie on grassy meads and pluck a new fruit every month from the tree that grows in the midst of the garden. No such lazy and degrading Eden could satisfy us for a moment, or for more than a moment. It is the very joy and charm of the Christian heaven that it will yield an ampler scope to all our powers; that we shall be still and for ever acquainting ourselves more fully with the works and wonders of God, still and for ever growing into a more complete and sustained harmony with his will, still and for ever developing and exercising new energies and faculties for serving Him in serving our fellows. The sweetest moments of our life on earth have been spent in acquiring knowledge, in learning wisdom, in shewing love and receiving it, in active enterprises to benefit our neighbours, and in the consciousness that we were serving and pleasing God our Father in all we learned and achieved. And it would be but a poor tale if we had to leave these pure and supreme joys behind us when we die. So far from leaving them behind us, we shall continue to enjoy them in purer nobler forms, being made like to those happy angels who excel in strength because they do the commandments of God and hearken to the voice of his word.

This, then, is the Christian conception of death: that it is an exodus to the land of life eternal, in which land all that is fair and good here will be seen and enjoyed in its ideal forms. When men come to us and ask: 'What is death? and what lies beyond it?' we are not driven to reply, 'Death is the end of all; you must look for nothing beyond it save to be cherished in the memory and affection of those whom you leave behind you.' And if we are not driven to the despair of that Atheism which doubts whether life is worth living and is quite sure that the grave is our goal, so neither are we limited to the narrow and irrational forecasts of many who are of the household of faith. We need not and cannot reply: 'Death will take you to a land of indolent and sensual delights in which, clothed in white and wearing a golden crown, you will wander through shady groves and beside purling streams, singing sweet songs and striking the sounding harp, incurious of all that may lie beyond, untroubled by the trouble of the lost.' We can appeal to all that is manly, to all that is highest, most loving, most noble and heroic, in the nature of man, and assure them that the narrow avenue of death will open out into a land in which they will for ever be learning new lessons of larger wisdom, for ever cultivating and developing all pure and noble energies, faculties, affections, for ever finding some new task in which they may at once serve their fellows and worship the God who is the Lord because He is the Minister of all.

Into that happy land may God gather us all in his good time; and, in the meantime, grant that the promise and hope of an exodus into it may pluck the sting from death, and lend a new sanctity and a new beauty to the life we now live in the flesh.

XII.

ON SERVING GOD WITH ONE SHOULDER.

'For then will I turn to the nations a pure lip, that they may all invoke the name of the Lord, and serve him with one shoulder.'
ZEPHANIAH iii. 9.

'*Then*'! *When?* In the day, as we learn from the previous Verse, in which God has risen up to pour out all the heat of his fury on the nations and kingdoms of the earth, until 'the whole earth be consumed by the fire of his zeal.'

Now there is no question which more frequently and deeply frets our hearts than this: What is the meaning, what the intention, of the innumerable miseries by which we are tormented? What is the true function of the sufferings of which the world is full? And there is no answer to that question which more commends itself to men who have had long and thoughtful experience of human life than this: The miseries of men are intended to purify and elevate them, to make them perfect; springing from their sins, they are designed to correct their sins, and to lead them to the love and pursuit of righteousness.

It would seem that God deals with us as the goldsmith deals with virgin ore. When the smith takes a piece of fine gold in hand that he may work it into artistic form and beauty, he tempers it with an alloy, and thus makes it hard enough to endure 'the file's tooth and the hammer's rap' and the keen edge of the graver. When the work is done, when the vessel is duly moulded, chased, embossed, he washes it in 'the proper fiery acid,' which eats out the base alloy, and leaves the pure gold untouched. No grain of the precious metal is lost; but its value is indefinitely enhanced by the artistic labour bestowed upon it. And thus God deals with us; thus He moulds our nature, in which the pure heaven-derived spirit is blended with the alloy of the baser 'carnal mind,' into 'vessels of honour.' The miseries and calamities which come upon us are but as the edge of the graving-tool, the rap of the hammer, the grating teeth of the file. By these He gradually and patiently carries out his conception of us, his purpose in us. And, at last, like the fiery acid which separates the base alloy from the pure gold, death comes to divide the carnal in us from the spiritual, and to reveal the beauty and value of the character which the Divine Artist has wrought in and upon us.

'Cure sin, and you cure sorrow,' say the reason and the conscience of man. *And the sorrow comes that the sin may be cured,* adds the Word of God. The miseries that spring from sin are intended to eradicate the sins from which they spring. All the fire of God's wrath against evil is to be poured out on the nations in order that He may 'turn to the nations a pure lip,' and lead them to serve Him 'with one shoulder.'

The Mercy of Judgment, then, is the Prophet's theme in the Verse before us. He is sure that God's intention in punishing men is to redeem them from their insincerities, their idolatries, their impurities; to work in them a pure heart, for 'out of the abundance of the heart the lip speaks,' and to draw them into that service in which alone they can truly rest. And he states his thesis in terms so bold and large as to warn us against a too literal interpretation of the words of isolated Scriptures. Read the eighth Verse of this Chapter as many read those passages in which the future punishment or destruction of the impenitent is affirmed, and what room do you leave for the gracious assurance of Verse nine? In the former Verse you read of an indignation, a fierce anger, to be poured out on 'the nations,' and 'the kingdoms,' of a fire in which 'all the earth' shall be devoured or consumed. What words could seem more final and conclusive? what words could more emphatically teach the utter and universal destruction of the whole sinful race? And yet, in the very next Verse, we learn that this terrible, and apparently final, destruction is to issue in *the redemption* of the whole race to the love and service of God—all men are to have a pure lip, all to serve the Lord with one shoulder! Let us be careful how we read the Scriptures, then; let us read them with the spirit and with the understanding, and not after the mere letter: let us read them as a whole, looking for the large general principles they contain, and not drawing out momentous doctrines from the narrow apertures of scattered or isolated texts.

But it is to the image of the final clause of my text —and they shall serve God *with one shoulder*—that I wish mainly to direct your attention. It is a very simple image or illustration, but it will yield us ample themes for thought.

The image the Prophet had in his mind was that of a number of men bearing a single burden. If they are to bear it without strain or distress, they must walk with even or level shoulders, no one of them shirking his part of the task, each of them keeping step with the rest: in short, they must stand and move as if they had but '*one* shoulder' among them. Only thus can they move freely and happily, and make the burden as little burdensome as possible to each and to all. This image, taken from common life, picked up, as it were, in the streets or highways, the Prophet transfers to the moral and spiritual domain. The law of God is a burden which all men have to bear; it rests on the shoulders of the whole world. Men can only bear it without strain or distress of spirit as each of them freely assumes it, as they all help each other to bear it, as they pace together under it with a willing and happy consent of obedience. It is for this end that we are judged and corrected of the Lord, viz., that we *may* serve Him with one shoulder, and thus make his yoke easy and his burden light.

Three thoughts are suggested by this image: (1) That the Divine Law is a burden which men are reluctant to assume; (2) that the true freedom consists in a willing assumption of this burden, a cheerful and unforced obedience to the Divine Law: and (3) that the happiness of obedience depends on its unanimity and universality; when *all* obey, obedience will be easy to all.

(1.) *The Law of God is a burden which men are reluctant to assume.* Is not that true? Does it need proof? Is it not notorious that of those who know and approve that law many decline to obey it, to make it the regulative power of their lives; while even those who are most profoundly convinced that the will of God, as expressed in his law, is a good and kind will, a will which moves in the light of an eternal Wisdom at the prompting of an infinite Love, too often fail in their obedience and prefer their own will to his? Do not we ourselves find it hard to cross our wills, though we know them to be erring and imperfect wills, driven to and fro by gusts of passion and caprice, in order to adopt the pure and stedfast Will that rules the universe? It *is* hard— hard even when that Will assumes its most gracious and inviting forms. The will of God is never so full of grace and attraction for us as when it is incarnated in the life of the man Christ Jesus, and breathes through the words of Him who came 'to publish to mankind the law of love.' When He who laid down his life for us says, 'Do this,' then, if ever, we try to do it. And yet even then it is hard. He Himself felt that it would be hard for us. In some of the tenderest words that fell from his lips He cried: 'Come unto me, all ye that labour and are heavy laden, and I will give you rest.' But the rest He has to offer is, after all, the rest of obedience. And this obedience, or the law we are to obey, He admits to be *a yoke* to our unruly passions, *a burden* to our stubborn necks. All he pleads is that *his* yoke is the easiest of yokes, his burden the lightest of burdens; and that by patiently enduring them we shall infallibly find rest to our souls.

And to our selfwill it is hard, and cannot but be hard, to submit even to the purest and tenderest will. Take any of the most distinctively Christian precepts, and you will see at once that, reasonable and beautiful as they are in themselves, there is nevertheless that in us which resents and rebels against them. *Love them that hate you; Bless them that curse you; Do good to them that injure you; Forgive them that trespass against you:* these are among the commandments which we have received of the Lord. They simply express ruling principles of his own daily life. As we listen to them we consent to them as good; as we see them incarnated in the lovely deeds of his perfect life we cannot sufficiently admire them. We can see that, were all men to obey them, heaven would come down to earth. We sigh and yearn for the time in which they will receive an universal obedience. But, none the less, we ourselves find it hard, almost impossible, to obey them to-day. We delight in the law of Christ after the inward man; but we find another law in our members, warring against the law of our mind. And how can we enter into 'rest' while this strife in our nature is maintained, while by the flesh we are drawn toward 'the law of sin,' and by the spirit toward 'the law of the Spirit of life?' We can only find rest as we impose a yoke on the flesh with its passions and lusts, and compel them to bear the burden of obedience to the higher law. In the flesh, or in the spirit, we *must* suffer. The only option before us is—in which? If the flesh conquer, the spirit groans and strives in a defeat which it will never acknowledge to be final; if the spirit conquer, the flesh *will* at times break out into flat mutiny and rebellion. In either case it is *we* who suffer; it is *our* spirit that frets in dishonourable and intolerable bondage, or it is *our* flesh that rebels against the yoke of the spirit.

Of course it is the flesh which ought to be subdued and made to serve. But that is a dreary household in which the servants are for ever trying to elude our vigilance, to thwart our will, to injure our best and dearest interests. And that is a dreary life in which 'the mind of the flesh,' all in us that holds by the visible and the temporal, has to be incessantly watched, coerced, held in with bit and bridle, lest it should debase and injure us. In such a life there can be no freedom, no dignity, no peace. The spirit, which has to maintain a sleepless vigilance and endeavour, is well-nigh as much a slave as the flesh which it watches. It can know no security, find no repose.

What shall we do, then, what can we do, that we may enter into rest? Shall we let the flesh have its way? Or, to put the question more fairly, shall we let these weak wavering wills of ours be the sport of the impulses, now good and now evil, which rise within us, and try to be content with yielding at one time to the flesh and at another time to the spirit? So base a content is, happily, impossible to us. We cannot be content while there is division, discord, in our life, while we are torn by conflicting impulses. We *must* get unity into our life, we must have one ruling aim to which all other and inferior aims are subordinated, before we can be at peace.

(2.) Nay, more: we must get freedom into our life if we are to get peace: and *we can only attain freedom as, with cheerful and unforced accord, we assume the burden of the Divine Law*, doing the will of God from the heart. Sooner or later self-will makes us hateful both to ourselves and to our neighbours. It renders us incapable both of social, and of spiritual, life. Let a man follow the vagrant and fluctuating impulses of his own complex nature, acknowledging no higher will than his own, no law which he is bound to obey, and he becomes a burden to himself and to all about him. You can see it at once in extreme cases. Let a lad think only of himself, of his own preferences and pleasures; let him take his own way, and insist on taking it even when, in order to take it, he must thwart the will of his parents, and make himself the tyrant of his schoolfellows and playmates;

let him strut, and domineer, and rebel, the mere fool of his own caprice, the mere toy of his own whims and cravings, and you see at once that, in asserting his freedom, he has sunk into a cruel bondage; that, in seeking pleasure, he has made himself utterly miserable. His very goodness is not good, because there is no law in it, and therefore no stability. His very love is all but worthless, for it is the offspring of caprice, and changes with his changing mood. And a wilful man is at least as much a slave as a wilful lad, and as great a nuisance. You cannot count on him. He cannot even count on himself. Till he curtails his natural liberty, he has no true liberty. Till he cheerfully yields to the restraints and respects the sanctions of law—the law of the land, the laws of business and of social intercourse—he is for ever clashing with his neighbours, for ever coming under their censure and incurring the penalties by which they enforce respect for established order and rule. He cannot make himself lord of the whole world. He cannot impose his will on his fellows and rivals, who consider that they have as clear a right to their will as he to his. Any man who sets himself against the world will soon find that the world has even a stronger will than he, and is more competent to enforce it. We *must* take up some burden, then. We must bear some yoke. We must submit to some law on pain of finding our hand against every man's, and every man's hand against us.

Here, again, only one option is before us. We cannot say that we will yield to no law; that choice is not open to us. All we can do is to choose the law to which we will yield. And if we take counsel only of reason and experience, even these will teach us that the law of God—and the law of man in so far as it expresses the will of God—is the law which it will be wise of us to accept. For, despite occasional appearances to the contrary, this is the law which really rules in human affairs. Other laws, adverse to the will of God, may gain a passing vogue and authority; but in the end, in the long run, the will of God prevails, and must prevail, over all the wills and laws and customs of men. So that, if we would enter into a true security and an enduring rest, we must make his will our will.

And even then our task is not complete. It is not enough that we *yield* to the will of God; we must heartily and cheerfully adopt it if we are to be free. Not only must we see that it will be prudent of us to make his will our law, since at last his will must be done; we must also passionately love that will if, in obeying it, we are to walk at liberty. For, as we have seen, obedience involves self-denial, self-sacrifice. To adopt another will than our own, to defer to it, to cross our passions and desires that we may keep it, is to bear a burden which will often seem heavy to us, to come under a yoke that will often seem hard. There is but one way in which we can make the hard yoke easy, and the heavy burden light. And, happily, it is a way with which we are all familiar; it is the excellent way of charity, of love. What pain will not a mother cheerfully endure for the sake of her child, even taking the strangest pleasure in the sacrifices she makes for it? What burden of toil and care will not the husband cheerfully carry for a beloved wife? When a true and pure affection has been kindled in the soul, the most difficult tasks grow easy. The most sacred of bonds is the very gate of liberty. And hence the incarnation and ministry of Christ are of such inexpressible value to us. The law of God never shews so fair as when we see it embodied in Him. The will of God is never so gracious and winning as when it flows from his lips. Apart from Him we learn, in time, that God's will must be done—to our hurt or to our advantage, in our condemnation or in our salvation. But, in Him, we learn that God's will *is* our salvation, that He loves us with an everlasting love, and can never cease to seek our welfare. And we love Him who so loved us as to live, and teach, and die for our instruction and redemption. Loving Him, we love the Will

He lived to do, and which He entreats us to do. That Will becomes beautiful to us, preferable to our own. It was obedience to that Will which made Christ what He was; and if obedience to that Will will make us like Him, how can we but resolve to do it at any cost? How can we fail to take delight in the labours and sacrifices by which we are conformed to Him and made partakers of his divine nature?

Thus we take up our freedom. We 'walk at large' precisely because we 'keep his commandments.' *Love* makes the burden light, the yoke easy; and, because we bear them willingly, we find rest to our souls.

(3.) But even so our rest is not perfect. *We have become a law unto ourselves by our cheerful adoption of the will of God. We are free, therefore.* But it does not follow that, because we are free we are also happy. *The happiness of obedience depends largely on the unanimity and the universality of the obedience.* Constrained by love, we gladly put our shoulder to the burden; but it is only when 'all' men serve God with one shoulder that all sense of distress and effort will pass away. And that for two reasons.

If we really love God and his law, we must also love men and yearn that they should keep his law. Till they share our freedom, it cannot be an altogether happy freedom. And, again, till they love

Him and do his will, they will put many hindrances in our path, strew in it many stones of stumbling and rocks of offence which cannot fail to make obedience difficult and painful to us. Without them we cannot be perfect. As yet, so to speak, the burden may press unduly on our shoulders because our neighbours do not faithfully bear their part of it; or because they are morally shorter than we are, or even because they are morally taller, or because they do not keep step with us. Only when the whole race stands under the burden as with *one* shoulder, and moves under it as with one foot, will all consciousness of the Divine Will as a burden disappear. Then, when our hearts are no longer torn with pity for the disobedient, and our progress is no longer impeded by the hindrances and temptations they cast in our way, the freedom of our obedience will become a happy freedom, and God's statutes will become our song in the house of our pilgrimage.

In this present world, at the stage we have reached as yet, much of the toil and distress of obedience arises from 'the contradiction of sinners.' Not only have we to bear other men's burdens as well as our own, not only have we to strain at the yoke for them as well as for ourselves; we have also to encounter their opposition, the scorn and contempt they feel, or affect, for those who live above the world and the world's law, and the temptations by which they seek to lure us from the path of duty.

Would that were all! But, alas! the Church, as well as the world, is often against us. Even those who gather in 'one place' are not always of 'one accord.' Even those who are of 'one heart' are not always of 'one way.' If at times we brace ourselves to a difficult course of duty, or resolve to speak the whole truth we know at all risks, or decide to serve God rather than man at all costs, it too often happens that the very first to meet us with counsels of prudence are of 'the household of faith.' If we are resolute, and *will* speak or do what we take to be God's will, they leave us to walk alone, to bear our burden alone, even if they do not add to the burden of obedience the still heavier burden of their opposition and dislike. The yoke galls us, not only because they will not put their necks to it, but also because they will fling their whole weight upon it, and make it almost too heavy to be borne. We have to carry *them* as well as our own proper burden. And thus our obedience is made so hard and painful to us that, were it not for the Father who seeth in secret and secretly upholds us, we should inevitably faint under the too heavy load. We have the freedom, but not the peace and happiness, of a divine service.

But when the Church serves God with one shoulder,

and, still more, when all 'the nations' serve Him with one shoulder; when the gracious promise is fulfilled: 'I will give them *one heart and one way*, that they may fear me for ever, for the good of them and of their children after them,' then, at last, the effort and the pain of obedience will be over, and we shall serve God with unbroken gladness because we and all men serve Him with a single and a perfect heart.

Even what is called 'an enlightened selfishness,' then, might well inspire us to take our full share in all endeavours to bring men, at home and abroad, to a saving knowledge of the truth as it is in Jesus, since we cannot enter into our full peace and joy until the whole family of man has taken up the yoke and burden of Christ. *That* is a poor motive and inspiration, however, for so noble a work, and I will not urge it upon you; for I trust you would still labour and yearn for the salvation of men even if you knew that when they took up the burden of obedience to the Divine Will, that burden would press still more painfully upon you. The true motive, the high motive is, that God, who is saving you, desires and intends the salvation of the whole world; that He pours out the indignation of his wrath on the evils which corrupt and degrade men only that He may create a clean heart and renew a right spirit within them; that He 'consumes' only that He may redeem the nations and the kingdoms. Let this picture hang in the study of your imagination, then, as an incentive to zeal in every good word and work,—the picture of a world searched through and through by purifying fire in order that God may turn to the nations a pure lip, that they may all invoke his Name, and serve Him as with one shoulder. If that will not at once reconcile you to the mercy of his judgments and stimulate your zeal in his service, I know not what will.

One word more and I have done. Who are those whom you most admire, in whom you recognize most of the spirit of Christ? Are they not the gentle and refined women who leave happy homes of which they are the light and joy to minister to the wants of the poor, the vicious, the suffering; who pass like ministering angels through the foul alleys of our great cities, or through the infected wards of hospitals, or through the carnage and perils of the camp, that they may carry succour and comfort to the wounded, the hopeless, the down-trodden, the diseased? Are they not the men who abandon all they love to announce the good news of eternal life to savage or brutalized races, to dwell with whom must be a kind of hell to their godly and sensitive spirits? And when these men and women die, killed before their time by their zeal and the horrors they have had to face in the service of their Master, and are taken to dwell with Him in heaven, *can* their natures suffer a change so gross that they will no longer pity the sinful, the outcast, the miserable, the lost? Can you believe that Florence Nightingale, William Knibb, John Williams, William Carey, David Livingstone, will be so absorbed in their own felicity that they will turn no single thought of pity on the poor souls down there in the pit and place of torment, and never once ask that they may go and share their pain in order that they may comfort them in their misery and teach them the secret of a nobler higher life?

Talk of 'dangerous doctrine'! What doctrine can be so dangerous as that which depicts a heaven which no man of a humane and noble spirit, no woman with a kindly pitiful heart, would care to enter, a heaven which makes us *less* merciful, less loving, less self-sacrificing than we are now? A *depraving* heaven! a heaven which makes men more selfish and not less selfish, the worse and not the better—who can believe in that, when the very earth itself is to be all flooded with righteousness and love and peace?

XIII.

WHY WE SUFFER.

'No doubt this man is a murderer, whom, though he hath escaped the sea, Justice suffereth not to live.'—Acts xxviii. 4.

I DO not know that this exclamation would have been less impressive, it certainly would not have been less natural, had the Maltese of St. Paul's time been 'barbarians' in our sense of the word. But they were not. Three civilisations at least had left their traces on the island,—that of Phœnicia, that of Carthage, and that of Rome. 'Barbarians,' as applied to them, meant no more than foreigners. They were a 'barbarous people' only in the sense in which St. Paul defines the term when he writes: 'If I know not *the meaning* of the language, I shall be unto him that speaketh a barbarian, and he that speaketh shall be a barbarian unto me.' They were barbarians only in the sense in which we should be barbarians in France or Germany if we did not understand the language spoken by the people among whom we sojourned.

The fact is that the conviction they expressed was universal. Neither barbarism nor civilisation had anything to do with it. It sprang from one of the primitive instincts of humanity. All men everywhere held that suffering implied sin, special suffering special sin. A Jew, no less than a pagan, a Roman, or a Greek, would have jumped to the same conclusion with these islanders of Malta, had they seen the venomous beast fasten on the hand of a man who had only just escaped shipwreck by the skin of his teeth. I doubt whether there was a man then on the earth who would not have thought or said: '*Justice* suffereth not this man to live, though he has just escaped death.' The very Apostles themselves, over a much less striking and dramatic instance than this, asked: 'Who did sin, this man or his parents, that he was born blind?' And I am by no means sure that any modern advance of thought has eradicated, or will eradicate, the stubborn instinct which teaches men to connect suffering with guilt, and even to see a Divine judgment in every adverse and painful accident. Even the most advanced thinkers admit, not only that there is some connection between sin and suffering, but also that the connection is one of cause and effect: while the great mass of men, who neither think nor theorise, instinctively associate the two and look for hidden guilt wherever they see conspicuous punishment. Even if we question the popular conclusion, or if we hold it only in a modified form, we shall readily grant that it *is* a natural and primitive instinct which leads men to connect the inward sin with the outward suffering, and that it is only by a resolute use of our reasoning faculty that we have been able to control it.

Admitting the instinct, we ought also to admit its testimony. For, surely, when Conscience insists on tracing human suffering to human sin, it bears a weighty testimony to truths of the utmost value. We are so made and so bred, it would appear, that we cannot, without a supreme effort, attribute the ordering of events to Chance or Accident. We feel instinctively that a Divine Nemesis manifests itself both in the order of the world at large and in the lot of individual men; and that, though our sins may be hidden from our fellows, or even praised by them, there is a Power in heaven which detects and will surely punish them. Before a man can get rid of this wholesome religious conviction—which does not in the least answer to Miss Bevington's ignorant and insulting definition of Religion as 'spiritual cakes and ale'—he must both unmake and remake himself: and even when he has thus radically changed himself, he will be very apt, despite the prevalent petticoat positivism, to revert to his original type.

For the conviction is a true one, though it often assumes questionable forms. It is true that all suffering springs from sin and bears witness against it, though it is not true either that we can always trace the suffering to its cause, or that the effects of a sin are always confined to the person who commits it. St. Paul traces death, for example, to sin; yet not every man's death to every man's sin. On the contrary he argues,—*one* sinned, *all* died. And it is at this point that men are apt, and always have been apt, to go wrong. The broad fact is true, that sin is the cause of suffering. But, like all large facts, it is capable of many interpretations. And men have commonly misinterpreted it. They have not been content to say: 'Sin is the cause of which suffering is an effect.' That is not sufficiently definite and precise. And so they have assumed that they can invariably trace the physical effect to its immediate ethical cause, and that the cause is invariably to be found in the conduct of those who suffer the effect. You know how impossible it was for our Lord Himself to dislodge these assumptions from the minds of the men of his own day. 'Suppose ye,' He said, 'that these Galileans were sinners above all the Galileans because they suffered such things?' Yes, that was exactly what they did suppose, and what they continued to suppose notwithstanding his 'I tell you, Nay.' Again He asked: 'Or these eighteen on whom the tower in Siloam fell, think ye that they were sinners above all men that dwelt here in Jerusalem?' And, again, this was precisely what they did think, never supposing for a moment that their own sins deserved a similar doom. An hour before the tower fell, many of them, I dare say, would have shrunk from placing themselves high above those on whom it crashed down. But the moment the tower fell that question was settled for them by God Himself. That they had escaped was a sufficient and a most gratifying proof of their moral superiority, though of course they were very sorry for the poor people who had been killed.

Let us learn what in all probability they did not learn even from the Great Teacher, that personal suffering is not always the result of personal sin; that family suffering is not always the result of family sin: and that even national sufferings are not always the result of national sins. Job suffered many strange calamities and indignities; yet Job was not a sinner above all the men of his time: God Himself bore witness to him that he was a perfect man and an upright, one who feared Jehovah and eschewed evil. Nay, if it were true that men always suffer for their own sins, and in proportion to their sins, we should be driven to the intolerable conclusion that the Greatest Sufferer the world has ever seen was also the Greatest Sinner the world has ever seen; that He who knew no sin was the very Chief of Sinners!

In our recoil from a conclusion so impossible, we naturally ask: What, then, are the causes, other than their personal sins, for which men suffer? And a twofold answer to that question is suggested by the instances at which we have already glanced. They suggest, (1) that we often suffer for our own good; and (2) that we often suffer for the good of others.

1. We often suffer, not for our guilt, but *for our good*. We are 'purged,' not because we do not bring forth fruit unto holiness, but that we may bring forth more fruit. The greater welfare of Job, for example, was both an intention, and an effect, of the sufferings inflicted on him. His cruel losses and pains came upon him, suggesting the still more cruel questions by which his heart was long agitated and torn, that he might gain larger and happier conceptions of God and of the providence of God, and a brighter and more inextinguishable hope both for himself and for mankind. In like manner St. Paul long writhed and groaned on 'the stake in his flesh,' in order that the unsuspected resources both of his own nature and of the grace of God might be developed in and upon him. And, still in the like manner, we are taught that the Man Christ Jesus 'learned by the things which He suffered,' tribulation

working experience even in Him; and that He was the more highly exalted, as assuredly He is at least in the thoughts and affections of men, because He humbled Himself to manhood, and to the sorrowful conditions of manhood—pain and grief and death.

2. Again, we often suffer, as for our own good, so also *for the good of others*. If Christ suffered more than other men, it was that, by suffering, He might become the Saviour of all men. If St. Paul long writhed in agony, like a man impaled, it was that the power and grace of God might shine the more conspicuously through him on the world around him. The affliction of Job was designed, not for his own teaching and welfare alone, but also for the teaching of his friends and neighbours, for *our* teaching even as well as theirs and his. Myriads of men have been the wiser and the better for what he endured, and have learned from him to see 'the end of the Lord' in afflicting them. 'Call no man happy till his death,' said the wise Greek; and Mrs. Browning has wisely added, 'Call no man *un*happy till his death.' And who that has followed the story of Job to its close would venture to call *him* unhappy?

Or take a case more on a level with our own conditions and experience. You all remember the man of whom the disciples asked: 'Master, who did sin, this man or his parents, that he was born blind?'

But have you sufficiently marked our Lord's answer to that question? How deliberate it was: 'Neither hath this man sinned, *nor* his parents,' shewing that He had considered both sides of the alternative placed before Him; and how bright with consolatory and hopeful suggestions: 'But that the works of God should be made manifest in him'—that he should become a notable example of the way in which the Divine Mercy penetrates and suffuses the sufferings of men, giving them an educational and disciplinary force not for the sufferers alone, but also for all who know them or hear of them. The blind man was blind, not because he was a sinner, but that he might first open his eyes on the Friend and Saviour of sinners, and get sight for his spirit as well as for his body. And through this man, unknown to us even by name, the enlightening and redeeming power of Christ has been set forth, in an impressive figure, to all the world. *This* was the intention, this the work, of God in him.

By calling our attention to him, Christ has taught us to look, in all our own sufferings, for some similar Divine intention and work. They may, or may not, be the consequences of our sins. They may, or may not, be intended for the correction of our sins. But they are always designed for the manifestation of some work of God which will promote our welfare and the welfare of those around us. And by the tone which our Lord took with his disciples as they speculated on the origin of this man's blindness He meant, I suspect, to give them, and us, the warning: 'When you consider the sufferings which men endure, do not lose yourselves in curious speculations on their origin, but rather find yourselves by recognizing their end, by adoring the power and grace by which God overrules them for good. Search for some Divine intention and work in them, some manifestation of the Divine wisdom and compassion. And when you consider your own afflictions, dwell, not on the loss and pain of them, but on the moral intention of them, on the moral discipline they may yield you, on the opportunity they afford you of shewing what the grace of God can do in you, how it can sustain you, and how, by enabling you to rejoice in tribulation also, it teaches you the divine art and mystery of extracting joy even from sorrow. You *must* bear the pain, the loss, which has come upon you; there is no escape from that: but why should you fling away the good of it, the very end and purpose for which it was sent, by refusing the discipline it may yield, by not permitting it to contribute whether to your own highest welfare or to the welfare of others?'

Now we all see, I think, that it would be well for us to take this warning. We can see that if, when we suffer, we were to fling away, as St. Paul flung off the venomous beast, all that is evil in suffering, all in it that tempts us to distrust or hopelessness or complaint, and to recognize the loving work and intention of God in it, we should be the gainers by it. And we can also see that, were we to take our suffering patiently, bravely, cheerfully, we should be teaching a valuable lesson and giving valuable help to our friends and neighbours; that even those who once thought we were sinners above other men because we suffered such things would come to think we were braver and better because we suffered them so patiently, and be led to ask whence we got our patience and our courage. For which of us has not been again and again impressed by the modest wisdom, the sweet cheerful submission, the tender consideration and charity of some great and habitual sufferer who had learned, and learned mainly in the school of pain and sorrow, to see God's intention and work in all that she suffered? Which of us has not known at least one couch that was a centre round which many gathered for wise tender counsel, and even for incentives to cheerfulness and hope? Which of us has not found at least one unfailing spring of sympathy and encouragement in white lips that were often wrung with pain and a heart that often throbbed with agony?

We *must* suffer, then; but we may *so* suffer as to get good from it, and to do good by it. This suffering for the good of others is, indeed, demanded of all who follow Christ. For if any man will follow Him, he must take up his cross: and of what is that cross the symbol but of the love that suffers, and is content to suffer, for the welfare of others?

Now do not put this thought away from you as though it did not bear on ordinary lives such as yours and mine. And do not suffer it to hang in your minds only in such hazy, general, and abstract forms as that it will not connect itself with your daily experience and tell on your daily conduct. There are many ways in which we may convince ourselves that to lose and suffer for the good or gain of others is a practical, and a practicable, law of the Christian life.

What, for example, is the very commonest form of affliction, the form in which no man can escape it, however strong or opulent he may be, however wise or good? It is, as you know, the pain we feel at the loss of those whom we love. That I must die is a solemn fact for me: but how much more heartrending and poignant is the fact that, before I die, I must lose some of the dearest companions I have known, and yearn in vain for the touch of a vanished hand and the sound of a voice that is still! And yet is it love, is it not rather self-love, that would call, or even keep, them back? Is it love, is it not rather self-love, which makes us so bitterly regret our loss of them that we refuse to be comforted? If, for them, to die is gain, shall we grudge them the gain because it involves loss for us, and yet call ourselves the servants and friends of Christ, who loved not Himself, but lived in and for others? There are those who think that to be inconsolable is a proof of love; but, surely, if they had more of the spirit of Christ, Love would teach them a joy in their friend's gain which would more than counterbalance their grief for their own loss. And, beyond all question, common as this kind of affliction is, it affords us a rare opportunity of bearing witness to the power and grace of God: for who would not admit a strange and mystic potency in Religion if, at such moments, it could bear our spirits up, and fill them with the fervours of an immortal love and an inconquerable hope?

True, Job on his ash-heap, and St. Paul on his stake, even the blind man in the Temple, and the Apostle when he bore the viper's fangs unmoved, had opportunities of glorifying God which do not come to most of us; but let no man say that he has *no* opportunity of glorifying Him, no opportunity of getting good or of doing good by the cheerful patience with which he endures suffering, unless indeed he is willing to admit that suffering is altogether unknown to him.

For any suffering, whatever the cause from which it springs, any loss, any pain, any sorrow may be so borne as to become a discipline in goodness to us, and a revelation to others of the power of trust in God to sustain the spirit of man, and to lift it above the changes and chances of this mortal life. Bear any loss, any pang, well, and you will benefit yourselves, and benefit your neighbours; and, in both, glorify God.

There are not many of us, I apprehend, who would deny that we may be the better for our tribulations, and may help to make men better by the courage with which we endure them. But there may be some of us who say sadly: 'I have had much to bear, and I have tried to bear it as well as I could; and yet *I* am none the better for it, nor can I see that any one else is the better for it.'

Well, of course, that may be so. You *may* have got little good from your trials; you may have done little good through them. And yet, all the same, God may have sent them to promote your welfare and that of the little world about you. But even He cannot make you good, or a cause of goodness in others, against your will, without your co-operation. Goodness is in the will, in the right direction of it; in the energy, and certainty, and stedfastness with which it is maintained in the right direction. A compelled goodness is no goodness. And the point you have to determine is, whether or not you have habitually and strenuously kept your will in accord with the will of God, whether or not you have recognized his intention, his work, in your trials, and bent yourself to it. Too often we see only the part which men and women play in the common yet fretting and exhausting trials of life—often an unjust and an unkindly part; and in our resentment of their injustice and unkindness we omit to note how justly and kindly God takes up their evil work and infuses a soul of goodness into it. If instead of dwelling on the ill-will and ill-temper, the irritating unkindnesses and dishonesties, of those about us—and these are the most common and fertile source of trial, we were to set ourselves to discover what part and meaning *God* has in them, what He permits them for, we should soon find that He intends them for our education and discipline in righteousness, in patience, in charity. And thus all the sting and meanness, if not all the pain, would be taken out of them. For if God intends them for our welfare, why should we complain of them or shrink from them? If He is providing us in them with opportunities of overcoming evil with good, of shewing that we are of a heavenly strain and temper, and of strengthening and establishing ourselves in righteousness, there is a kindly and noble intention in them which we may well adopt, with which it is worth our while to co-operate. If the Cross we are to bear is not some rare and heroic misery—as for most of us it is not, but the petty details and trials of the daily round and common task; if in enduring *these* bravely we 'take up our cross daily,' then these petty trials assume a high dignity, and we may shew a true nobility of nature, a true Christian wisdom and courage, in bearing them with composure and fortitude.

On the other hand, it does not follow that, because we do not see that we are getting any good out of our trials, or doing any good by the patience with which we confront them, that no good comes of them. There are a good many things which we don't see, and even a good many which are not visible to us. God sees much that escapes our glance. And, for us, all good work is slow work, while much of it lies beyond our range. The task of renewing our souls in holiness and love is a long and gradual task; so long that, for long, there is not much to be seen; so gradual that the advances it makes are well-nigh imperceptible. But of this we may be sure, that, if we are honestly trying to get a little better by the things we suffer, and to make our neighbours a little better by the constancy and courage and cheerfulness with which we suffer them, there is a real growth of goodness in our souls, however gradual it may be; and we are putting our hands to a good work to which God has also put his hands; and the work *is* telling and advancing, let who will deny it, and even though we ourselves are never quite sure of it.

XIV.

AARON'S APOLOGY.

'I cast it into the fire, and there came out this calf.'
EXODUS xxxii. 24.

IF it is strange that so good a man as Aaron should stoop to a subterfuge so false as this, it is still more strange that a man so capable should stoop to a subterfuge so silly, contemptible, and ludicrously absurd. Who could be deceived by it even for a moment? And how came a man of his mark, so ready with his tongue too, to sink to the level of a surprised and foolish maid-servant lying over her broken dish or milk-pot? His rude work of art had cost him no small labour and pains. He had had to collect from the willing tribes their ear-rings and ornaments of gold, to melt and fuse them, to run the mass into a mould, to fashion it with a graving-tool. He had deliberated on the form he should give it, and determined to make it like one of the animal gods—the sacred bull-calf—with which he and the Israelites had been familiar in Egypt. And yet when he is charged with his offence, instead of pleading that he had but sought to pacify the mutinous tribes by giving them an image of the Divine Power; instead of frankly and manfully confessing his sin—which would have been far better, he is weak and silly enough to plead: 'I cast the gold into the fire, and there came out this calf,' as if the fire were to blame, not he, as if the form assumed by the gold was the pure result of accident over which he had no control, and for which, therefore, he could not be held responsible! It is the lie of a schoolboy or a slave; we resent it and condemn it almost as much for its lack of wit and invention as for its lack of truth.

One is almost ashamed to hint at any apology for such a self-condemning excuse as this. But in common fairness we ought perhaps to remember that Aaron was a born orator, and that the specifically oratorical temperament is a singularly nervous and sensitive temperament. There are few gifts which Englishmen more admire than eloquence; but there are few which are more perilous. A man speaks better than his fellows mainly because he is more easily and deeply moved than they are. He sways them because he is himself swayed more quickly and powerfully by the influences by which both he and they are touched. He can utter their thought more richly and expressively than they can utter it, because he is more instantly and profoundly impressed by it than they are. And how should a man be sensitive to good thoughts and influences without also being sensitive to those which are evil? Action and reaction are opposite and *equal*. The man who swings far in one direction will probably swing as far in the opposite direction, unless some powerful moral check be applied. The temperament which stands fluttering in poise, and is lightly stirred by every breath, is only too likely to become the sport of all the winds that blow. I think I have observed, too, that men who can speak well, better than their neighbours, when they have prepared and braced themselves for the effort, often speak more foolishly and weakly when taken at unawares, and are far less shrewd and capable when summoned to meet a sudden and grave emergency. We can understand, therefore, how Aaron, with his sensitive impressionable temperament, who had instantly responded to the imperative cry of the people, 'Up, make us a God to go before us!' would also instantly cower before Moses as he strode, white with righteous indignation, through the camp, and be cut to the very heart by the fierce irony of his demand: 'How have this people sinned against *thee*, that thou shouldest bring so great a sin upon them?' We can at least partly understand how the eloquent orator, taken by surprise, struck dumb with shame and fear would be likely, as soon as he could speak at all, to falter out whatever silly excuse came uppermost.

And yet silly and contemptible as Aaron's apology for himself is, how true it is to human nature! Let no man scorn and condemn him as a sinner, or even as an idiot, beyond his fellows, or even deem it impossible that under any pressure *he* should be driven to adopt an excuse so paltry and absurd. Strange as it may sound, and much as many would resent the charge, we all of us resemble Aaron at his worst, even if we also resemble him at his best; his words are but as a glass in which every man may see himself. In various ways we all recognize the rule of Accident, and throw the blame of our faults and sins upon it. There can hardly be a man or a woman on the earth who does not at times plead the force of Accident in self-excuse, and say in one of many idioms: 'I cast this or that into the fire, and, lo, there came out this calf!'

Aaron's excuse, as I have already hinted, is the standing excuse of at least one large class among us. Servants use it every day. Who has not heard them plead? 'Please, ma'am, I couldn't help it; it broke in my hands,' as if it were not they, but the wilful jug or dish which was responsible for the fracture, or some malign fate which mocks at human endeavour and care. 'It was an accident' has been their sigh ever since domestic service became an institution among us. But is the plea confined to them? Do you not also hear it from the lips of every child? '*I didn't do it,*'—they are all quite sure of that; though, if they did not do it, it would be hard indeed to say who did.

Here are two large classes, then, to whom Aaron's excuse is familiar; and to one of these classes we all belonged in our time. But are there no more? Most of you will remember that inimitable scene in *Adam Bede* in which Mrs. Poyser, while rating the clumsy Molly for her broken jug of beer, herself drops a still more precious jug from her angry fingers, and exclaims: 'Did anybody ever see the like? The jugs are *bewitched*, I think.' You will remember how she proceeds to argue that 'there's times when the crockery seems alive, an' flies out o' your hand like a bird,' and concludes, philosophically enough, that '*what is to be* broke *will* be broke.' Possibly most of us have known mistresses who, while indignantly repudiating the common excuse of their maids, have nevertheless condescended to employ it in their own behalf. And what bankrupt tradesman, or broken merchant, or fraudulent banker is there who does not plead the same, or a similar, excuse? It is hardly ever *their* fault that they cannot pay twenty shillings in the pound; it is their *misfortune.* 'Things have gone against them.' 'Circumstances over which they have no control have been their ruin'—not their own rashness, or dishonest discounts, or risky speculations. They put their capital into that shop, that firm, that bank, and, lo, there came out this ugly calf of bankruptcy! But you must not blame them; it is the furnace that was in fault.

And if mistresses no less than their maids, and men of business no less than their wives, attribute to accident, mischance, or a malignant and mysterious Fate, results of which the cause might be found much nearer home, scholars no less than men of business, men of science no less than scholars, Christian commentators no less than men of science, too often betake themselves to the same egregious line of argument and excuse.

Scholars, for example, who have devoted their lives to the study of classical literature, will take up such a poem as that of Homer, and gravely contend that it had no author; that it is simply a collection of antique legends, recited by rhapsodists in the cities of Greece, which gradually shaped themselves, or were shaped by Accident, into the fair and wondrous unity that now commands the admiration of the world: in short, they maintain that Pisistratus, or some unknown editor, cast a number of stray legends and ballads into a pot; and, lo, there came out this Iliad! In like manner, there are men of science who attribute the origin of the harmonious universe to the same potent but unknown cause. According to them, it was not made by anyone; it made itself: it is the work, not of Design and Intention, not of one creative overruling Mind, but of Evolution or Accident. An indefinite number of atoms, with a single force capable of taking many forms—and where these came from Heaven itself does not know—were flung loose into space—by whom or what it is impossible to discover; and, lo, out of their action and interaction there came forth this Cosmos! So, again, there are critics and commentators who affirm that the Christian Story assumed its present form in the same strange accidental way. Brief memoirs may have been current in the primitive Church and fragmentary traditions; but John wrote no record of 'the Word that came and dwelt among us,' nor Luke, nor Mark, nor Matthew. It was not at the earliest till the second century after Christ, when the literary art was at its lowest in the Church and the air was full of fables and heresies, that those Sacred Narratives were produced which even as works of historical art are still unmatched: but *then*,—just then of all times when there was hardly a living man capable of writing a book that would live—the ancient fables, memoirs, traditions were flung into an unknown crucible by an unknown hand; and, by some unparalleled miracle, there came forth these Gospels!—which let him believe who can; but he whose credulity is so ample that he can swallow this calf, or camel, of Criticism certainly need not strain at any gnat which he may find, or imagine, in the chalice which the Church offers to his lips.

It is not, however, in this province of human thought and action that I would have you linger. There are illustrations and repetitions and modifications of Aaron's Apology which touch us closer home. The man who is a sinner—as which of us is not?—has it perpetually on his lips. Like the mischievous boy, or the clumsy maid, his cry is: 'I couldn't help it; I didn't do it; it broke of itself: it fell to pieces in my hands.' How often, when arraigned at the bar of Conscience or taken to task by Authority, have we urged that we really could not help ourselves; that, to use Mrs. Poyser's word, we were 'bewitched' by some evil and malignant power: that it was impossible to keep the law we had transgressed, and that 'what is to be broken' will and must be broken? 'A hot temper leaps o'er a cold decree.' With passions so hot and strong as mine, with a natural and hereditary bias to evil, exposed to temptations so numerous and so nicely adjusted to my temperament, why should I be blamed, why should I overmuch blame myself, if now and then I *have* overleaped the cold and strict requirements of the law. Such as I am, in such a world as this, with a passionate craving for immediate enjoyment, exposed to forces so powerful and so constant in their operation, hampered by conditions so inauspicious, how could I do otherwise than I have done? Is it my fault that, with desire and opportunity conspiring against me, I have sometimes been overmastered or betrayed by them, and broken a commandment which no man has always kept?

In various forms, answering to our various temperaments and conditions, we have all, I suppose, defended or excused ourselves thus. And, no doubt, even the best of us, even those of us who sincerely love righteousness and pursue it, are tempted at times to use St. Paul's words in quite another sense to his, and say: 'Now it is no more *I* that do it, but *Sin* that dwelleth in me.'

When we consider all this, my brethren, when we see how much our own excuses resemble theirs, there should surely be some allowance, some kindly amusement even, in the smile with which we listen to the poor housemaid's cry, 'It broke itself;' nor should we too fiercely and scornfully condemn even Aaron's apology for himself. Fellow feeling should make us kind. The universality of the excuse should set us on reflecting whether after all there may not be some modicum of truth in it. And, if we reflect, we shall find, I think, that, in whatever form we meet it, it is not wholly false. Accident, or what we call accident, has a real though limited power over our lives and deeds. It is quite true that accidents only seldom happen to the careful; and that if our servants were more thoughtful and attentive and painstaking they would not break so much as they do. But is it not also true that there is a kind of malice in our fate at times, that by some inscrutable law accident succeeds to accident, that the most dexterous and careful of us seem to turn clumsy for a while, so that if we break or spoil one thing we almost expect that one or two more will be spoiled or broken before the favourable turn comes? Are we not all liable to the influences of heat and cold and still more subtle and recondite atmospheric variations, of slight changes of health or disease in our own bodies, of the still more mysterious changes of our moods and tempers, of the monotony or variety of our life, of solitude and of society,—so liable to them that, while at times all goes well and happily with us, at other times we seem to take hold of everything by the wrong handle and all goes ill with us? And if we are conscious of these changes in ourselves, and know them to be inevitable, not to be surmounted by any effort, not to be avoided by any care, why should we expect our servants always to avoid them and to live in a serene atmosphere in which accidents shall be impossible to them?

There *are* bad times in trade, with which a man cannot successfully contend. Things *do* sometimes go wrong with him, so that he is called to confront conditions too hard and cruel. It is *not* by his own default that every bankrupt gets into the *Gazette;* and before we blame the man who fails we ought to be sure that he is not a victim to circumstances over which he had no sufficient control.

There *are* traces of what seem different hands in the Iliad, there are discrepancies in the Gospels, there are facts in Nature and in human life, which in each of these cases render the theory of one creative and designing Mind difficult and in a certain sense questionable; and some men *are* so made as to feel these difficulties more keenly than others. We should pity rather than blame them if they are oppressed by the doubts these difficulties breed, and only blame, while we pity, them when they wilfully hug their doubts, and propound theories obviously inadequate or absurd.

And, in like manner, there *is* that in us and around us which in various degrees, answering to our several natures and conditions, makes our sins not all, or not altogether, our own. Do not suffer any creed or dogma to becloud your moral sense, or even your common sense, I beseech you. In so far as you or I sin because of an evil bias we have received from Adam or from any other of our forefathers, *they* are responsible for our sins; they must answer for them, not we. But—and do not forget *this* application of the same principle—in so far as we ourselves weaken and debase the nature we transmit to our children by sinful indulgences, *we*, and not they, shall have to answer for their offences. Confessedly we enter an impenetrable cloud of mystery here,—a mystery not at all lightened by our belief in 'original sin,' or our confession of universal sinfulness: but, however dark our way may be, of this we may be sure that, under the just rule of the just God, every man must bear his own burden and answer for his own transgressions —his own, and not another's. If Adam is to blame for any sin of mine—though, I confess, *my* conscience never accuses *him*—he must bear the blame of it. If I am to blame for any sin of yours, which only too likely I may be, I must bear the blame of it, and not you. And if, by neglect of the world, any lad is suckled and trained in vice and crime, the world must bear much of the blame of any crimes that he commits, and you and I will have to take our share of the blame.

This is the sense in which it is true that men may not be always, or altogether, responsible for their sins, in which their sins are not their own. This, at least, is one sense; and the holy Apostle hints at another and still higher sense in the words: 'Now, then, it is no more I that do it, but sin that dwelleth in me,'— words far too profound and difficult, however, to be taken up at the close of a discourse.

Practically our wisdom is to make no allowance for any sin of our own, but to make as much allowance as we honestly can for the sins of our neighbours.

'And how much is that?'

Well, Aaron's excuse for himself has reminded us of a good many excuses as irrational and absurd as his which men make to this day. And we have seen and acknowledged that there is some element of truth in them; that what we call Accident does play a certain part in our life and the lives of our fellows. But though, in the abstract, we cannot define this mysterious power, or determine exactly how far we are subject to it, in conduct and practice we have no great difficulty in dealing with it. We make allowance for our servants; we admit that even the most careful must meet with an accident sometimes, and that there are times even when a small series of such accidents are almost certain to tread on each other's heels. Nevertheless, if, after due trial, we find that a servant has contracted a constant and incorrigible habit of breaking whatever is breakable, we promptly dismiss her as *too* unfortunate for us, or as abnormally clumsy, or as wilfully negligent. We make allowance, too, for the accidents of commerce; we confess that now and then a man may fail honourably because he fails through no fault of his own. But if we meet with a man who has failed in almost everything he has undertaken, and who has spent half his time in the Court of Insolvency and its purlieus, we are in no hurry to associate ourselves with him or to assist him; nay, unless he can bring surprisingly good evidence to the contrary, we set him down as a lazy vagabond or an unscrupulous rogue. Just so we make, or ought to make, allowance for a man who is 'overtaken by a sin.' We admit, or should admit, that every man lies perilously open to temptation of some kind. Without for a moment pretending that his sin is not a sin, or assuming that his sin must be hushed up 'because he is a Christian brother, and any exposure of him might bring a scandal on the holy name of Religion,' we ought nevertheless to feel that there are dark possibilities in every man's nature, mysterious inherited taints of blood and will, inscrutable forces of evil, at work within and around us all, and not to condemn him as lost beyond hope, or even as utterly unworthy of the Christian fellowship.

if he repent and amend. It should be our aim, rather, to 'restore such an one in the spirit of meekness, considering ourselves, lest we also be tempted.' But, on the other hand, if a man is an habitual and notorious sinner, if some fresh scandal is for ever cropping up about his feet; if he has no sense of shame, makes no confession of sin, gives no proof of amendment, are we to suffer such an one to plead: 'I cannot help it, I am so made:' or, 'I am singularly unfortunate, and am always being made out worse than I am?' Are we to allow *him* to cast his guilt on the back of Accident, to attribute it to circumstances, to predisposition, to temperament, or to pose himself as a victim of misfortune and a mysterious ill-luck? Are we to suffer him to plead: 'The gold'—in this case *brass* might be the more appropriate metal—'was cast into the furnace, and, lo, there came out this calf'? Not till we keep a servant who breaks everything entrusted to her clumsy hands. Not till we give credit to the habitual bankrupt. Till then, we can only say to him, as Moses said to Aaron: 'How have we sinned against *you*, that you should bring this great shame on us?'

And for ourselves, my brethren, let us have done with this poor subterfuge, which we know to be, for us at least, a mere refuge of lies even as we run into it. Let us refuse to plead the weakness of our nature or the strength of temptation, to insinuate, if we do not openly allege, that creatures such as we are in such conditions as ours cannot hope to resist and overcome evil, when we know very well that there is no transgression into which we have fallen which we might not have escaped had we resisted it with all our force, and taken the help which God was waiting to bestow.

That is not a healthy spiritual mood which prompts us even to palliate our sins before Almighty God. It becomes us rather to cast ourselves before Him with the confession, 'Father we have sinned before heaven and against thee,' and the prayer, 'Create in us a clean heart, O God, and renew a right spirit within us.'

XV.

THE PARABLE OF THE TALENTS.

'The kingdom of heaven is as a man travelling into a far country, who called his own servants and delivered unto them his goods. And unto one he gave five talents, to another two, and to another one; to every man according to his several ability; and straightway took his journey,' &c., &c., &c.—ST. MATTHEW xxv. 14–30.

THE historical conditions which gave shape to the framework of this Parable present no difficulty; there are few of us to whom they are not familiar. We all know, or easily may know, that in our Lord's time there were two ways of 'dealing with property in the absence of the owner. The more primitive and patriarchal way was for the absentee to make his slaves his agents. They were to till his land and sell the produce, or to use the money he left with them as capital in trading. In such cases there was often, of course, an understanding that they should receive part of the profits, though, being slaves, there could be no formal contract to that effect. The other way was to take advantage of the banking, money-changing, money-lending system of which the

Phœnicians were the inventors, and which at the time was in full operation throughout the Roman Empire. The bankers received money on deposit and paid interest on it, and then lent it at a higher percentage, or employed it in trade or in farming the revenues of a province. This was therefore the natural resource, as investment in stocks or in companies is with us, for those who had not leisure or energy to engage in business.'* The faithful servants of the Parable used their lord's goods in the first way, trading with them and making them more; the slothful servant ought to have dealt with them in the second way, putting his money with the bankers that, when his lord returned, he might receive his own again with interest.

If the outward form of the Parable presents no difficulty, so neither does its inner and main drift. As we read it we understand at once that it is a picture of human life, and of the sentence which the Divine Judge will one day pass upon it. Nevertheless there are some points in the Parable on which we need to pause and reflect if we would reach their full meaning and bring it home to our consciences and hearts.

1. First of all, and very obviously, the Parable

---

* Professor Plumptre *in loco:* Ellicott's New Testament.

assumes that all who call Christ 'Lord and Master' will find *some* work to do for Him, and even some distinctively spiritual and religious work. For, of course, the 'goods' which He delivers to his servants, and with which He expects them to trade are 'the things'—the truths and treasures—'of his kingdom.' What He demands of us, and of every one of us, is that we exemplify and enforce the truths we have learned from Him, that we shew the courage of our convictions, that we use the gifts and graces of his Spirit, not for our own culture and comfort alone, but also for the good of our fellows, that we make known the revelation of the Divine Love which He was and made; that, by our own pursuit of them, we induce our neighbours to follow after righteousness, charity, peace: in short, that in some way, in the best way open to us, we take an active and diligent part in the endeavour to enlighten, better, and redeem the world.

Not only does the Parable assume that we each one of us have some portion of the 'goods' of Christ entrusted to us, and some capacity for using them; it also implies that we each of us have precisely that portion which we are capable of using, as much as we can use, and even more than we are always willing to use. As Napoleon's rule was 'The tools to the man who can use them,' so the law of distribution in the Divine Kingdom is 'To every man *according to* his *several ability,*' according, that is, to the ability which *severs* or distinguishes him from his neighbours. The Master of us all does not condemn us all to one form, or one kind, of service, though He will have no servant who does not in some way serve Him. He recognizes the immense variety of our powers, gifts, dispositions, and finds scope for them all.

And, however inequitably *this* world's goods may be divided, a moment's reflection will suffice to shew that in the spiritual realm every man may take and do as much as he can. Who is to hinder us from being as self-denying, as lowly in spirit, as charitable and kindly as we care to be? If we have a special faculty for apprehending and teaching the truth, what is there to prevent us, if only we ourselves are willing and resolved to endure the toils and sacrifices involved in the exercise of that high faculty, from using and cultivating it? Or if we are strong in affection and sympathy, if we have a special gift for entering into the sorrows of our neighbours and of comforting them, again what is there to hinder us? And so with every other spiritual capacity and gift. Whatever it may be, we may find room for it, ample room and verge, in the service of God. Whatever we can learn, we may learn; whatever we can appropriate, we may appropriate; whatever we can do, we may do; whatever we can give, we may give. Our 'ability' is the only measure, the only limit, of our right. We are welcome to all that we can take, to all that we can use.

And our ability is the only measure and limit of our *duty* as well as of our right. Our Master and Lord *expects* us to take as much as we can take from Him, and to do as much for Him as we can do,—to take ten talents if we can use ten, five if we can use five, two if we can use two, and to be content with one if we can only use one. But we must all take *something*, and employ it for Him. So much He demands of us all, and demands it of us both for our own sake and for that of the world,—that we may grow in capacity, in gifts, in serviceableness, and that the world may be the better and the happier for us.

2. The Parable affirms that the term of service is to be followed by a day of judgment, in which every man's work will be tried, and either approved or condemned. And this is a point to which we give too little heed. Not that we doubt it. There are few articles in our creed to which we more easily and generally assent than that which affirms that God will come to judge the world by that Man whom He has appointed. And yet how seldom do we reflect on the fact, that the Lord whom we serve will one day sit in judgment on our service! How seldom is our life, and the work of our life, affected by the fact that

a day is coming in which we shall hear what He thinks of us and of our works, in which our place and the measure of our reward will depend on the quality of the service we have rendered Him! And yet Christ the Judge is well-nigh as familiar a figure in the New Testament as Christ the Saviour. How many of our Lord's parables, for instance, close with a picture of that solemn session in which quick and dead, righteous and wicked, will be assembled before his bar, to receive according to the deeds done in the body, whether these be good or whether they be bad. And in the Epistles that final judgment is no less prominent than in the Gospels. In a memorable and famous passage, for example, St. Paul tells us that, whenever the earthly home of his tabernacle is dissolved, he has, and knows that he will pass into, a heavenly and eternal home, not made with hands. He is sure that, for him, to be absent from the body is to be present with the Lord; and therefore he longs to escape from the frail and hindering tent of his mortality. But there is one thing he longs for even more than this; and it is that, whether in the body or out of the body, he may be approved by Christ. 'We labour,' he says,* 'that, whether present or absent, we may be accepted of him: for we must *all*

---

* 2 Corinthians v. 1–10.

appear before the judgment-seat of Christ, that *every man* may receive the things done in the body, according to that he hath done, whether it be good or bad.' In fine, he recognizes the laws of continuity and evolution on which Science insists, affirms that the future life of men will be an equitable pro-duction and development of their present life ; and, in full accordance with our inborn sense of justice, which demands that men should receive the natural and due reward of their deeds, declares that they must and will receive it. No man could be more sure than Paul was that he would be saved by Christ ; and yet he was equally sure that he should be *judged* by Christ. He has no fear that Christ will condemn him ; but he is gravely anxious lest Christ should not approve of his service. That his *work* should be accepted, as well as himself, was indeed his main anxiety and endeavour.

Let us remember, then, that *we* may be accepted, while yet *our work* is condemned. We may be 'saved so as by fire '—pulled out of the fire in which the wood, hay, and stubble of our works are burned up. Many a man, many a saint, many a theologian and divine, has thought to serve God by actions, and even by long courses of action, which were alien and opposed to the will of God. St. Paul himself had once thought to do God service by making havoc of the Church. No wonder, therefore, that he was habitually and painfully bent on making his later service right,—right in form, right in motive, right in spirit, and anxious to know, after all his toils and sacrifices, what his Lord and Judge thought of his service. *We* are at least as liable to error as he was. And if we take no thought for our service, if we never suspect that we may be working in ways that are not good, if we are not bent on doing our best for God and man, and are troubled by no fear lest we should have missed our mark, we can hardly hope that our work will pass the scrutiny of Christ and be approved by Him. Since, then, it will help to make us thoughtful and modest, help to set us right and keep us right in action, in motive, and in the animating spirit of our service, let us bear in mind that we too must stand before his judgment-seat, and receive from Him a just, and therefore a merciful, recompense of the deeds we have done in the body, both good and bad. We do well to think much and often of what Christ has done for us; we shall do better still if we also think much and often of what we are doing for Him.

3. The Parable teaches that the reward of faithful service will be an enlarged capacity and scope for service. To each of the servants who had traded with his goods and made them more the lord said: 'Thou has been faithful in a few things, I will make

thee ruler over many things.' They had not displayed any very singular fidelity or heroism, I dare say; and no doubt they had had their moments of indolence, negligence, and self-pleasing: but, on the whole, they had been honest, active, loyal, and had done the best they could, with their capacities, in their conditions, exposed to their temptations. And the Master we serve is neither hard nor austere. If, in the main, we have been diligent, faithful, earnest in our use of his gifts and our endeavours to serve Him, though doubtless we shall suffer loss for every negligence and mistake, He will nevertheless acknowledge us to be good and faithful servants: He will reward us openly and generously for toils and sacrifices of which the world, and perhaps the Church, took no note; and reward us in the way most grateful to us—by giving us an increased ability to serve Him, and a keener delight in his service, by calling us to serve Him in 'many things' instead of in 'few.'

Now this welcome and familiar thought is of special value in a time like this, when men are charging the Gospel with pandering to a base selfishness by its constant promise of reward; for it furnishes us with a cogent and complete answer to that charge. No doubt there is a base and selfish hunger for reward,—and those are not always most free from it who most loudly condemn it; but it is not very common, I think, either in the Church or in the world. Most men who wish to rise into larger and happier conditions intend to make a good use of them, or what they conceive to be a good use, should their wish be gratified. And there is nothing wrong, nothing selfish, in wishing to be better off in many ways if we honestly intend to use our larger means for worthy ends. The charge of selfishness is a very common one; but, after all, is there not a great deal of unselfishness in the world? Is not very much of the best work that is done in it done for nothing, or for a wage miserably incommensurate with its deserts? However that may be, the *Christian* reward is above suspicion. If we understand it at all, we not only labour and long for it in order that we may use it for worthy ends, but we know that it is of a kind which absolutely cannot be used for unworthy and selfish ends. In our Parable, for instance, as in many passages of the New Testament, we are taught that the reward of good work, of faithful service, is power and opportunity to do more and better work, to serve God and man on a larger scale, in a nobler way: and how can such a reward as that be prostituted to ignoble and selfish purposes? In other passages the reward of good and faithful service is described as a growing likeness to God which will gradually make us righteous as He is righteous, pure as He is pure, and even perfect as He is perfect. And to grow like Him who lives not unto Himself, who rules all by serving all, is surely a reward for which we may yearn and strain without any base or selfish taint. Nay, he who does *not* long for it may well suspect himself of some hidden baseness or insincerity. He who does not crave to become more righteous than he is, more pure, more gentle and kind, may well fear lest his pursuit of righteousness and goodness should prove to be as insincere as ineffective. The more bent we are on serving God and man the more ardently we must long for the coming of a time in which our capacity for serving them will be enlarged and refined. If we have any likeness to God our Father, we cannot be content until we are 'satisfied' with his likeness.

4. The Parable implies that the spirit and character of our service will depend on our conception of the Divine Character and Spirit. We are not expressly told, indeed, that the faithful and industrious servants thought well of their master; we are left to infer that from their cheerful diligence and their fidelity to him. But we are expressly told that the slothful and wicked servant thought ill of him, and was bold enough to tell him so to his face: 'I knew thee, that thou art a hard man, reaping where thou hast not sown, and gathering where thou hast

not strewed.' And though this conception, or misconception of his master, as a stiff and bitter man, capable of plundering his neighbours' fields and barns, was in part an afterthought, an invention of the moment, a mere fetch to excuse his own disloyalty, yet no doubt it was in part a true expression of his real thought about him. No doubt he did think of him as likely to demand more than his due, and to expect more of him than he could possibly render,—just as many men now are quite prepared to maintain that even God Himself demands an impossible purity of us, or an impossible unselfishness, or an impossible superiority to the common habits and aims of the world around us. Shocking and startling as the fact is when we consider it, it is yet true that a man may think badly even of God!

Every day, and in every age, we may see how the conceptions men frame of God give form to their service of Him, or drive them to revolt from his service. Most of us probably have known men who sincerely held God to be what the slothful servant proclaimed his master to be. Even this horrible caricature of the Lord who sustains and rules the kindly universe has been and is entertained, and He is set forth as hard and austere, as reaping where He has not sown, gathering where He has not strewed; as damning men for the sinful nature they inherited from their fathers, or for not responding to a call which never reached them, or for not yielding to a ministry never vouchsafed them: or even as decreeing them to an everlasting misery before they were born 'for the praise of his glorious justice.' And from men who thus misconceive the just God and Saviour, who, not content with making Him altogether such an one as themselves, make Him unfathomably worse and baser than themselves, how can we expect any earnest and sustained efforts to bring back to God a world which they hold Him to have condemned, or to shew much love for the brother whom they suppose God to hate?

But apart from these gross caricatures of the Divine Character and Will, we need to remember that our conceptions of God, even when they are in great measure true, determine the kind of service we render Him; and that in proportion as they are defective they make our service incomplete. We often meet with men, for example, who, with much faith in God, a sincere delight in worshipping Him, nevertheless lack a strict conscientiousness; in their intercourse with their fellows they do not leave an impression of an integrity that never swerves, of an honour that will take no stain: and hence they do not serve the world as they might, they do not do as much as they ought to make righteousness an efficient and ruling power in the affairs of men. They do not feel the claims of justice, or do not feel them quickly and profoundly; and hence when movements are on foot in which questions of public duty are involved, and the rights of men or of classes of men are advocated, they stand aloof. And, very commonly, justice is not so dear to them as it should be, nor righteousness so lustrous and attractive, mainly because they have conceived of God as a tender and forgiving Saviour rather than as a just Ruler and Judge of men. They are easily drawn toward works of pity and compassion, for in these they are sure that they have the sanction and approval of God; but they do not sufficiently realize the righteousness of God, his care for righteousness and love of it, and hence they do not readily respond to the claims of 'mere justice,' or take their due part in endeavours to put down wrong and oppression.

And, in like manner, those who are very sensitive to the claims of justice, and are eager to see right done in the world and wrong put down, often lack tenderness; and lack it because to them God is mainly an upright Judge, a righteous Ruler, and not a pitiful and forgiving Friend.

In many ways, in short, our conceptions of the Divine Character determine the quality of our service. And, therefore, it will be our wisdom to frame the truest and largest conceptions of Him that we can, to embrace in our thoughts of Him both his righteousness and his love, both his compassion and his justice. For though all honest service will find acceptance with Him, yet in the searching scrutiny to which all our works are to be exposed at the great reckoning, those who have served Him best will be most approved, and be rewarded with the largest capacities and the amplest opportunities for future service.

5. The Parable suggests that those who have but slender capacities for service may turn them to the best account by associating themselves with others and helping in a common work. 'If,' says the lord in the Parable to the wicked and slothful servant, 'you knew that by and of yourself you could do nothing to please me, why did you not at least put my money with the bankers that I might have received mine own again with interest?' And, whatever else or more that may mean, it surely must mean that those who know little of God, or of the best methods of serving Him, would do well to take up some recognized and established form of service, put themselves under the guidance of wiser and more experienced men than themselves, and contribute to enterprises which they could neither originate nor conduct. Most of us *do* thus put our

Master's money with the bankers. Much of the charitable and religious work we do, we do in methods and through organizations originated by abler men. We subscribe to schools, churches, societies which aim at ameliorating the physical and social conditions of men, or at diffusing a knowledge of the Christian Faith throughout the world; or we help to *work* some of these organizations, contributing time and energy to them as well as money. Now and then, doubtless, men, and even Christian men, are to be met who are too conscious of the defects of every existing organization to take part in any of them, while they are also too slenderly gifted or too little in earnest to devise better methods of service. Now and then, too, men, and even Christian men, are to be met who, though they are too weak to originate anything or to work alone, are too strong in self-conceit to work with others or to be content with a subordinate and inconspicuous part. But, as a rule, we are most of us content to cast our contributions into some common bank, and to leave the management of it with the bankers. And if we are capable of nothing more, our kindly Judge and Saviour will accept even this at our hand, and say perhaps that we have done wisely in not attempting more. But the implication of the Parable is, I think, that most of us could do more if we tried, and would do more if we were good and faithful servants. There is some direct and immediate work which most of us might do if we cared to do it; there must be at least a few people about us whom we might influence in various ways for good, or help to reclaim if they have gone astray. And what we can do in this way, Christ expects us to do: and surely we shall all wish that we had done it when we come to lay our work before Him and to hear what He thinks of it.

6. Finally, the Parable implies that the rewards both of faithful service and of unfaithfulness and sloth are not arbitrary, but fair, reasonable, inevitable. 'To every one that hath shall be given, and he shall have abundance; but from him that hath not shall be taken away even that which he hath.' Paradoxical as the words sound, how clear and true is the thought which lies beneath them. For does not every faculty we possess grow by use, and decay, or even die out, by disuse and neglect? Think what an infinite variety of abilities and aptitudes every child that is born into the world brings with him. You may make 'anything' of him. You may train him to any one of the thousand handicrafts, trades, callings, professions by which men earn their bread, though each of these demands special capacities specially trained. All depends on the faculties you select and develop by the culture you give him. These

grow by use; the others die out or remain dormant for lack of use. And when his special faculty, or group of faculties, is developed, do they not continue to grow in force and delicacy so long as he continues to employ them? If he has gained manual dexterity by working in wood or leather, stone or metal, does not his hand grow ever more dexterous? If he *has*, and uses what he has, *is* not more given unto him? And if he *has not*, does it not grow ever more impossible for him to acquire a dexterous and masterly use of the faculty he has neglected? If a man has learned one foreign language, does he not find it easier to learn another, and still another? whereas if he has learned none, if he has suffered this faculty to 'fust' in him unused till he is advanced in years, will he find it possible to acquire any foreign tongue with ease, or even at last to acquire it at all? It is true, then, that in every province of manual or mental dexterity the law holds good: to him that hath it is given and given ever more abundantly, while from him that hath not even that which he had is taken away.

Nor is it otherwise in the moral sphere. It cannot be otherwise. If a man has exercised himself to apprehend truth and enjoy it, must not his apprehensions and love of it grow ever larger, stronger, finer? If a man has practised himself in the love and obedience of righteousness, must not his faculty for doing that which is right increase by what it feeds upon? If a man has long ruled and denied himself, does not mere habit render the task of self-rule easier to him? If a man has long cherished pure and kindly affections, is it not reasonable, and even inevitable, that his love for God and man should become more true and deep and tender? And, on the other hand, if a man has wilfully closed his eyes against truth, if he has preferred self-indulgence to self-restraint, and greed and sloth to a diligent service of righteousness, must not his capacity for evil increase and his capacity for good diminish?

It is not, then, by any caprice on the part of our Divine Ruler and Judge that, if we have been faithful in few things, we shall receive many things, and that, if we have been unfaithful in little, we shall lose even the little we once had: on the contrary, it is the clear and logical result of our very nature and of the conditions under which it works.

To what end, indeed, should God give us *more* than we can use and enjoy? And we can only use and enjoy more even of that which is good as we learn to use and enjoy that which we already possess. Even God Himself cannot smuggle us into heaven through some back-door of secret and sovereign grace; for we can only be in heaven as we are made meet for it.

And how can He make us meet, *i.e.* how can He make us good and faithful, against our will? Our wills must blend and work with his before we can be approved and blessed by Him. Only as we grow like the Lord can we enter into the joy of the Lord.

XVI.

THE PARABLE OF THE SHEEP AND THE GOATS.

'When the Son of Man shall come in his glory, and all the holy angels with him, then shall he sit upon the throne of his glory; and before him shall be gathered all nations: and he shall separate them one from another, as a shepherd divideth his sheep from the goats: and he shall set the sheep on his right hand, but the goats on the left.' &c., &c., &c.—ST. MATTHEW xxv. 31-46.

THE Son of Man here claims to be the King and the Judge of 'all nations.' A wonderful claim, surely, for 'mere man' to make! For what man is there who knows *all* men? What man is there who knows *one* man altogether; knows him well enough to judge him fairly, even though that one should be himself? What man is there by whom we any one of us would like to be judged? What man is there who would make due allowance for the frailties of our nature, for our hereditary bias, for the temptations to which we are exposed, the subtle and fatal conspiracies of occasion with desire, for our struggles against evils to which we have nevertheless succumbed, for the endeavours after goodness in which we were nevertheless defeated, for the bitter shame and remorse with which we look back on our failures and our sins? Can any one but the Omniscient God judge us fairly? Must not He, then, who claims to be our Judge, and the Judge of all men, claim to be God, claim to share his omniscience, his disinterested and impartial justice, his loving kindness and tender mercy? And if the Man Christ Jesus, 'the best man who e'er wore flesh about him,' advance this claim, shall we traverse or resist it?

Before we resist, before we so much as question it, let us at least remember that the claim is as gracious as it is marvellous. For if only One who partakes the Divine Nature can so know men as to judge them fairly, is not One who is also partaker of our human nature the more likely to judge us tenderly? 'God knoweth our frame,' indeed; but the Son of Man has inhabited our frame. Like us at all points, He has been tried at all points as we are. He knows, by personal experience, what we are, and what we can do; what gifts we have received and what use we are capable of making of them; to what temptations we lie open, and how far we are able to resist them. He knows the frailties of that part of our complex nature which is but dust, and the capacities of that part of our nature which is spiritual and divine. And therefore He is able, not only to succour but to *judge* us. This, indeed, seems to be the thought which underlies and explains his own mysterious saying concerning Himself: 'The Father hath given him authority to execute judgment also, *because he is Son of Man*,' as if his humanity gave Him a new claim and the most decisive qualification for the office and function of Judge.

And what better Judge could we have or desire? a Judge human and yet divine; divine, and therefore above the infirmities which warp our judgment of each other; and yet human, and therefore touched with a feeling of our infirmities which prompts and enables Him to make due allowance for us all.

In the Discourse which St. Matthew here records for our instruction the judgment of the Son of Man is set forth under three figures or parables. In the parable of the Ten Virgins we are taught that we shall be judged by our foresight, by our promptitude in seizing opportunities, by our preparedness for the great and happy change of death or our unpreparedness for it. In the parable of the Talents we are taught that we shall be judged by our diligent use of the gifts severally entrusted to us, or our lack of diligence. And in this parable of the Sheep and the Goats we are taught that we shall be judged by the active benevolence which has moved us to relieve the distresses of our fellows, or by our want of it.

Nor are even these the only tests by which we are to be tried. We are to be justified or condemned by our words as well as by our deeds; by our inward emotions, dispositions, motives, as well as by our words; by the faith without which it is impossible to please God, by the hopefulness which leads us to look for better things to come, by the charity which is even greater than hope or faith. In short, as we learn from the teaching of Christ and his Apostles, every appropriate criterion is to be applied to us; whatever in the whole round of thought and emotion, speech and action, motive and aim, indicates character will be accepted as evidence for or against us, and will influence or modify the sentence pronounced upon us. The good impulses and kindly deeds of the bad will not be forgotten, nor will the bad impulses and unkindly actions of the good be overlooked. And, no doubt, every kind of test, from the most simple to the most subtle and elaborate, will be applied to us, in order that we ourselves may see ourselves as we really are, and be constrained to ratify the verdict of the Judge.

1. The first and simplest thought we have to impress on our minds, then, is, that at, or after, death our whole life will be scrutinized, revised, judged; and that the sum of all our thoughts, affections, volitions, actions—our *character*, in short—will determine the

condition or state on which we shall then enter; every man 'going to *his own* place,' the place for which he has fitted himself and into which he will *fit*. The thought is a simple one; it is consonant with the teaching of Science, and of Conscience, no less than with the plain declarations of the Word of God. Nevertheless, it needs to be again and again impressed upon us. In the throng and noise and hurry of our life we too much, and too often, forget it; and even when we remember it, and profess to believe it, we do not suffer it to exert its due influence whether on our thoughts or our lives. Most of us, no doubt, reflect seriously at times that our life, with all that it inherits, is a sacred trust of which we are bound to make the best use we can, of our use of which we must one day give account, by our use of which our condition will be determined in the world to come. But do we habitually refer to this solemn fact and reckon on it? Does the fact that we are bound to make the best possible use of our gifts and opportunities, and that we shall have to account for the use we have made of them, influence and control us in our business transactions, for example, or in the management of our property, or in the education and placing of our children, or in the attachments we form, the company we keep, and the style in which we live?

It *ought*, if it be true. And who can question its

truth? Science tells us that at every moment our life is but the sum and outcome of all that has gone before; that our future is and must be determined by our past. In affirming a judgment to come, therefore, Religion does but confirm the teachings of Science and project them into the future. Conscience, too, the universal conscience of man, pronounces it to be just and right that every man should receive according to his deeds, both good and bad, whether in this world or in any other. History, again, loves to track the steps of that impartial and beneficent Nemesis which dogs the feet of men, smiting even the mightiest criminal with the retribution he has provoked, and bringing a late yet ample reward to lowly virtue, or valiant struggles for the right, or an heroic endurance of wrong. And Nature, while just to our deserts, shews a love and bounty beyond our deserts, permitting every man to reap *as* he sows, and yet *more* than he sows, and scattering around us sweet flowers and wholesome fruits whose seeds did not fall from our hands nor from any hands visible to us. So that in proclaiming a judgment in which every man shall receive his due, and yet, through the great mercy of God, far more and better than his due, Scripture does but echo and ratify the teachings of Nature and Science, of History and of Conscience.

We *ought*, therefore, to believe in a judgment to

come; we ought to let our belief in it influence and determine our various courses of thought and action.

2. Nay, more, we ought *to rejoice* in this belief. What craving strikes its root more deeply in our nature than the craving for justice, the desire that we should get our due and that all men should get theirs? Are we not for ever being judged—judged wrongfully, partially, inequitably—by men and yet compelled to submit to their inadequate and erroneous judgments of us? Must it not be an unspeakable blessing and comfort for us, then, to be removed, as we shall be at death, from their ignorant censures and unjust rule into the rule and judgment, into 'the pure eyes and perfect witness,' of the just yet gracious God?

The ancient Psalmist, vexed by the tyranny of Oriental despots, burst into a very rapture of song at the mere thought of being taken into the hand of God: 'Let the sea roar and the fulness thereof, the world and they that dwell therein; let the floods clap their hands, let the mountains be joyful together before the Lord; for he cometh—he cometh *to judge* the earth: with righteousness will *he* judge the world and the people with equity.' And why should the mere hope of the advent of God the Judge fill the Psalmist's heart with a tumult of gladness which only the great world with its seas and floods, its woods and mountains, could adequately express, while yet the assurance of that Advent and Epiphany only saddens or alarms us? If we loved righteousness as we ought to love it, and longed to see it established in the earth; if we believed in God as we of all men ought to believe in Him, and in the blended mercy and equity of his judgments; if we realized that our lives are to be scanned and our sentence pronounced by that gentle and kindly Son of Man who once walked the earth and wore our flesh about Him, instead of shrinking and trembling at the thought of a Divine judgment and rule, we too should rejoice in it with a joy unspeakable and full of glory.

The first lesson we learn from this Parable is, then, that we shall all be judged when we die by the Son of Man; and the second, that we ought to be very glad that we shall be judged, and judged by Him.

3. But there are many other lessons to be learned from this Chapter, and notably this: that *the deeds* we have done in the body will go far to determine our sentence.

We have seen that every possible and appropriate test will be applied to us in the great assize; that whatever indicates character, whether it be found in our words or thoughts, or in our motives, emotions, aims, will be accepted as evidence for or against us. But we need to mark that, throughout this Chapter, the main stress is laid on what we *do*. The Virgins of the first Parable have to keep their lamps burning and their vessels charged with oil, and to be ready for the Bridegroom come when he may. The Servants of the second Parable have to trade with the talents committed to them, and to make them 'more' by a wise and diligent use of them. And in *this* Parable men are rewarded for the practical and active benevolence with which they have ministered to those who were in distress, or are condemned for their lack of it. So that, throughout, it is active endeavour, it is our deeds, which are made the first and ruling test.

And is not that just? If 'deeds speak louder than words,' ought not our deeds to have more to say for us or against us than our words? If no inward impulse, no movement of mind or heart be complete till it is clothed in action, if good impulses and kindly dispositions are only made permanent and regnant as we habitually act on them, should not our actions tell for more than the fluctuating impulses and inclinations which do not rise into action, and pass through action into habit? And yet there are many good people who depend more on their 'frames' and inward moods than on the toils and sacrifices of active enterprise. There are many who, because they cherish kindly and tender emotions, or prayerful and devout emotions, account that they shall be approved by the Judge. There are many even who expect and urge their neighbours to do much for the Church, or for the poor, the ignorant, the afflicted, who do very little themselves,—many who, as George Eliot's village preacher quaintly put it, are like the wood-pigeon which for ever flutes out 'do,' 'do,' but never begins to do anything itself. Let us remember, then, that Christ demands action, endeavour, enterprise of all who love Him, and will judge us not so much by our emotions, or even by our exhortations, as by our deeds.

4. Let us still further remember that there is one form or kind of activity to which Christ our Judge attaches a special and preëminent value. The Parable of the Sheep and the Goats contains his most elaborate and solemn description of the Judgment. And on what do the issues of that judgment turn here? Simply on the fact of whether or not we have ministered to the hungry and thirsty, the naked and the sick. If we have done that, He takes our service as service done to Himself. Why? Partly, no doubt, because, we have been doing what He Himself would have done had He stood in our place. But, mainly, because in his love and his pity He has so identified Himself with every man, and especially with the afflicted and distressed, that any kindness shewn to them is virtually kindness shewn to Him.

It would almost seem, indeed, that mere kindness of itself, when at least it is an active kindness, makes men his 'brethren,' even though they are not his brethren by faith and conscious personal love. For in this Parable He speaks to certain 'righteous' persons as if they were not his brethren, but had only ministered to 'one of the least of *these* my brethren;' and yet He bestows on them the reward of 'brethren' and admits them to the kingdom of his Father. In his sight an active benevolence is of such value that it amounts to 'righteousness,' and is a sufficient proof of brotherhood with Him.

And, when we come to think of it, we may easily understand how that should be. For what, according to Christ, is the whole duty of the Gospel as well as the end of the Law? It is that we love God with all our heart and our neighbour as ourself. *God loves us*,—that is the whole doctrine of the Gospel: *let us love God*,—this is its whole morality. And does not St. John teach and assure us that we cannot love the God whom we have not seen, unless we love the brother whom we have seen? To love our neighbour on earth proves that, consciously or unconsciously, we love our Father in heaven. And he who loves God and man,—shall not he be accepted and blessed by the Judge? The very end to secure which the Gospel was given has been reached in him, even though he be ignorant of the Gospel, even though the Gospel should be incredible to him.

Now from this thought we get a most comfortable hope for some in our own day who, in their despair of reaching a settled faith, have devoted themselves to a life of charity, a life of service; who have sought rest for their weary spirits in tending the sick, the poor, the wronged; whose days are spent in hospitals, asylums, workhouses, prisons, or in provinces stricken by famine or devastated by war. In ministering to the simplest and most primitive wants of men they have discovered a duty the obligation of which they could not doubt, and in the discharge of this duty they have found a welcome calm and peace for their perturbed spirits. And shall not Christ the Judge say even to these also?—'Inasmuch as ye did it to the least of my brethren, ye did it unto me.'

5. For, finally, let us observe that in our Parable both the righteous and the unrighteous are taken by surprise. The former did not know that it was *Christ* to whom they ministered, nor the latter that it was Christ whom they passed by. Both can say, and say with genuine astonishment: 'When saw we *Thee* hungry or athirst, naked, or sick, or in prison?' The one had not been moved by any theological belief, nor the other by any theoretical unbelief. The 'righteous' had simply acted on the kindly and gracious

impulses of their hearts—it was that which made them righteous; and the wicked had simply trampled down those impulses, so making themselves wicked.

And in this thought there lie two suggestions each of which is, I think, very instructive and pathetic. The first is that the judgment pronounced on our life and work by the Son of Man may turn on points we did not anticipate: and the other is that the Judge will be apt to see in our actions far more than we consciously put into them, and to reward us for them far beyond our deserts.

Those whom Christ here pronounces blessed of his Father evidently set little store on the works of 'common humanity' which they had performed; *they*, possibly, were fearing lest the Judge should condemn them because their creed, or their knowledge of Him, had been terribly imperfect: and those whom He pronounces accursed may, perhaps, have been confidently looking for approval because they knew Him so well and their creed was so 'sound;' they may never have dreamed that by their want of common humanity they had provoked his anger and demonstrated that, whatever their creed, they had no genuine faith in God. And, very certainly, if we are trusting in any faith which does not work by love, *we* shall be amazed to find ourselves rejected by the merciful Judge eternal: while, if we are doing kindness and shewing mercy to our neighbours in despair of ever learning a higher duty or a larger truth, we may be no less amazed to find that He whom we did not know knew us,—knew, and approved.

But there is no need to set faith and works in opposition. The great truth of this passage is that if there be *any* good thing in us, or in any part of us—in our faith, in our dispositions and affections, in our motives, words, actions, aims; if we have tried to think wisely and largely and to give our neighbours the benefit of our thinking; if we have cherished kindly feelings and a self-forgetting love; if we have striven to keep ourselves free, and to set our neighbours free, from clamorous and selfish desires; if we have studied how we could serve men in our business life, in our home life, by our devotion to high and noble ends; or if we have gone about doing good, ministering to the necessities of the poor, the ignorant, the sick, the sorrowful: in whatever form or degree we have done the right and possessed ourselves of that which is good, Christ the Judge will discover it by the application of some appropriate test, value it at its true worth, nay, even beyond its worth in any eyes but his; and, in rewarding us for it, will use good measure, pressed down, shaken together, and yet running over.

Here, then, are five great truths suggested by this

Parable and Discourse which we shall do well to lay up and ponder in our hearts: (1.) That we must all appear before the judgment seat of Christ *to have our lives revised by Him:* (2.) That *we ought to be very glad that we shall be judged,* and especially that we shall be judged *by Him:* (3.) That, as deeds are the most reliable and complete indications of character, it is mainly *by what we have done* that He will judge us: (4.) That by deeds of one kind, *by ministering to the primitive and common wants of men,* by an active and benign benevolence, we most of all commend ourselves to Him: and (5) that, though He may apply to us some tests of character which will *take us by surprise, his aim will be to discover whatever there may be of good in us, in order that He may reward it with a generosity unstinted and divine.*

XVII.

THE PARABLE OF THE TEN VIRGINS.

'Then shall the kingdom of heaven be likened unto ten virgins, who took their lamps, and went forth to meet the bridegroom. And five of them were wise, and five were foolish,' &c., &c., &c.—St. Matthew xxv. 1-13.

For all so simple as it sounds this Parable is, probably, the most difficult of which we have any record, as it is certainly one of the most terrible in its suggestions. There is much in it which seems alien and opposed to the gracious spirit of the Friend and Saviour of men; much which, on the common hypothesis, it is impossible to interpret; much which, on any hypothesis, it is difficult to handle fairly. Put your heart into your mind, and then put your mind to this picture or parable, and you will be startled and shocked again and again. And yet the outward form of the Parable presents no difficulty; while even its inner spirit and intention, strange to say, seem to excite no feeling of horror and aversion in most of those who have had to expound it.

The scene here depicted is one that any traveller in

the East may come across to this day; and to most of the travellers who have witnessed it, it appears to suggest nothing more than the accuracy and beauty of our Lord's description. One accomplished writer and traveller, for example, has this passage:[*] 'At a marriage, the procession of which I saw, some years ago, the bridegroom came from a distance, and the bride lived at Serampore, to which place the bridegroom was to come by water. After waiting two or three hours, at length, near midnight, it was announced, as if in the very words of Scripture, "Behold, the bridegroom cometh, go ye out to meet him." All the persons employed now lighted their lamps, and ran with them in their hands, to fill up their stations in the procession. Some of them had lost their lights and were unprepared; but it was too late to seek them, and the cavalcade moved forward to the house of the bride, at which place the company entered a large and splendidly illuminated area before the house, covered with an awning, where a great multitude of friends, dressed in their best apparel, were seated on mats. The bridegroom was carried in, and placed on a superb seat in the midst of the company, where he rested for a short time, and then went into the house, the door of which was imme-

---

[*] W. Ward. Quoted by Dr. Morison, *in loco*.

diately shut, and guarded by sepoys. I and others expostulated with the doorkeepers, but in vain. Never was I so struck with our Lord's beautiful parable as at this moment: *and the door was shut.* I was exceedingly anxious to be present while the marriage formulas were repeated, but was obliged to depart disappointed.'

Beautiful parable! and special beauty of that touch, *and the door was shut!* That is not precisely the impression such an incident would have left on a mind occupied with the grave and momentous realities set forth in the Parable, instead of being pre-occupied with its literary form and 'exceedingly anxious' to hear the 'marriage formulas of the Hindoos.' To one who has long been haunted by its suggestions of despair, who in his waking and dreaming thoughts has heard that dreadful 'door' slam to for years, and listened to its echoes rolling and reverberating down the long corridors of endless time,—heard it and trembled for himself, heard it and been shaken with a still deeper pity and apprehension for the millions around him—it is not the beauty of the Parable that strikes him, but the terror of it, the vast, horrible, unending tragedy implied in it.

1. Nor is this the only difficulty involved in the Parable, or in the common interpretation of it. Most of the Commentators whom I have consulted tell us

that in this Parable of the Virgins we are to see Christ's judgment of the members, or nominal members, of his body the Church; the wise Virgins standing for his true disciples, and the foolish Virgins for his false or pretended disciples; while in the Parable of the Talents we are to see his judgment on the ministers of that Church, and in the Parable of the Sheep and the Goats his judgment of the world at large, and especially of the heathen world. Now I am not prepared to affirm that there is no truth in this scheme of interpretation, nor have I the slightest wish to turn the edge of any warning addressed whether to the Church or to the ministers of the Church. All I want to do is to ask: Does this interpretation cover and explain all the facts of the Parable? There are five wise and five foolish Virgins in it. Are we then to conclude that in the last day it will be proved that there have been as many false as true disciples of Christ, that *one half* of the very Church itself will be consigned to eternal perdition? Is that the way in which the Redeemer of mankind is to 'see of the travail of his soul, and to be *satisfied*?' The five foolish Virgins are represented as friends of the bridegroom bent on doing him honour; as having so much oil in their lamps that their lamps were only just 'going out' when, after their long vigil, the bridegroom came; as being willing and anxious, even then, to beg or buy more oil for their lamps; as knocking earnestly at the closed door for admission and entreating to be let in. Is that a picture which instantly and naturally calls up before our minds the hypocrites who merely make a false show of religion, who have possessed themselves of the mere form of godliness without its power? Are we to believe that any love will be rejected by the Saviour, that any service or intention of service will be passed by by the Judge of men? or that He will for ever exclude from his kingdom any who really desire to enter it?

The wise, or, rather, the 'prudent' Virgins are represented as refusing to help their imprudent sisters, as packing them off to buy from them that sell when they knew that it was too late, that the shops would be shut, or that before their companions could return the bridal train would have swept into the palace. Is that in the spirit of true disciples of Him who gave Himself up for us all? Can you so much as conceive of *Him* as saying to any seeker after life: 'I cannot give to you, lest I should not have enough for myself'? Can you even conceive of Him as sitting down to his wedding-feast with a composed and cheerful mind while poor souls, who thought to do Him honour, were shut out in the cold and the dark, knocking and begging for entrance in vain, weeping in vain? or as saying 'I know you not' to any who wanted to know Him? Would it not be infinitely more in accordance with all you know of Him if, springing from his seat, and leaving his bride to follow at her best speed, He hurried to the door at the first sound of appeal, to rebuke the servants who had so miserably mistaken his mind as to close it against any who would come in, and to give a tender cordial welcome to as many as were willing to eat and drink with Him? If I know Him at all, I for one would far rather stand with the poor foolish things weeping outside in the dark, than with the Pharisees of the door-mat who had shut them out.

I do not say that these difficulties are insuperable, though I confess I see no way either over or through them; I say simply that they *are* difficulties, and difficulties which attach to the main facts and incidents of the Parable, and not to its mere details,— such for example, as the lamps, and the oil, and the vessels, and the traders in oil, on all of which points no little scholarship and ingenuity have been wasted.

And these difficulties grow as we remember that, whereas in this Parable one in every two is represented as rejected by the Judge, in the very next Parable, that of the Talents, only one in three is assumed to fail, while in the third Parable, that of the Sheep and the Goats, a vast multitude is represented as approved by the Judge simply on account of services which they had unconsciously rendered to Him,—not knowing that it was He whom they had served, not intending and striving, as these poor Virgins did, to do Him honour. From these later Parables indeed we learn what may help us here— and that is the reason why I asked you to take them out of their natural order and study them first—that in the Judgment many tests will be applied to us, every appropriate test; and that the object of the Judge will be to discover our true character, to make it manifest, in order that if there is any good in us it may be cherished and rewarded, and if any evil that it may be condemned and punished. Ministers are members of the Church, and members of the Church are men. Tried as ministers, we may be shewn to have failed, and yet not necessarily to have failed in our private relation to the Church. Tried as members of the Church, we may be shewn to have failed, and yet, as men, we may have displayed that active kindness to our neighbours which will lead the Judge to say: 'Inasmuch as ye did it to the least of these my brethren, ye did it unto me;' or even: 'Come ye blessed of my Father, inherit the Kingdom prepared for you from the foundation of the world.'

Now this thought of itself, that the Parable is one of a series, and only sets forth one test among many, robs it of half its difficulties. Read in this light, we see at once that we must not infer from it the perdition of half the Church, nor of half the world; we leave room for the final salvation even of the imprudent, since the imprudent and uncalculating are often very kindly and self-sacrificing: and we are no longer driven to think of the Judge as rejecting any who love Him and have tried to serve Him, however imperfect their service may have been.

2. In some measure, at least, we may thus reconcile this Parable with the other teaching, and with the just and merciful spirit, of Christ our Saviour and our Judge. But we are still very far from having discharged all severity from it, all thoughts and suggestions of terror. We shall never do *that;* we should not hope to do it. For how should Christ be the Truth indeed if his words were untrue to our experience of human life? And life is often very hard; there is an inexorable severity in it which no words can soften or explain away. And it is to one of the austerest aspects of our life, projected into the future—*prolonged* into it—to which, as I believe, our Lord here calls our thoughts.

We all know that there are grave conjectures, critical emergencies, auspicious opportunities, in our lives which, if we recognize and use them, alter and raise the whole current of our after-life; while, if we fail to see and to seize upon them, they never return to us, or only return in some different form, and commonly in some form in which we find it still more difficult to recognize and employ them. Most of us can recall opportunities of this kind that we have had, and lost—opportunities of acquiring knowledge, or rising into a happier or establishing ourselves in a securer position; opportunities of winning distinction or winning affection, of gaining mental or moral culture, or of practising ourselves in the more difficult virtues; opportunities which we either saw too late, or, seeing in time, nevertheless suffered to slip by unused for lack of courage, or lack of promptitude, or from mere indolence, preoccupation, neglect. We all admit that it is not prudent, that it is not wise, to live as if no opportunities, no 'chances' of this sort would come to us. They come to all men. Yet since no man can tell when, or in what form, they will come *to him*, we confess that it is our wisdom and our duty to prepare for them, to be on the look out for them, to train and accomplish ourselves as thoroughly and as variously as we can, in order that we may both have the more opportunities of this kind and be the more ready to seize upon them. Even if we have missed some of these golden opportunities—and I am very sure that even as I speak many of you are thinking ruefully of chances you have lost,—we do not allow that a man should leave off looking for them or preparing for them. While there is life there is hope. We call no man either 'happy' or 'unhappy' till his death. Some 'chances' are gone indeed, and we shall never get them back; but others may come in their place. And hence we exhort each other not to despair, but to watch and to be ready. Nay, we even teach one another that our very failures, wisely handled, may help to prepare us for the next auspicious occasion, and to set a higher value upon it. 'There is a tide in the affairs of men,' we say, 'which, taken at the flood, leads on to fortune:' and the tides rise at least once every day, and there are even more flood-tides than one in the year.

At the same time we admit, with our great Poet, that there are cases in which, if the tide be once missed, all the after life is 'bound in shallows and in miseries.' A man who, because he has missed a favourable conjuncture, begins to despair of himself, may only too easily fall into habits, or sins, from the evil effects of which there is no redemption at least in the present life. For if opportunities come to us by seizing which we may make great gain, temptations come to us to which if we once submit we may do ourselves an irreparable injury. There are stains which no tears can remove; there are faults and crimes which no penitence can atone. At any moment we may speak a few words, or do a single deed, which will permanently darken our whole life, and other lives as well as our own, clouding them with 'mist and a weeping rain:' There are sins—and these not always the worst—which so damage both men and women in their own eyes or in the eyes of the world around them that, if they once fall into them, they can never be the same again whether in character or in reputation; just as there are chances which, if they are once lost, are lost for ever.

And yet even the most disastrous failures *may* be retrieved—not in the eyes of the world indeed, but in the eyes of Him who is to judge the world. Penitence, meek and patient submission to the inevitable results of sin, faith in the Goodness and Love, which are 'more than all our sins,' personal amendment and care for others, may redeem even the most miserable and self-condemned life from final and ruinous failure. At times we see those who have fallen under the ban of conscience, as well as the censure of the world, out of very weakness growing strong, finding in loss itself a gain to match, and driven by their very failures in this life to fit themselves for a fairer and happier life in the world to come. *Sometimes*, but not often; for the worst of utter failure is that we are apt to give in to it, to despair of retrieving ourselves, to contract habits which still further damage and depress us.

Human life, then, stands thick with conjunctures for which we prove to be unprepared, with opportunities which we fail to see or fail to improve, with chances which, once missed, never recur, although they may be succeeded by others. And *death*—such seems to be the teaching of our Parable—will be such a crisis to many; an opportunity which they are unprepared to seize and to turn to good account. The spiritual world on which they will then enter is one that has been seldom in their thoughts, one in which they have not trained themselves to be at home and to take delight. Stripped of all that they really knew and cared for, they will find themselves lost, naked, poor indeed; and then it will be too late to make ready. The whole tone and bent of the spirit cannot be changed in an instant. To the merely natural man, the man who has only studied his appetites, or his business, or his social success, the spiritual world must at first be as uncongenial, as alien, as the world of thought and culture and refinement to the most clownish and ignorant of mankind. What charm can there be in purity to the impure, or in righteousness to the unrighteous, or in charity to the selfish, or even in wisdom to the foolish?

When, therefore, our Lord says (Verse 46), 'These shall go away into eternal punishment,' *i.e.* into the punishment of the eternal world, He is pronouncing no arbitrary sentence, no angry and resentful award; He is simply foretelling the natural and inevitable result of the moral conditions of men who have lived in and for the things which are seen and temporal rather than in and for the things which are unseen and eternal. *To be in* the world that is spiritual and eternal must of itself be a punishment to the sensual and selfish, to those whose thoughts and wishes and aims are bounded by sense and time. That world cannot but seem to them a foreign world, to which they cannot suddenly adjust themselves, or even a hostile world to which they can hardly hope to be reconciled.

They have missed their chance; they have lost the sovereign and supreme opportunity of life; and they must long rue the consequences of their folly, their imprudence, their sin.

3. But have they missed their *last* chance? is the door which they have shut in their own face shut against them for ever? We have no right to say that it is. To say that is to be wise above what is written. Nor do I see how we can say it without denying to the self-condemned the very nature of man, and to God the love which He has revealed in Jesus Christ his Son. *The punishments of eternity are no more necessarily to be borne to all eternity than the punishments of time are necessarily to be borne through the*

whole duration of time. Man is essentially a spirit: and therefore so long as he remains a man, he must at least be *capable* of being trained to appreciate and enjoy the spiritual world, to be at home in it. And it may be that 'the punishments of eternity' will afford him the very discipline he needs, just as the punishments of time often teach him to make a better use of time. We too often take the redeeming work of Christ as a single action of Divine Love, a solitary irrepeatable instance of it, rather than as the crowning revelation of a Love that always *was* and always *will be*, a Love which can know no change and no diminution. If God be love, if that be his essential quality, how can we doubt that so long as man remains a spirit and is capable of spiritual training, the Love of God, the Love which is God, will be bent on training him for the highest service and blessedness of which he is capable? How can we doubt that the Eternal Father will pursue his erring child with the discipline by which he may yet be brought back to Himself and made at home in his Father's house? If there are some passages in the New Testament which seem to imply that the fate of men is irrevocably fixed at the Judgment, there are many more which imply that it is the Divine purpose to redeem them all, and to quicken in all the rapture of a spiritual and perfect life. And if we *believe* in God, and in the revelation He has made of Himself in the truth and grace of Christ, are we not compelled to grasp the larger hope, sure that even our largest thoughts of Him must fall far short of the divine reality?

Yes, my brethren, we may cherish hope for all men, even for ourselves; but, with hope, let us also cherish a wholesome fear or awe. The rigours and punishments of time are sharp enough; but if, when these have failed to correct and redeem us, we are to be exposed to 'the punishments of eternity,' how sharp must those be if we are to be really penetrated by them and made plastic to the saving will of God? He little knows himself or God who, because he hopes that he is not to be for ever damned, risks the life to come, and buries himself in a living death from which all the artillery of Heaven will very hardly awaken him. Love is a fire: and to be searched through and through by the pure cleansing fire of Divine Love is a doom before which even the boldest must quail. Now the Spirit of God comes to you in all benign and gracious forms, wooing and inviting you to turn and live. Will you fling away your chance, and wait till He comes in forms of judgment and of terror which heart of man cannot so much as conceive?

4. Finally, we of the Church need especially to

be on the watch, and to prepare ourselves to stand before the bar of Christ: for I suppose there is at least so much of truth in the current interpretation of this Parable as may well suggest to us that 'judgment will *begin* at the House of God,' and that of all things a formal religion, an indolent and imprudent piety, is the most hardening and degrading. Whether the five imprudent Virgins stand, or do not stand, for false disciples, for those who have a form of godliness without its power, there can be no doubt that many who assume themselves to be very religious grow so familiar with forms of worship, and so busy themselves in the mere administration and routine of the Christian Fellowship, that they are in no little danger of dropping into a narrow mechanical round in which they lose insight, outlook, forecast, and miss the opportunities of quickened and larger life which God sends them. It was *the Church* of Christ's day which, absorbed in ritual and traditional routine, missed the supreme opportunity of all time, and put the very Lord and Giver of life to death. It was *the Church* of Luther's day that, not knowing the hour of its visitation, rejected the truth with which *he* was charged, and would have put him also to death if they could. And it is at least a large section of *the Church* which is to-day turning a deaf ear to the new truths of the day—truths of Science and of Criticism, for instance—and resenting any vital and springing forms of doctrine which would disturb their slumbers and compel them to readjust and enlarge their conceptions of duty and worship.

In our private lives we all know how difficult it is to remain watchful and alert, to keep ready for the Bridegroom come how and when He may; to welcome new forms and ministries, or to go on finding new life and incentive in forms and ministries with which we have grown familiar; to strike out new paths of service, or to walk in the old paths without forgetting that they *are* paths, and should lead us somewhere. To us, therefore, as to all, but especially to us of the Church, the warning is requisite which our Lord Himself drew from his Parable. 'Watch, therefore, for ye know neither the day, nor the hour, wherein the Son of Man cometh.' For whenever He comes and calls for us, we shall surely wish that, to the very end, we had done our best for Him, and for the Church, and for the world.

XVIII.

ST. PETER'S SIFTING AND CONVERSION.

1.—THE PROLOGUE IN HEAVEN.

'And the Lord said, Simon, Simon, behold Satan hath desired to have you, that he may sift you as wheat; but I have prayed for thee, that thy faith fail not: and when thou art converted, strengthen thy brethren.'—ST. LUKE xxii. 31, 32.

WHEN we read that marvellous Prologue to the Book of Job which has inspired more than one of our modern poets with his loftiest verse, we are apt to say: 'Sublime as it is, it is only poetry after all. We are not to suppose that Jehovah ever held a court at which Satan appeared among the sons of God to malign the character and motives of the patriarch of Uz, to ask and obtain that he might be delivered into his hands, and put to test after test of the utmost severity, in order that his selfishness and impiety might be made apparent. All that,' we say, 'is but the dramatic form in which the Poet clothed certain abstract conceptions of the Providence of God, and of the discipline by which He perfects the sons whom He will afterward receive into glory.'

Nor can there be any doubt that we have some ground, good ground even, for this conclusion. The sacred realities of the spiritual world are too large and lofty, too pure and august, to be compassed by human thought or expressed in human words. In our highest flights we do but skim the mountain tops; the heavens are still as far beyond us as when we 'considered' them from the plain.

We have no truer name for God than Father, for example; and yet if God be our father, He must be our father in a far other and deeper sense than the father of our flesh, or than Adam even, who is the father of us all. Our best and highest conceptions of spiritual entities and spiritual relations must of necessity be inadequate so long as the spirit in us is hampered and confined by this 'mortal coil.' But it does not follow that our conceptions, because they are inadequate, must therefore be inaccurate and misleading—very few conceptions, indeed, even though they be scientific conceptions of natural laws are adequate; *i.e.* very few of them cover all the facts, or are already perfect. They may be true, so far as they go, just as the thoughts of a child about his father and the world his father inhabits may be true, though they must of necessity be partial and incomplete. That is to say, there may be, there are, spiritual realities and relations answering to our conceptions, though, until that which is perfect is come, we can but know them in part, can but see them as in a glass darkly, can but measure and define the shadows cast by the eternal substances rather than the very substances themselves. Still, where there is shadow there must be substance; and from the shadow, if only we think enough about it, we may draw a true and helpful prevision of what the reality is like.

So that if, on the one hand, we must admit that in the Hebrew Poet's description of the scenes in heaven we have only dim shadows of heavenly realities and transactions, we must, on the other hand, be careful not to deny that these shadows are cast by heavenly substances; if we admit that he gives a dramatic form to his conceptions of the spiritual world, we must be careful how we deny that there *is* a spiritual world, and even a spiritual world answering to his and our conceptions of it. If every drama does not set forth an actual story, at least every drama worthy of the name does set forth some of the actual relations which subsist among men, and is based on occurrences which have really taken place; it teaches and moves us only in proportion as it is true to nature, true to fact.

In *this* sense, at least, we have many reasons for believing that the Prologue of the Book of Job is true to nature, that it is not a mere fiction which we owe simply to the 'fine frenzy' of some unknown Hebrew of genius; but, at lowest, a fiction founded on facts, a parable which truly, though imperfectly, sets forth real spiritual relations. The very form of it even is not peculiar to the Book of Job, but runs through the Scriptures of a thousand years. In 1 Kings xxii. 19-22, for example, we read that, when the Kings of Israel and Judah had been well-nigh persuaded by false prophets to deliver an assault on Ramoth-Gilead, the true prophet Micaiah dissuaded them from it in words which instantly remind us of the opening Verses of Job: 'I saw the Lord sitting on his throne, and all the host of heaven standing by him on his right hand and on his left. And the Lord said, Who will persuade Ahab that he may go up and fall at Ramoth-Gilead? And one said in this manner, and another said in that manner. And there came forth the spirit, and stood before the Lord, and said, *I* will entice him. And the Lord said unto him, Wherewith? And he said, I will go forth, and I will be a lying spirit in the mouth of all his prophets. And He said, Thou shalt both entice him, and prevail. Go forth and do it.' So, again, in Zechariah iii. 1-5, the Prophet represents himself as seeing Joshua the high priest standing before Jehovah, and 'the Satan,' *i.e.* the accusing spirit, standing at his right hand to resist or accuse him. Now Joshua was clothed with filthy garments—the filthy garments representing his own sins and the sins of Israel of which Satan had accused him and them at the Divine bar. But Jehovah bids his ministers 'take away the filthy garments from him' and clothe him in new robes as for a feast, and to set 'a fair mitre' on his head, graciously assuring him meanwhile: 'I cause thine iniquity to pass away from thee, and I will clothe thee in festive raiment.' And so, once more, we read in the Book of the Revelation (Chap. xii. 7-10) of a war in heaven, in which Michael and his angels fought against the Dragon and his angels, and drove them down out of heaven,—even the great Dragon, 'that old serpent, called the Devil and Satan, who deceiveth the whole world.' And no sooner is the victory won than a loud voice is heard in heaven saying, 'Now is come the salvation, and the strength, and the kingdom of our God, and the power of his Christ; for the accuser of our brethren is cast down, who accused them before God day and night.'

Now it is easy to say that all these are poetic and prophetic visions which must not be taken too literally; that they simply set forth in a dramatic form the conflict of good with evil, and the victories in which evil is, or is to be, overcome of good. It is natural—to a certain extent, within certain limits, it is right—that we should say so. But we must not forget that behind every drama there is a true story; that every parable is based on actual facts and relations, and sets forth other and higher facts and relations: and that poetry itself is but the truth of life thrown into elevated and beautiful and ideal forms. Nor must we omit to note how strangely persistent *this* special dramatic form is; how this picture of an evil spirit accusing and enticing men to their ruin, and of good spirits who withstand him and come to their assistance and strengthen them to withstand and overcome the evil one, lives on, and reappears in the pages of Scripture, from the very first to the very last, from the temptation in Paradise to the final war and victory in Heaven. If there were not much more in it than we commonly suppose, if this 'dramatic representation' were not much closer to the facts and forms of spiritual life, it surely would not so often appear and reappear in the writings of those holy men who have taught us nearly all we know of that higher world in which alone we truly live. They may have seen only 'in a glass darkly;' but at all events they saw more, and more clearly, than we do. They may have 'known but in part;' but their part was at least a larger one than ours commonly is. And I really do not know why we should even try to impoverish the spiritual world which they have made so rich, by banishing from it the bright heroic forms with which they have filled it, and replacing them with thin colourless abstractions which have no power to stir our blood.

Nay, more: I do not see how we *can* thus impoverish and dispeople it: for these noble spiritual forms, which as yet we have only caught glimpses of in the visions of the prophets, also invade the realm of history; they move among actual men, and take an intimate and inextricable part in the grandest historical scenes the world has witnessed. Unless we are prepared to dissect the very life out of the Gospel Narratives, to take some fragments of those sacred annals as recording actual facts, and other fragments, which yet stand in the closest vital relation with the former, as recording only the dreams and dramatic inventions of men who warn us of the transition from one to the other by no change of style or tone, even the slightest, it seems impossible for us to deny that the facts and occurrences of human life have their heavenly correspondences and counterparts in the spiritual world, and even their original causes and springs. It is not simply that, according to the Evangelists, the dark figure of Satan throws its shadow across Gethsemane and Golgotha, and that troops of angels, 'legions of angels,' stand waiting for the word of the Son of Man. The fates of common men, of men like ourselves, the temptations, the defeats, the victories, the toils and sufferings of Judas and Peter and John, and of many more, are also affected by the same supernal and infernal influences. There are scenes in heaven by which *they* are influenced no less than Christ Himself, and which correspond to and determine the scenes afterwards enacted in their earthly lives.

Take, for instance, the scene recorded in my text, and consider how it is woven into the very stuff of the Narrative, so that you cannot tear it out without tearing the very Gospel itself into pieces. In its present form, as given in our Authorized Version, the meaning and effect of the passage are somewhat blunted. It should run thus: 'Simon, Simon, behold Satan *obtained* you, that he might sift you like wheat; but I *prayed* for thee, that thy faith fail not: and when thou art converted, confirm thy brethren.' Now observe, first, that the pronoun 'you' in this passage is in the plural, while the pronoun 'thee' is singular; and that the effect of this use of the singular and plural pronouns is this: 'Satan obtained *you all*,' *i.e.* all the disciples, 'that he may sift *you all* like wheat; but I prayed for *thee*'— thee, Peter—'that *thy* faith fail not: and *thou*, when *thou* art converted, strengthen *them*.' Observe, secondly, that the verbs translated 'obtain' in 'Satan *obtained* you,' and 'prayed' in I '*prayed* for thee,' are in the Greek tense which denotes 'acts belonging entirely to the past.' So that our Lord is not speaking of the present moment, but of some bygone occasion of which He does not give the date. Observe, thirdly, that the Greek verb of the phrase 'Satan *obtained* you' implies and suggests the terrific figure, 'Satan has *drawn*, or *dragged*, you out of the hand of God into his own hand:' that is to say, he has been permitted by God to put forth his hand upon you, to do his worst and utmost against you. So that what this solemn warning really means and implies is that there had been a scene in heaven like that depicted in the Prologue to the Book of Job. On some great day Satan had come to present himself among the Sons of God. He had impugned the sincerity, questioned the disinterested piety, of the twelve men who stood nearest to Christ. He had undertaken, if he might expose them to a decisive test, to prove that they did not follow Christ 'for nought;' that they would forsake Him and deny Him to his face rather than follow Him to prison and to death. And he had *obtained* them. God had put them, and all that they had, into his hand, lifting from them the protection of his own Divine hand, in order that they might be tried to the uttermost and that the world might know what manner of men they were. But Christ, present at this heavenly session in spirit,—for the Son of Man who 'came down from heaven' was, as He Himself affirmed,* 'in heaven' even while He was on earth—Christ had prayed for them; prayed that none of them should fail Him save 'the son of perdition;' prayed especially that the faith of Peter, the leader of the Twelve, should not utterly perish in the hour and power of darkness, in order that, when he recovered from his own partial failure, he might recover and confirm his brethren.

All this is clearly implied or asserted in the Verses before us. And the implication is so strange, so momentous, it involves so many mysteries and difficulties, it is so alien to the modes of modern thought that, if the passage stood alone, we might be tempted to evade its plain and obvious force. We might say: 'It is but a poetic device, a dramatic representation, not an exposition of actual facts and occurrences;' we might doubt whether this solitary passage were not the interpretation, the gloss, of some ancient commentator which had gradually crept into the text: we might even argue that, if good men so conceived of the springs of moral action in the first century, we are not bound so to conceive of them now. But it becomes very difficult for us to take this line of

---

* St. John iii. 13.

argument, or evasion, when we observe how the conception of my text dominates this whole section of the Gospel story, is referred to again and again, and is even confirmed in the most impressive way by our Lord Himself. It is not only in one passage, but in many, that we trace the influence of this scene in heaven on the affairs and destinies of men upon the earth.

Glance at a few of these passages that you may judge of their accumulated force.

When certain Greeks came to see Jesus a few days before He was crucified, He rejoiced in spirit, and cried,* 'Now is the crisis of this world; *now shall the prince of this world be cast down!*' As He sat at the Last Supper with his disciples, no sooner was supper served than, we are told, '*the devil put it into the heart of Judas Iscariot to betray him.*'† *This*, however, was only the first inception, the first injection, of that evil purpose; for by-and-bye we read,‡ when the supper was wellnigh ended, and Jesus had given the sop to Judas as a sign of who it was that should betray Him: 'After the sop, *Satan entered into him*,' following his own evil suggestion, and taking full possession of the traitor's heart,—thus *obtaining* him in very deed. As they passed from the upper room,

---

* St. John xii. 31. † Ibid xiii. 2. ‡ Ibid xiii. 27.

and went on their way to the garden at the foot of Olivet, our Lord, tremulously sensitive to all spiritual influences, warned his disciples, '*The prince of this world cometh*'—cometh, that is, to renew his temptation, to put us to the proof once more; '*but in me he hath nothing.*'* In Himself He had the sure forecast of victory, knowing that in this final conflict the Prince of this world would be dethroned and cast down; but He cannot be so sure of *them*, so sure that the Prince of this world will find nothing in them on which he can lay hold. Nay, He is sorrowfully aware that in them there *is* that by which the Evil One can strongly lay hold upon them, and move them to what, for a day or two, seems an utter failure of loyalty and faith. And so, when they have entered the Garden, and He advances to his own conflict and agony alone, He bids † them, '*Pray that ye enter not into temptation.*' The temptation is coming; so far as *that*, Satan has obtained them; and they too must fight their battle alone: but He beseeches them that they do not give place to the devil, that they do not yield to the temptation with which the Prince of this world is about to assail them. If, thanks to his warning, they did not yield to temptation in the Garden, at least they yielded to sorrow and to the

---

* St. John xiv. 30.   † St. Luke xxii. 40.

exhaustion produced by sorrow. And so, once more, as they are about to leave the Garden, his thoughts still intent on 'the sifting' they are to undergo, He rouses them with the words: 'Why sleep ye? *Rise and pray, lest ye enter into temptation,*' lest even yet ye be overcome of the adversary.* Nor is it without interest and meaning for us to observe that even our Lord Himself, as in the temptation in the wilderness, so also in this severer temptation and agony in the Garden was succoured by the coming of '*an angel out of heaven to strengthen him;*'† the spiritual world being moved about Him on its superior and heavenly as well as on its inferior and infernal side. Even amid all the bustle and violence of his arrest, moreover, He does not forget his encounter with Satan before the throne of God; to the chief priests who came out against Him as against a thief He says ‡ with patient dignity: 'This is your hour, *and the power of darkness.*'

In fine, it is impossible to study the history of the closing hours in the life of our Lord without everywhere meeting traces of that Scene in Heaven so briefly yet graphically described in my text. Let what will happen, nothing puts it long out of the mind, or even out of the words, of Christ:—as, indeed,

---

* St. Luke xxii. 46.   † Ibid xxii. 43.   ‡ Ibid xxii. 53.

how should it, when the very essence of his history during these hours was precisely the conflict with the Power of Evil and the conquest over it? He never forgets that Satan has 'obtained' both Him and his disciples that he may try and sift them to the core; and even while accomplishing his own warfare and enduring his own agony, the Son of Man is sufficiently at leisure from Himself to mark how his disciples bear themselves in the conflict, to warn them of their peril, and to animate them to renewed endeavour. As He had prayed for them in heaven, so He seems to be ever praying on earth that they may only be sifted 'like as corn is sifted in a sieve,' and that not 'the least grain may fall upon the earth.' Tried they must be, or how can they be followers of Him? but his one care and hope for them is that, however sharply they may be tried, they may finally be approved of God; that, though pursued, they may not be overtaken, or, if overtaken, may be rescued from the jaws of the lion 'who goeth about seeking whom he may devour.'

Now I confess I do not see how we are to set aside this conception of correspondences and pre-intimations in the heavenly world of the spiritual experiences of men upon the earth, when we find it not only giving shape to the prologue of a great poem like the Book of Job, and to the visions of the Old and New

Testament prophets, but also entering into the very substance of Gospel history, and moulding the thoughts and actions of our Lord and his Apostles; when we find the holy Evangelists speaking as simply and naturally of Satan as of Judas or Caiaphas, and of the 'angel out of heaven' who ministered to Christ in Gethsemane as of the women who embalmed his body and laid it in the tomb. If we accept these holy men as our teachers at all, we accept them on the distinct ground that the unseen spiritual world was more familiar to them than it is to us; that they saw more of it than we see, knew more of it than we know, and were more fully 'moved' by the Spirit of all wisdom and knowledge. And what they saw was —Heaven in the closest commerce and fellowship with earth: the principalities and powers of the spiritual or substantial universe striving against men and striving for men, plying them with temptations, and helping them to withstand temptation: while the great Lord of the Universe sat high above all, controlling all the powers whether of good or of evil, and compelling all to subserve the purpose of his fatherly and redeeming love: Christ ever pleading with Him on behalf of the tempted, the tried, the fallen, and ever revealing to us in his watchful sympathy and affectionate care the care and sympathy of our kind Father in heaven.

And why should we even try to shut our eyes on this grand vision, to refine it away into bloodless abstractions, to persuade ourselves that it is but a dramatic presentation of truths and relations which we could grasp in no other form? Does not Science itself emphatically teach us both that the universe is one, so that nothing can happen in the remotest star by which we are not presently affected; and that all this visible world is but a passing show, a transient manifestation and projection, of forces invisible, of things not seen or see-able by the mortal eye? Why, then, may we not believe in a spiritual world as populous, nay, more vast, and populous, and bright, than the world we grasp by sense, and believe also that the beings and forces of that world act and react on us even more potently than the forces and persons of the world we see? Does it not add a new dignity, and a new solemnity, to our life to conceive of it as the theatre in which not only our own passions and impulses are wrought out, but in which also the universal conflict between the powers of good and evil is being carried to its happy and triumphant close?

That our faith is weak, and needs the aid of Imagination, with its airy but picturesque and graphic shapes, is proved by the whole pre-Christian history of man, in which we see him *inventing* the spiritual personages and relations he could not find out to perfection. If it is our happiness that the spiritual world has, at least in part, been unveiled to us, with its armies and hierarchies of ministering spirits, of which even those that are evil can but sift the grain in us from the chaff, while the good bend eyes of sympathy upon us, and bear us in their hands lest at any time we trip against a stone, and cast round us shields on which the fiery darts of the wicked one are quenched, let us not doubt or deny their ministry even as we profit by it; let us rather rejoice that they *are* sent to minister to the heirs of salvation.

And above all, I think, we should value this revelation of the heavenly world because it brings home to us, home to our imaginations and hearts, the gracious providence of God. Held simply as bare doctrine, that providence is of the utmost value to us. But if, instead of simply regarding it as an indefinite protecting force, we believe in myriads of strong and busy spirits, who delight to run on the errands of their King and ours, who are with us in every hour and power of darkness to strengthen and to sustain us, and with us in every hour of light, bringing the light to us and augmenting it by their presence and sympathy, then surely the Divine Providence becomes very real and very welcome to us, so that we can trust it and lean upon it. And best of all is it to feel that God Himself so cares for us, and so concerns Himself for us, that our lives are not left to the pressure of accident or of circumstance, nor to be shaped simply by our own hands or the hands of our fellows, but are discussed and shaped in the very council-chamber of Heaven itself; that our trials are appointed for us by the deliberate wisdom of the great Saviour and Father and King, and so appointed that all things evil may be searched and sifted out of us: and that heavenly succours and ministries are vouchsafed us in order that, when we are succoured, we may succour those who are still tempted, that when we ourselves are converted, we in our turn may convert and confirm our brethren.

XIX.

ST. PETER'S SIFTING AND CONVERSION.

2.—THE SCENE ON EARTH.

'And the Lord said, Simon, Simon, behold Satan obtained you that he may sift you like wheat; but I prayed for thee, that thy faith fail not: and when thou art converted, strengthen thy brethren.'
ST. LUKE XXII. 31, 32.

ST. PETER is so human, his character presents so singular and yet so common an admixture of strength and weakness, that of all the Apostles we know him best and like him best. Of some of them we know so little, and even that little is so little characteristic, that we can hardly be said to know them at all. And, on the other hand, those whose characters are strongly marked,—James, for instance, and John, and Paul—are of so heroic a make, or they soar so high above us, that we are conscious rather of their immeasurable superiority than of their likeness to us; they move through an orbit so large and lofty, with a rectitude so undeviating, that we 'look up' to them rather than look round for them, regard them as far off from us, not nigh, as having reached a height which we can hardly hope to attain. But it is not so with Peter, great as he is. *He* is on our level, travels by the path we tread, wanders from it and stumbles in it as we ourselves wander and stumble. His very faults endear him to us hardly less than his virtues. They are so exquisitely natural, so closely akin to the faults of which we are conscious in ourselves, there is so much *man* in them and even so much *boy*, that fellow feeling makes us kind and lenient in our judgment of them, and of him. His impulsiveness and self-confidence, the facility with which he yields to the various influences brought to bear on him, his passionate vehemence alike in evil and in good, his forwardness and loquacity, his promptness to speak and to strike, all serve to engage our interest, our compassion, our sympathy, and render us more at home with him than with men of a nature more finely balanced and composed. We could better spare a better man. There is nothing mean and petty in his faults. They spring from his quick sensibilities, his indomitable energy, his large and generous confidence in himself and in those whom he loves. His very failings lean to virtue's side; for the most part they are but virtuous impulses or emotions carried to excess.

Such natures are very lovable, but they lie open to many perils. They move so easily and yet so vehemently that they are in constant danger of losing their balance and toppling over into disastrous fracture. A man readily touched by spiritual influences and responding to them strongly, is as accessible to evil influences as to good, and may yield to them as utterly,—as we know that St. Peter did, at least for a time.

But though the impulsive self-confident temperament has special dangers of its own, it does not follow that, on the whole, it is more perilous than other temperaments cast in a different mould. Certainly St. Peter did not fall lower, nor so low, in the hour and power of darkness as his fellows, albeit the common impression is that he did. Their promises of loyalty to Christ were as confident as his; their infidelity to their vow was earlier and in some sense even more shameful than his. When Christ warned the Eleven, 'All ye shall be offended in me this night,' if Peter was the first to say, 'Though I should die with thee, I will not deny thee,' yet we are expressly told that so 'likewise said they *all*.' If Peter denied Him in the hall of judgment, *they* did not even follow Him to the hall, did not stop to be questioned,—denying Him in deeds, which speak louder than words, even before Peter denied Him with oaths and curses. If when He was led away captive by the soldiers they '*all* forsook Him and fled,' St. Peter was the first to arrest himself in that shameful flight; and while *they* scattered every one to his own, he at least followed Jesus 'afar off,' to see what would be done unto Him. In short, they fell before Peter fell, and more utterly than he fell, as Jesus had said they would. For what He really recorded and foretold in my text was that, while Satan had obtained permission to try and sift them all, Christ had prayed that Peter's faith might not wholly fail, that he might be the first to recover from their common fall in order that, when he was converted, he might strengthen his brethren.

If, then, we have thought of St. Peter as weaker and worse than his brethren, we have done him a grave injustice, and must henceforth think of him as the last to forsake his Master, and the first to reclimb the heights of faith, to which he drew up his brethren after him.

Last Sunday we studied the Scene in Heaven in which Satan 'obtained' the disciples that he might test and prove them, while Christ 'prayed' for Peter that, however heavily his faith might be tested and strained, it might not snap and part. And it will be well, I think, that we should now consider the earthly counterpart of that scene in heaven, and mark (1) what it was that was sifted out of Peter, and (2) how it was sifted out of him.

1. The secret may be told in a few words. The cause and spring of the most obvious defects in the Apostle's character was that large and assured confidence in himself which made him so quick to speak, so prompt to act. But, throughout Scripture, as in human nature, self-confidence is opposed to faith, or confidence in God. Everywhere, too, we are told that God dwells only in the humble, lowly, contrite heart. So that if God was to take up his abode with Peter, if the impulsive and vehement strength of the man was to be schooled into stedfastness and hallowed by the indwelling of the Holy Ghost, in order that, being himself divinely moved and led, he might rightly lead the Apostolic Company during those first critical months in which the foundations of the Church were laid,—then, obviously, his self-confidence must be purged out of him, and replaced by the humility with which God delights to dwell. On no other terms could he be fitted for the work to which he was called. And therefore it was that Satan 'obtained' him, obtained, *i.e.* permission to sift and purge self-trust out of him. If the process was severe, the task and honour for which it prepared him were great; and greatness is not to be achieved on easy terms. If we are tempted to think the process too severe, let us ask ourselves whether any milder process would have sufficed.

The point is one which it is easy to decide. We all know men who are 'very much of their own opinion,' and who have a very good opinion of themselves; self-confident men, always ready with their advice and their censure, however difficult and complicated that may be of which they speak, and however ignorant of it they may be: men who believe, apparently, that all the world is out of joint and that they were born to set it right; men who assume to teach, to judge, to rebuke even those whom, when pushed, they acknowledge to be far wiser and better than themselves,—just as Peter rebuked Christ, and said, 'This be far from thee, Lord!' Is it easy, when this self-confidence has been much and long indulged, to purge it from them? We all know that it is hard, so hard as often to seem impossible. We have seen such men tried in many ways, brayed as in a mortar: the advice they gave has been followed and shewn to be disastrous, or their censures have been disregarded with manifest impunity; their own affairs have fallen into ruin about them while they were affecting to guide the counsels of the nation: shame has invaded their families and homes through their sins or their neglect; they have been publicly censured and disgraced: and yet, when all was done, we have seen them carrying their chins as high as ever, and heard them take the same 'Sir Oracle' tone, bating no jot of confidence in their own wisdom and importance. Of all qualities self-confidence is perhaps the last which we most of us lose; of all virtues humility the last that we acquire.

We need not wonder, therefore, to find St. Peter exposed to a most penetrating and fiery trial. For, strange to say, his self-confidence, though it had been so often rebuked, comes out more conspicuously than ever in the last moments he was to spend with the Son of Man; the need for sifting grows most apparent as Satan draws near to sift him.

On the very night on which Jesus was betrayed, for example, and as they gathered round the table at which they were to eat and drink with Him for the last time, Peter and his brethren contended among themselves which of them should be greatest. The couches on which they reclined at the Last Supper each held four or five, and each, according to Eastern custom, had its highest and its lowest place. Possibly it was in claiming the better places on these couches that the contention broke out, if it was not rather in the strife as to which of them should wash the others' feet. The petty and shameful strife was silenced by the gracious rebuke of Christ. But the flush and excitement of it seem to have left their traces on Peter's mind: for when, to enforce his lesson of humility, Jesus rose and girded Himself with a towel, and began to wash their feet, Peter first exclaims, 'Thou shalt never wash my feet!' and then, 'Not my feet only, but also my hands and my head!' No doubt the impulses which moved him to these exclamations were fine; but impulses which lead a man to correct the Divine Wisdom now in this way, and now in that, betray a blind and impetuous self-reliance, however fine they may be in themselves. Emotions, however good, become evil, they become both signs and portents of evil, when they run to excess. The wish to be near Christ, and to stand high in his love, is good; but it becomes evil when it grows into a wish to be nearer than others, and to stand higher than they. The reverence which prompted Peter to cry, 'Wash not my feet,' was good, and the love which prompted him to cry, 'Not my feet only,' was good; but reverence becomes irreverent, and love unloving, when they lead us to assume that we know what is meet and right better than our Master and Lord, and still to suggest a something lacking in the way He takes with us.

However good his motives and impulses, then, it is easy to see that even at the Lord's Supper Peter was in his most imperiou sand self-confident mood. And the impression grows on us as we follow him to Gethsemane. In the Garden he shews that he trusts more in his own loyalty than in the wisdom and

x

grace of his Master. 'Though all men should be offended in thee, yet will not I!' he cries. And when the Lord repeats the warning, Peter only 'speaks the more vehemently, saying, If I should *die* with thee, I will not *in anywise* deny thee!' Even when he falls asleep in the Garden, so belying his vehement protestations of loyalty and love, and proving that he could not 'watch an hour' for Him with whom he thought he was ready to go both to prison and to death, his confidence in himself is no whit abated. Startled from his untimely slumbers by the clash of arms, and the glare of torches, 'Simon Peter, having a sword, drew it,' and smote off the ear of the High Priest's servant,—nothing doubting but that that was the right course to take, since it was the first that suggested itself to his mind. He looks to his Master for no sign, waits for no command, or he would not have fallen into that sin. Christ has to undo his evil work, to rebuke his spirit. Peter is put to shame, but not to a saving shame. As his Master will not let him fight, he runs away, forsaking the Friend for whom he had professed himself ready even to die. But, as he runs, he remembers himself; his natural boldness returns: he detaches himself from the other fugitives, and follows Jesus, though 'afar off.' When he reaches the Palace, however, instead of pressing to his Master's side, as who should say, 'I at least will be true to Him,' he lingers in the open court outside the judgment hall, and joins the soldiers round the fire, casting in his lot with the very men who had arrested his Lord instead of with the Lord Himself. And, here, when he is questioned, he again and again denies Him, affirming in the broad Galilean accents which betray him, 'I know not the Man.' Nay, with his constitutional passion and vehemence, he backs his denial with oaths and curses, calling Heaven to witness that he has no lot nor part in the kingdom of heaven.

It is a cruel spectacle, one of the saddest on which the stars have ever looked down,—a brave man turned coward, a true man turned liar, a strong man weeping bitterly over the very sin which of all sins might well have seemed impossible to him! But would anything short of this open and shameful fall, this fracture at his strongest point, have sufficed to purge him of that self-confidence which we have seen to be so potent and so active in him up to the very instant of his fall? And if nothing else would have so suddenly and sharply sifted it out of him, and wrought into him the humility which fitted him to receive the Holy Ghost and to found the Church which Christ was about to redeem with his precious blood, shall we complain of the severity of the process by which he was purged from a dangerous self-trust and made meet for a task so honourable and blessed? Shall we not rather ask that we too may be sifted even by the most searching trials, if we too may thus be made partakers of the Holy Ghost, and be qualified for a Divine service?

2. So far, then, we have seen how Satan obtained Peter, that he might sift him. But if Satan obtained, Christ *prayed* for him, and even *obtained* him in a far higher sense; for he obtained that Peter should *only* be 'sifted,' and that the sifting should issue in his 'conversion.' It is to this second part of the process that we have now to turn our thoughts. For the conversion of the Apostle was no less gradual, and no less complete and wonderful, than his fall. I must tell the story of it very briefly, but, happily, it is familiar to you, so that few words will suffice.

St. Peter's 'conversion' began at the very moment when he had fallen lowest. For it was when he denied his Lord for the last time that Jesus turned and 'looked' upon him; and this look was the turning-point in the great crisis of his life. Jesus does not *speak* to him; words are not necessary; and even in the very depth of his fall Christ is too tender of Peter to confirm the suspicion of the bystanders and to prove him the disciple he has denied himself to be. He simply *looks* at him, bends on him, we may well believe, a glance of blended pity, reproach, and love. But that look is sufficient. As he met it Peter 'called to mind the word that Jesus had said to him; and *when he thought thereon*'—or, literally, '*flinging himself* on' that word—'he wept' 'wept bitterly.' And there we have the very man. With passionate vehemence he flings himself as on the sharp edges of his Master's gracious warning and rebuke, bruises himself against them, rends and tears himself upon them, till the difficult tears of a strong man in his agony are wrung from him.

The man is all broken with remorse. He cannot face his old comrades, for, though their sin has been as great as his, to him no sin seems comparable with his. He creeps to a solitary hiding-place where he may weep alone, and see no reflection of his shame from other eyes; and here he remains during the days that Jesus slumbered in the tomb. Of all the Apostolic Company only John seems to have suspected where he was, to have sought him out, and to have spent an hour with him when he could leave Mary, *his* mother now.

Now when men have fallen into a great sin, a great shame, a great misery, we all know how apt they are, as they brood over it, to recall the similar sins of which they have been guilty, to deepen their anguish by tracing back their recent offence through previous offences which paved the way for their last and crowning transgression. We may be sure, therefore, that in his solitude and grief Peter would compel himself to dwell on the many occasions on which he had been betrayed by his self-confident temper into sin and shame. He would recall, for instance, how boldly he had once cast himself on to the heaving waters of the Galilean lake, only to lose courage and faith, only to sink and perish but for the grace of Christ. He would remember how, while he had been the first to confess Jesus the Christ of God, no sooner did Jesus begin to speak of his death and of the glory that should follow than he had rudely broken in upon Him with, 'There shall no such thing happen unto thee!' And, as he flung himself on these sorrowful remembrances, he would feel that his recent sin was but a repetition and an exaggeration of former sins; that what he had to mourn over was not simply this faithless action or that, but a radical weakness of nature, a self-reliance which was perpetually leading him astray and landing him in open guilt and shame.

Such thoughts as these were natural to his position, and we might reasonably conclude that he brooded over them even if there were nothing in the Sacred Record to suggest the fact. But there is much. For as the Divine discipline always answers to our needs, the gracious discipline now accorded to Peter indicates his needs, and his needs the thoughts on which he had been sorrowfully brooding.

Mark what that discipline is. Not only does the risen Lord bid Mary Magdalene go tell his 'disciples *and Peter*' that He has broken from a grave which could not hold him; not only does He confirm this special and tender sign of grace by appearing to Cephas *before* He appears to the Twelve; but having touched Peter's heart with these proofs of a love stronger than death, a love not to be alienated even by infidelity and desertion; having thus shed the light of hope into the darkness of his remorse and despair, and turned his remorse into a humble and healing contrition, our Lord proceeds to convert him, and to prove him converted, by leading him to unsay all his foolish boasts, and to retrieve all the failures which had sprung from too much confidence in himself, too little trust in God his Saviour.

Take an instance or two—we have no time for more —of this process of conversion. When the Apostles returned into Galilee, where Jesus had promised to show Himself to them again, Peter with his old energy and impatience of inaction, determines to work while he waits for the coming of the Master. 'I go a fishing,' he cries; and the rest, or some of them, go with him. They toil all night, and catch nothing. But in the morning a Stranger accosts them from the shore, tells them where to shoot the net, and now they take a multitude of fishes. The wonder recalls a previous wonder. 'That must be Jesus,' thinks John: and looking stedfastly through the morning haze, he cries, 'It *is* the Lord!' Then Peter, we are told, girded himself with his thick rough coat, 'for he was naked,' *i.e.* stripped to his shirt, and cast himself *into*, or *onto*, the sea. The Greek preposition will bear either meaning; and, as men do not hamper themselves with thick heavy garments when they mean to swim,—and still less when they have to swim two hundred cubits, *i.e.* one hundred yards; as, if Peter meant swimming, he would have been more likely to strip off his coat than to gird it on, we may fairly conclude that what he intended was to repeat his old experiment, to walk on the waters into which he had once sunk. And now, animated by no boastful self-trust, by no over-weening ambition to outdo and outdare his brethren, but drawn by Christ and his passionate love for Christ, that he may be marked out as the leader and captain of his brethren, he retrieves his former failure: he comes safely to the shore, and is thus taught how much mightier are humility and trust than self-confidence and vainglory.

When he reaches the shore a further trial awaits him. On the night of the Betrayal he had boasted of a love beyond that of his brethren: 'Though all (*i.e.*

all *these*) should be offended, yet will not I.' And this vain boast had been followed by no less than three open and shameful denials of his Lord. These false steps have now to be retraced, these failures retrieved. Hence, when they had broken their fast, Jesus turns to Peter with the question, 'Simon, son of Jonas, lovest thou me *more than these?*' 'Do you still hold by your boast?' But Simon has not been sifted in vain. There is a tone of shame and disavowal in his simple reply, 'Lord, thou knowest that I love thee,—not more than these perhaps; I no longer measure myself against them; they may love Thee more and better than I: still I love thee, and thou knowest that I love Thee.' Three times the question is repeated, till Peter is 'grieved;' for he does not see, what we see plainly enough, that, as he had been guilty of three denials, so our Lord is constraining him to undo them, as far as they can be undone, by witnessing three good confessions. Once Peter's grief would have been anger had he been thrice asked, 'Lovest thou me?' He would have exploded into vainglorious vaunts, if he had not rebuked the Lord for suspecting his fidelity. But there is no anger, no boasting, no vainglorious self-confidence now. All *that* has been sifted out of him; and he answers only with a quiet appeal to the Searcher of all hearts: 'Lord, thou knowest all things, and thou knowest that I love thee.'

As he has become a new man, not only is he thrice reinstated in the pastoral office but, a new promise is made him, a new path is marked out for him; as you will instantly see if you compare the fragment of a conversation between Peter and Christ before the Sifting, with the fragment of a conversation between them after the Conversion. The first runs thus:—

'Whither I go, thou canst not follow me now.'

'Lord, why cannot I follow thee now? I will lay down my life for thy sake.'

'Wilt thou lay down thy life for my sake? Verily, I say unto thee, A cock shall not crow till thou hast denied me thrice.'

In the second conversation Jesus says to his sifted and converted Disciple:

'Verily, verily, I say unto thee, When thou wast younger thou didst gird thyself, and walk whither thou wouldst; but when thou art grown old thou shalt stretch forth thy hands and another shall gird thee, and shall carry thee whither thou wouldst not.'

'This spake he, signifying by what death he should glorify God. And having thus spoken, he saith unto him, Follow thou me.'

Is not that a striking contrast? The circle has completed itself and run full home at last. Christ now foretells for Peter, not an open and shameful denial of his Master, but a public and honourable death for his Master. It is no longer, 'Thou wilt not lay down thy life for my sake,' but 'Thou *shalt* lay down thy life for me.' It is no longer, 'Thou canst not follow me,' but, 'Follow thou me.' And this striking change and contrast indicates that at last Peter was fully 'converted,'—converted from rashness to sobriety, from vainglory to humility, from self-confidence to self-distrust and steadfast trust in God. Every step of his fall has been retraced, every failure retrieved. He is now prepared to become the temple and organ of the Holy Ghost, the Solid Rock of the Church on which the waves of change and temptation will beat in vain.

This story of St. Peter's Sifting and Conversion suggests many valuable lessons on the scope and function of Evil and the true meaning of Conversion, on which I must not enter now, though I hope to call your attention to them soon. For the present let us only note, for our encouragement, the Divine order which runs through the Apostle's life and stamps it with an impressive unity. Though we know so much of Peter, yet how little we know! All that the New Testament records of him, might be printed in a few pages. And as we glance over this brief but pregnant record, it seems at first as if there were no unity in it, no plan. Few men have been more impulsive than he, more apt to rise to the spur of occasion, to act without forethought, or any settled and consistent scheme. To him himself, probably, his life seemed as clouded and confused as our lives often seem to us, —a *petty* maze without a plan, a series of disconnected inconsistent fragments, full of accident, disorder, self-contradiction. And yet, as we study even our brief record of his life, we see that, if Peter had no plan for himself, God had a plan for him. Event meets and answers event, false steps are retrod, broken threads are taken up and worked in, triumphs of faith are set over against failures in faith, denials are retrieved by confessions; the evil in the man is sifted out of him, the good cultivated, consolidated, made permanent; and in and through all this strange and mingled discipline we see the grace of God at work to prepare him for the most honourable service and the highest blessedness.

Let us be sure, then, that God has a plan for us no less than for Peter, a plan which dominates all our fugitive impulses, and changeful passions, and broken purposes, and unconnected deeds. Our lives are not the accidental and purposeless fragments they often seem to us to be. God is so disposing them as that we may be sifted from all evil, converted to all goodness, his end for us being that we may become perfect and entire, lacking nothing.

XX.

ST. PETER'S SIFTING AND CONVERSION.

3.—THE SCOPE AND FUNCTION OF EVIL AS ILLUSTRATED BY THE SIFTING OF ST. PETER.

'Simon, Simon, behold, Satan obtained you, that he may sift you like wheat; but I prayed for thee, that thy faith fail not: and when thou art converted, strengthen thy brethren.'—St. LUKE xxii. 31, 32.

So Satan is not a mere myth then! not simply a Jewish, nor even simply a human, conception of the origin and power of evil! He who is true, He who is the Truth, here explicitly affirms the existence, not of evil only, but of an Evil Spirit who seeks to obtain men that he may use them for his own sinister ends. Many good persons, indeed, utterly refuse to believe in the existence of the devil, and seem to derive much satisfaction and comfort from the refusal. But if we take the holy men who were moved by the Holy Ghost for our teachers, I do not see how we are to get over the fact that the existence and activity of the devil are explicitly affirmed or implicitly assumed in all their writings. Nor do I see how any reasonable man should derive comfort from questioning or denying the existence of a Spirit who tempts and betrays men to their hurt. If, by denying the existence of the devil, we could put away evil from our hearts or banish it from the world, then, indeed, there would be no comfort like it. But we cannot do that. However we may account for its presence, evil is *here*, in our hearts, in our lives, in the world around us. It were as easy to jump off our own shadow as to escape it. And, often, it takes the most monstrous and incredible forms. Women have been known to stab their husbands as they caressed them; priests to poison their flocks in the Sacramental wine; parents to train their children to vice and crime; despots to sacrifice the lives and welfare of myriads to their ambition or their caprice. And where is the comfort of denying the existence of the devil while we are obliged to admit the existence of a Messalina, a Borgia, a Medici, or of a Pharaoh, a Herod, a Nero, a Napoleon, or even while we find so many deadly evils lurking in our own hearts? We are men and women; and if we are to have any comfort as we think of men and women whose names are a byword of infamy, it surely does not lie in denying that they were tempted by that Evil Spirit who is very potent with such as they; but, rather, in confessing and insisting on it, in affirming that their enormous wickedness did not spring wholly and solely from a purely human source. Instead of doubting or denying the existence and power of the Prince of this world, it were surely wiser of us, and more profitable to ascertain what the Bible really asserts concerning the nature and limits of his power; and to detach from the Biblical teaching the traditional and Miltonic legends: for, beyond a doubt, the popular conception of 'the Archangel fallen' is derived rather from Milton's great poem than from the teaching of Holy Writ.

1. The word 'satan,' then, means 'adversary,' the word 'devil' one who 'sets at variance,' one who turns friends into foes by falsely accusing them to each other. By the very names assigned him in Scripture, therefore, the Evil Spirit is marked out as the Adversary of God and man, and as endeavouring, by falsely accusing the one to the other, to set God against man and man against God. In full accordance with the implication carried in his very names, he is represented as *slandering God to Eve*, alleging that He had prohibited the tree of knowledge to our first parents only lest they should become as wise as He Himself: and as *slandering Job to God*, alleging that he served God not from love, but only for what he could get thereby. And this, according to the Bible, is his constant method. His chief power to

harm us lies in his being able to suggest false interpretations of the facts of life, to awaken distrust of God by persuading us that He asks more of us than we can give, lays upon us more than we are able to bear; that He forbids innocent pleasures, exacts unnecessary sacrifices, commands impossible duties.

Practically, this power of suggesting false interpretations of the facts of life, and especially of our relations with God our Father, is the point of chief moment in the ministry of Satan. But, theoretically, the chief point lies, perhaps, in the fact that his ministry *is* a ministry; that even Satan is under law to God, and is compelled to serve the cause he hates, and to promote the welfare of those whom he would fain destroy. In many of the Pagan mythologies the Evil Power is put on a level with the Good Power, or practically above it; but in the Bible the Evil Spirit, so far from being co-ordinate with God, is strictly subordinated to Him; his task is fixed, his scope limited: he has to appear before Jehovah and to give account of himself to Him; he must 'obtain' men before he can so much as sift them; and, save by our own default, he can *only* sift the chaff in us from the wheat, the worthless and transitory from the precious and abiding: the evil he does is permitted only that it may lead in a larger good.

This, in general, is the teaching of the Bible on the

work and ministry of Satan. He is the slave of the Great Husbandman; he holds the sieve, or shakes the sieve, in which good is separated from evil, the wheat from the chaff: and, because he hates the wheat, and would shake it all into chaff if he could, he has only the bran for his pains, the wheat being safely gathered into the garner of God,—*every grain of it*, according to that ancient and gracious promise: 'I will sift the house of Israel among all nations, like as corn is sifted in a sieve; yet shall not the least grain fall to the ground.' *

2. From this Biblical point of view it is easy to form some conception of the Sifting of St. Peter. We are expressly told that Satan had '*obtained*' him; *i.e.* he had challenged or demanded Peter of God, as of old he challenged Job. He had slanderously accused the Apostle of interested motives, of following Christ, not because he loved either Him or the truth He taught, but for what he hoped to get from Him and to gain by Him. And he had received permission to put Peter to the proof, to shake him to and fro in the sieve. Acccordingly, he sets himself to undermine Peter's faith; for, said Christ, 'I prayed for thee, *that thy faith fail not.*' This, then, was to be the point of attack. Peter's faith was to be tested, tried, and, if possible, overcome.

---

* Amos ix. 9.

To undermine his faith, Satan rouses and flatters the self-confidence which was Peter's besetting sin, the self-trust which is the very opposite of trust in God, and which we have seen to be so strangely and exorbitantly active in him as the hour and power of darkness drew nigh. Then, when Peter has fallen, through self-confidence, into sins which seem at variance with his very nature, and set his nature at variance with itself; when the true man has turned liar, and the brave man coward, and the loyal disciple has denied his Master with oaths and curses, how easy would it be for the adversary to suggest to him, first, that Jesus of Nazareth could not be the Christ of God or He would never have been allowed to fall into the hands of men; and then, touching him still closer home, to suggest that, if Jesus were indeed the Christ of God, so much the worse for Peter: how easy to argue, 'He can never forgive you for you have denied Him; He will never own you, for you have disowned Him;' and, again, 'You could never have loved Him sincerely, or you would not have denied Him.' We may be sure, I think, that, having obtained him, Satan would sift Peter in some such ways as these, slandering Peter to God, and Christ to Peter, and even Peter to himself, that he might drive him to conclusions of despair.

And yet, through the strange mercy of God, all

that Satan did for Peter's ruin turned out for his salvation; all that he did against him turned out for him. What was really sifted out of Peter was not his faith, but the self-confidence which, because it marred and at times subverted his faith, unfitted him to become the organ and minister of the Holy Ghost. Shaken to and fro like as corn is shaken in a sieve, not the least grain was suffered to fall to the ground, but only the chaff which unfitted the wheat in his nature for the service of God and man. So that, if we may draw so large an inference from a single case, it would seem that there really is some truth in the quaint homely saying: 'God keeps a devil, as some men keep a dog; not to bite and devour his children, but to frighten from them, or to frighten them from, whatever would endanger or harm them.'

And surely we cannot err in taking Peter's as a leading case, as a crucial instance, of the scope and function of Evil. For we ourselves are not ignorant of Satan's devices. He has tried these very wiles on us, slandering God to us, and even slandering us to ourselves in those rare moods in which we think as much worse of ourselves as in our common moods we think better of ourselves than we ought,—suggesting that by our sins we had placed ourselves beyond the reach of mercy; or that our natures were so weak and worthless that, despite our best endeavours, we should slip from sin to sin, and fall to fall, until we were utterly undone. How often, and how keenly, have we been tormented by these evil suggestions, these despairing apprehensions and forebodings! And yet they are all *lies*—lies from beginning to end. They are the mere devices, the damnable inventions, of God's adversary and ours, the slanders by which he seeks to sap and shake our faith. The mercy of God—blessed be God for his mercy!—is 'more than all our sins.' There is no child of man, however low he may have fallen, whom God is not able, and willing, and even seeking, to save. And He has many ways of saving us,—none more common than this way of sifting, of allowing us to pass into an hour and power of darkness, to fall into some sin so great, so unlike our customary sins, that we can no longer cloak our sinfulness from our own eyes or dissemble it from the world. If we will play with the serpent, He lets the serpent bite us, that we may hate it. If we will toy with the fire, He lets the fire burn us, that we may get to a safer distance from it. If we will gather chaff about us, He suffers us to be shaken like as corn is shaken in a sieve, that what is good in us may be detached from that which is evil.

This, then, is our first consolation as we contemplate the inscrutable mystery of Evil: that, if Satan be against us, God is for us; that, if Satan hopes and intends to sift the good out of us, God will not permit him to do more than sift the evil out of us, and so prepare us for a larger good.

3. But there is another consolation for us: there are many more, had we time to enter upon them. For, mark, Satan must 'obtain' Peter before he can so much as sift him. That is to say, Evil itself is under the control of God. If Satan goes to and fro, and up and down, in the earth, he can but move within limits prescribed for him by the Divine wisdom and righteousness and love. It does not lie at his pleasure even to sift whom he will, how he will. He can do nothing, for us or against us, save as God permits. And God is good. He will not suffer us to be tried beyond our strength. He does not. For which of us can honestly say that he has ever yet encountered a single temptation which he might not have overcome had he met it with all his force? When we fail, when we are defeated, that which most of all embitters our defeat is the conviction that we might have conquered had we tried, that we must have conquered had our hearts been fully set on righteousness and had we taken the aid which God was waiting to bestow.

'But what is the necessity for this incessant conflict? Why are we for ever being put to the proof? Why may we not know a little peace?'

The answer is plain. We must *conquer* peace before we can enjoy it. We must become wholly good before we can be at rest. So long as there is any evil in us, how can that which is good in us but strive against it and seek to cast it out? Not till we are perfect can we hope to escape strife. So long as any imperfection cleaves to us, it must be sifted out of us.

Would you have it otherwise? Would you have the very wheat in you left to rust and rot into mere chaff rather than submit to the pain of having the dust and chaff shaken off you? If wheat were sentient, no doubt it would dislike the discomfort of being shaken to and fro in the sieve. But if wheat were wise as well as sentient, and knew that the very end of its being was that it should become pure grain, would it shrink from the sieve? would it not, rather, leap into it, and cry out to be shaken, that so it might the sooner become perfect? And we, my brethren, are we so foolish that we can only complain of the kindly though painful process by which our baser are separated from our better parts? If we can only become good, good to the very core, and fit for the use whether of God or of man, as we shed our imperfections and shake off our sins, shall we not rather rejoice in the discipline, in the 'divers tribulations,' by which we are purged from evil and made meet for the kingdom and service of God?

4. Finally, there is still another and a great comfort for us as we confront the great mystery of Evil. It is much to know, as we may know if we accept the teaching of Christ, that, if the Evil Spirit is against us, the Spirit of all Good is for us. It is much to know that Satan himself is under law to God, and can only go so far as He permits. It is much to know that even when the Evil Spirit obtains us and sets himself to destroy us, he can but sift the evil out of us, and so further our salvation. But it is even more and better to learn that many of our severest trials and siftings happen, not simply for our own sakes, but also and mainly for the good of others, that they may be the better for what God has made good in us. It was not because Job was a worse man, but because he was a better and a stronger man, than his neighbours that he was more severely tried. And if *he* gained much by the trial, if he learned the very lessons he needed to be taught, his friends, his tribe, and all the world down to this day, were also taught by his trials and enriched by his gains. Peter, again, was not a weaker man than his fellows, but a stronger; he stood after they had fallen, and recovered from his fall before they recovered from theirs. *Therefore* he was more severely and exhaustively sifted than they were. Nor was it only for his own sake, only that the Peter in him might conquer

the Simon in him, that he was so terribly and searchingly tried; but also that 'when he was converted, he might strengthen his brethren.' And who that compares the Apostle's life before his Sifting with his life after his Conversion does not see that this strange crisis in his history made a new man of him, and gave him a new power among and over his fellows, purging him from the rashness, the self-confidence, the vaingloriousness which had often quickened the selfsame faults in them? If he himself was a better man for it, were not they also the better for the change in him?

And, indeed, if we are of those who study the interior changes which pass upon men, we shall all confess, I suppose, that in so far as we ourselves have any influence with our fellows, and that influence tells for good, we have acquired it in the main from the trials we have suffered, and by which the crudenesses and harshnesses of our character have been mellowed, and from which we have learned a larger patience, a higher wisdom, a wider charity. Men, says Shelley,

> are cradled into poetry by wrong:
> They learn in suffering what they teach in song.

And that is just as true of piety as it is of poetry. If you discover in an author, or a preacher, for example, a noticeable access of spiritual power, if you find his words answering more and more closely to your deepest inward experience and exerting a happier and more potent influence upon you, you may pretty certainly conclude that that new power has cost him somewhat dear; that it has come to him through conflicts, siftings, griefs, of which you would have known nothing but for their invigorating and refining effects on his work. If as you talk with a Christian neighbour, you presently become aware of a deepened tone of piety, if you feel that he is very unworldly and unselfish, very cheerful when days are dark, very patient under wrong and pain, very kindly and charitable in his judgments of men, very fearless in the prospect of death, you will run but little risk in concluding that he has been keenly tried, sharply sifted; that it is because he has been painfully 'converted' from much which was evil or imperfect in him that he is now strong enough to strengthen his brethren.

But if these trials and siftings make us pure and strong, strong for our fellows as well as for ourselves, who that has any touch of generosity and a noble mind will not gladly endure them? We cannot serve men merely by wishing to serve them. Before we can effectually assist them we must go into training; we must endure hardness; we must be sifted from our natural selfishness and self-confidence and impatience and folly; we must suffer as they suffer, and more than they suffer; we must be comforted with a comfort they have not known: in short, we must pass through a wider and deeper experience both of evil and of good, if we are to comfort and strengthen them. For if when we ourselves are troubled on every side some slight shallow person, on whom we can hardly but look down, brings us the trite consolations which he deems appropriate to the occasion, we know very well that, so far from comforting and strengthening us, he simply irritates and weakens us. It is only those who have had a wider experience and more searching trials than our own, and have met them with a more resolute constancy, who can really help and console us. How, then, can *we* hope to strengthen our brethren except as we ourselves have been sifted and converted again and again?

Here, then, is help for us just where we most need help. As we confront the great mystery of Evil, we may and must feel that we can never hope to solve it; that the further we penetrate into it the more impenetrable are the shadows that fall around us. And, yet does not Christ throw a sufficient light into this thick darkness when He tells us that Evil is but as a sieve in which we are shaken to and fro like as wheat is sifted, and that, whatever may become of the chaff, not even the least grain shall fall to the ground? For all practical purposes do we not know enough if we know that evil is under law to God, that its scope is limited by Him, and that its true function is to sift our imperfections out of us that we may be the stronger for service and the happier in it? If we hold fast to this teaching, we need have no doubt, no fear. We need not—if I may use words so hackneyed that they have lost all freshness, while yet they are difficult to replace and seem impossible to amend—stretch lame hands of faith to what we feel is Lord of all, and grope and gather dust and chaff, and faintly trust the larger hope. We may know, we may be sure that, somehow, good *will* be the final goal of ill:

> 'That nothing walks with aimless feet;
> That not one life shall be destroyed
> Or cast as rubbish to the void,
> When God hath made the pile complete.'

We may know, we may be sure that, however we and our fellows may suffer from this world's unkindly weather, the highest good of which they are capable will come, at last, to all, 'and every winter change to spring,' and every spring pass into the eternal summer of the eternal Righteousness and Love.

XXI.

ST. PETER'S SIFTING AND CONVERSION.

4.—CONVERSION AS ILLUSTRATED BY THE CONVERSION OF ST. PETER.

'When thou art converted, strengthen thy brethren.'
ST. LUKE xxii. 32.

Does a man need to be converted *after* his conversion? At all events St. Peter did; and if he did, why may not we?

Rightly considered, Conversion is not a single and momentary act, but a continuous, multiform, and lifelong process. And yet, especially in those sections of the Church which arrogate to themselves the style and title of Evangelical—too often on the *lucus a non lucendo* principle, because they have no real 'evangel' to preach, or a very little one—Conversion is held to be a sudden and radical change of heart, an instant transition from 'a state of nature' to 'a state of grace,' which is never repeated and never needs repetition. It is only a minority which understands that men need many conversions before they can be wholly reconciled to God and made meet for the kingdom of heaven. Nevertheless, this,—this, and not that,—is the teaching of the New Testament, as we may see from the sentence we have just read. For who can deny that, when our Lord warned him of an approaching conversion, St. Peter was already what is commonly understood by a converted man? Long before this he had left all to follow Christ,—home, handicraft, the goodwill of his neighbours—to come under the ban of the Synagogue, the rabbis, the Pharisees, the priests. Long before this, too, he had witnessed the good confession: 'Thou art the Christ, the Son of the Living God,' and had received this testimony from the Lord: 'Blessed art thou, Simon Barjona, for flesh and blood hath not revealed this to thee, but my Father who is in heaven.' Which of us has shewn so strong a faith, or can adduce so clear an assurance of acceptance with God? If Peter was not converted, if he had not become a child of God and an inheritor of the kingdom of heaven, who has? Yet it is to this converted man that Jesus says: '*When* thou art converted, strengthen thy brethren!'

But perhaps it is our Version that is in fault; perhaps the Greek would tell a different tale. No, the word used here ($\dot{\epsilon}\pi\iota\sigma\tau\rho\dot{\epsilon}\phi\omega$) is the word constantly used for 'conversion' in the Greek Testament; it is the very word used by Peter himself when, on the day of Pentecost, he exhorted the multitude that had murdered Christ: 'Repent, and be ye *converted*, that your sins may be blotted out;' it is the very word used by St. James in the well-known passage: 'He who *converteth* a sinner from the error of his ways shall save a soul from death, and hide a multitude of sins.' In short, it is the one word which the New Testament sets apart throughout to the office of denoting that spiritual change, or process, by which men are turned from darkness to light, from evil to good, from the bondage of sin to the service of righteousness. Here, indeed, lies the whole difficulty, such as it is; for the New Testament does unquestionably pronounce him 'converted' who has once passed through this happy change, and yet it also affirms that this happy change may or must be repeated again and again before Conversion is complete.

How, then, are we to solve the difficulty? Nothing is easier, for it is purely a difficulty of our own making. The very moment that we conceive of Conversion, not simply as a sudden and momentary act, but also as a gradual, iterated, lifelong process, the difficulty is solved, and we see that Conversion may occur many times and take many forms. And to this conception we are led both by our own experience, in which the transition from evil to good is only too slow and gradual, and by the word we use to denote that transition, no less than by the express teaching of Christ Himself. For, as the Greek word (epistrophē) means a *turning back* upon God, so the word 'conversion' denotes a *turning with*, or *toward* some person or force, instead of *turning from*, or *against*, it. Our conversion to God, therefore, means simply that we turn back to, or turn toward, the God from whom we have too often turned away; that we turn with the influences of his grace and Spirit instead of turning against them. So that *whenever* we yield to the Divine Influence, instead of resisting it, we are converted; and whenever we yield to it, *for the first time*, that is our first conversion.

But when *do* we yield to it for the first time? Most of us would be puzzled, I suppose, and even unable, to say: for most of *us* became very early aware of two great conflicting forces or powers at work within us and around us, of which we felt that only the good force had an imperative claim upon us, though it would often have been more pleasant for the moment to yield to the evil force. Most of us, too, I dare say, can remember the peculiar glow of satisfaction which warmed our breast when, in those early years, we denied ourselves some inviting evil—some temptation to falsehood or laziness, disobedience or selfishness—that we might do what we felt to be right or good or kind. *That* was our first conversion; then, first, we voluntarily turned with God and toward Him, and entered the heaven that lay about our infancy. From that time onward our life has been a strangely-blended sequence of sins and of conversions from sin, a chequered series of occasions on which we have yielded ourselves to the gracious influences with which God has surrounded us or have ungraciously resisted them. So that most of us passed through many conversions before, in the technical or theological sense of the word, we were 'converted' at all.

Even this conversion, moreover, our conversion in the theological sense of that term, may have taken one of two forms, answered to one of two types; for, as we all know, there are two main types or forms which this great spiritual change assumes. There is the gradual and continuous type; there is also the sudden and—if I may use the word—catastrophic type: one man rising into the distinctively spiritual life by changes which are almost imperceptible, while another breaks into it by a change so sudden and violent that it assumes the proportions of a moral cataclysm or catastrophe.

Cases of either kind are probably familiar to us all. While we were still children most of us, as I have said, now turned toward God, and now turned away from Him, on the spur of a thousand slight occasions. Suppose, then, the child of pious parents, with many inherited predispositions to that which is good, to grow up in a pious home, such as, thank God, we can most of us remember, in which he is surrounded with sweet and wholesome influences on every side. Is it not probable that, though he will often slip, and sometimes fall, into sin, he will gradually form a habit of yielding to these gracious influences, that he will at least acquire a sincere reverence for all that is good? At last—say, in early manhood—he comes to know what all this means, to feel that through all God has been guiding and training him for his service, and that it is high time he voluntarily consecrated himself to that service. Accordingly he associates himself with those who are like-minded with himself, enters the Christian fellowship, takes the Christian sacrament or sacraments,* and talks with the Christian people about him. At first he is probably a little disappointed with them, but, above all, with himself. He is conscious of no radical and sweeping change in his own character, no budding saintship, no such elevation of spirit and added power of obedience and delight in God as he

---

* In my own Community we only administer *baptism* on a voluntary confession of faith.

had anticipated. Unless he fall into wise hands, he begins perhaps to doubt whether he has been really converted, whether his experience answers to the Christian type. Possibly he tries himself by all manner of inappropriate tests, by the experience of friends who have had a wholly different training to his own, or even by the history of Oriental Jews who stormed through their grand passionate lives three or four thousand years ago. Poor lad! How should *he* know any deep radical change whose brief life has been a succession of gentle changes, each of which has brought him nearer to God? How should *he* feel what they feel who, after years of habitual and gross iniquity, are suddenly seized by great spiritual convictions, and swung right round as in a moment,—*he*, who has never altogether turned his back on goodness, but has been drawn on toward it step by step? If we believe in the sinfulness of man and the redeeming grace of God, what other proof do we need, what better proof can we have, of the genuineness of his conversion than this: that he has turned toward God, and is walking with God?

On the other hand, here is a lad who, though he too has had his higher moods and better impulses, has grown, by force of an evil inheritance and an evil training, or by the wild passionate tumult of an unbalanced nature, into a habit of resisting such gracious influences as he has known. He runs the riot of the senses, follows his lusts, till he sinks into a reckless godless reprobate. Or he may be 'a thoroughly respectable man;' only he has forgotten God: he has become insensible or indocile to spiritual influences, and lives only for himself, only for his own ease, his own ends, his own aggrandisement. At last he loses his wealth,—O, happy loss!— or his character, or his health, and finds that he is no longer sufficient to himself. Some great truth *finds* him, comes home to him in the hour of his loss and weakness, some strong conviction seizes upon him; he becomes conscious of the poverty of his previous aims; he is smitten with bitter compunction and remorse; out of the depths he cries to God for mercy and help: and he is drawn up out of the mire; his feet are set on the rock; he finds rest and peace. Is not this a conversion? It is a most true and happy conversion—so far as it goes; for the whole man is changed, changed in the central and animating motive and bent of his life. *He* turns toward and with God who had long turned from and against Him. A great spiritual revolution has swept through his nature. In all probability he will never experience any other change so radical, so startling, so wonderful as this.

What then? Is his experience to be elevated into

a standard by which the very different spiritual experiences of men differently placed and trained are to be tried? He himself, if he has really turned to God, will be the last man to think so. He will know that his case is not the rule, at least in Christian lands, but the exception; that his conversion is a singular and marvellous instance of the Divine Grace.

Are we to suppose that his conversion is more thorough and complete—that it answers to a higher type—than that of the man who has been trained to love God and goodness from his youth? The probabilities are a thousand to one that it is much less complete, that it answers to a lower and less permanent type; that he has much more to learn and to unlearn, much more to alter and renounce; that the power of evil habit will render obedience to the Divine law much more difficult and painful to him, and temptation much more seductive and perilous.

Are we to assume that *this* conversion will be his last? It is no more the last than it is the first. A thousand times yet he will grieve and resist the Spirit of God, and be constrained to yield to it; he will turn from God, and be taught to turn with Him. Like Peter, he will need to be afresh converted,—converted from impatience to patience, from rashness to sobriety, from disloyalty to constancy, from self-confidence to faith, from vaingloriousness to humility.

Not till his soul moves with the will of God at every moment, and at every turn, will his conversion be complete.

Of these two main types of Conversion, the gradual and the sudden, the continuous and the spasmodic, we may find an illustration in the biographies of the two chief Apostles, St. Peter and St. Paul.

Peter seems to have been a good Jew before he became a good Christian, one of the faithful souls who were looking for the Consolation of Israel while they walked in all the ordinances and commandments blameless. When the Baptist broke on the astonished Jewish world to announce that the Messiah and the kingdom of heaven were at hand, Peter, who had long since been sincerely converted to God, was converted anew by the preaching of the Baptist, converted to a closer walk with God, a more earnest hope of the crowning manifestation of the Divine righteousness and love. No sooner does John, as he sees Jesus coming to him, cry, 'Behold the Lamb of God which taketh away the sins of the world!' than Peter, still conscious of many sins from which he longs to be delivered, follows Jesus that he may learn of Him. He companies with Him for weeks and months before Jesus of Nazareth so grows upon him that he can confess from the depths of his heart: 'Thou art the Christ, the Son of the Living God.' All the while he had been walking with Jesus the Father in heaven had been teaching him, until at last he has learned, not from flesh and blood, but from the immediate influence of the Divine Spirit on his spirit, that God was in Christ, reconciling the world unto Himself. Even yet he has much to learn, falls into many and grievous sins, passes through many painful conversions; but through all he is being gradually trained to turn wholly with God, to yield himself absolutely to the Divine hand. Here, then, we have a continuous and progressive conversion, not without its crises and catastrophes indeed, but still, in the main, slow and gradual in its advance towards completion.

St. Paul's conversion is of the other and opposite type. As good a Jew as Peter, if not a still more punctilious observer of the law that came by Moses, and more accomplished in the righteousness of that law, verily thinking to do God service even when he was fighting against the kingdom of God, Paul first met with the Christian Faith when it seemed to him but as one of the idle novelties after which the idle and credulous multitude is always eager to run, or, at best, as an instance of that fanatical attachment to an imposing personality to which Oriental races are liable, and by which so much had been done, even in his own time and by his own race, to imperil the national welfare and independence. And when, after the Resurrection, he found that faith, or fanaticism, not only infecting the base multitude with the swiftness and force of a contagion, but invading the very Synagogue, culling its recruits mainly from this sacred precinct, selecting for its champions the most ardent and accomplished rabbis,—how could he but resolve, now that it had foemen worthy of his steel, to enter the lists against the new Faith and those who upheld it? To his surprise and chagrin he meets, in Stephen, more than his match, and finds himself wholly 'unable to resist the wisdom and the spirit with which he spake.' His hatred of the Faith is sharpened by the mortification of public defeat, defeat with his own weapons, on his own ground. For in the temperament of St. Paul there was an obvious self-consciousness, and even self-assertiveness, though it was strangely penetrated by shafts of the most pathetic humility, surcharged and suffused with the most impassioned hues of friendship and of love. It was only too likely that, with a nature such as his, he would brood over his defeat, and suffer the shame and rage of it to intensify his previous hatred and contempt for the Faith everywhere spoken against, until, breathing out threatenings and slaughters, he set himself to stamp it out.

It was in this fierce and hostile mood that he was encountered and struck down by the power of Christ on the road to Damascus, and at the same time melted and won by the grace of Christ. His conversion was a catastrophe which cut his life into two distinct halves, the influence of which we can trace in all he wrote and said after this profound and decisive change was wrought upon him. How unlike was it to that of St. Peter! Yet was it not a most true conversion? It was as true as that of Peter himself. But it was not Paul's first conversion, nor was it his last. He had still much to learn, and much to unlearn, much in himself to resist, and much in God to yield to and receive. We have no more right to measure and test his conversion by that of Peter than we have to test that of Peter by the conversion of Paul. Both were won to God and accepted of Him, though they were led to Him by such different roads and their conversion took such different forms.

Now, my brethren, if all this were a mere question of words and names, we might very safely be indifferent to it; but, so far from being a merely verbal question, it is of the gravest practical importance. For want of a true conception of what Conversion is and of the different forms it assumes, innumerable mischiefs have been wrought in the Church and are still wrought in it or by it every day. Few of us who visit the sick and dying, or have either to meet the inquiries of the newly awakened religious life or to minister to minds diseased by persistent brooding over isolated texts and dogmas, can have failed to meet instances in which timid or inexperienced souls have been driven, from a trembling yet growing faith, to utter despair, by those who will accept no evidence of the reality of the spiritual life save a sudden and violent inception. How often have we been moved to an indignation too deep for words by the narrow bigots who condemn all whose religious experience does not tally with the base coarse pattern which they have evolved from their own rude experience of spiritual things; who refuse to admit any to be truly converted to God who cannot fix the exact date of their conversion, and prove it to be as sudden and vehement as the change through which they themselves have passed or fancy they have passed! I have myself seen again and again, even in these comparatively enlightened years, and some of you must also have seen, anxious and delicate-minded women lying on their deathbeds, whose weary hearts were beginning to find peace through trust in the saving mercy of God as revealed in Jesus Christ his Son, rudely flung back into the misery of despair by this inexorable demand for the date and evidence of their conversion, and that not by ignorant enthusiasts alone, or loud-mouthed converts from the gutter—to whom much may be pardoned when they are sincere, but also by men trained in our universities, and who spoke with all the authority of 'pastor of the parish.'

How shall I sufficiently impress upon you the utter absurdity, as well as the frightful cruelty, of this demand? Perhaps I can in no way impress it more instantly and deeply than by putting what these men call 'the Gospel' into a parable such as cannot fail to suggest by contrast, the homely tales in which our Lord Himself conveyed the good news of the Kingdom. Listen, then.

A certain man had two sons. And the younger of them went into a far country, and spent all that he had in riotous living. When he had spent all, and began to be in want, he bethought himself of his father's house and his father's love. And when he came to himself, he said, I will arise and go to my father, and will tell him how wicked I have been, how sorry I am, and I will ask him to let me be one of his hired servants, since I am no more worthy to be called his son. So he arose and came to his father. And when he was a great way off, he stopped, and looked, but he could see nothing of his father, nothing but the house, and even that was locked and barred against him. But, though his heart turned cold with fear, he crept on, and on, until he reached the door, and rapped, faintly at first, then loudly, upon it. After a great while his father half opened the door. Father, he cried, I have sinned, I have sinned; but I have suffered, and I am sorry for my sins. I am dying of want and fear. Have pity on me, and take me in. But the father said, You are no longer a son of mine; and if you would be so much as a servant, you must tell me the very moment, and all the circumstances of the moment, in which you first thought of asking so great and unmerited a boon. *Can* you tell me *now*, this instant? And the prodigal replied, O father, the thought has been growing up in me ever since I knew how wicked I had been; but I cannot honestly say I know when I first became conscious of it. All I know is that I have sinned, that I am sorry and in want, that I long even for the lowest place in my old home. You may go, then, said the father, and you need not trouble yourself to come again. This is no place for such as you. And so the door was shut and barred once more, and the poor lad was left to die in the darkness and the cold.

And this is the Gospel! It may be the gospel according to Beelzebub, but it is *not* the Gospel of God, or of Christ, although it be preached from a thousand throats, and though I myself have known many tender souls who have been driven by it to madness or despair.

Nor is this horrible perversion and caricature of the grace of God the only, though it be the most frightful, consequence of that misconception of Conversion which still darkens many a pulpit, many a heart. Another injurious result of it is that many young persons who have been reared in Christian homes, and whose hearts have been gradually drawn to God, fear to join the Christian fellowship and to take the Christian sacraments because they have never experienced any sudden and violent change of heart. If I speak to any such, let me say to them: You have already been converted many times. So often as you have turned *to* God instead of away from Him, *with* Him instead of against him, you have been converted from your sins. But if you are still doubtful and apprehensive, let the past go, and tell me this: How stands it with you *now?* Do you now believe that God is good, and wants you to become good by trusting in his goodness? Do you believe that, in his love, the Son of the Living God took away the sin of the world, that He might redeem *you* from all sin? Are you conscious of any impulse, any influence, which inclines you to respond to that love and to enter his service? If you are, the Spirit of all Goodness is striving with you at this very moment, and if you turn with it and yield yourself to it, *this* will be the happy moment of your conversion, as I pray God it may be, and you may now enter the kingdom of heaven.

Another injurious consequence of the common conception of Conversion is that those who can remember a time of profound spiritual excitement, in which they felt and responded to 'the powers of the world to come,' are apt to rely on it as a sufficient proof of their Christian character and standing long after it has passed, and they have ceased to watch and strive and pray. Their faith in spiritual realities is not intense, nor their obedience steadfast, nor their lives unselfish and unworldly, nor their hope bright, nor their charity wide and fervent; but they deem that all is well with them because they were once 'converted.' My brethren, there is no safety in that. We need a daily conversion, a lifelong conversion, from impurity to holiness, from worldliness to spirituality, from selfishness to love. So long as there is any evil in us we need to be changed, turned, purged, to have the evil sifted out of us; just as Peter, long after that moment of supreme spiritual agitation in which he confessed Jesus to be the Son of God and the Saviour of the world, needed to be converted to a truer, higher, and more steadfast faith in Him.

Nor must I omit to remind those of you who have been gradually drawn into the kingdom and service and love of God that, though your Conversion has been very genuine, and though in your daily life of duty and obedience you may be giving the best proof that you are accepted of Him, yet, *as a rule*, men do not become wholly or greatly good except through severe trial, vehement effort, and at times a conflict which tries and strains every fibre of the soul. Paul's life of faith in Christ *began* with a catastrophe; Peter's with a gentle 'Come and see,' or, at the latest, with the good confession 'Thou art the Son of God' which had been slowly taking form in his heart and mind. But even to Peter the catastrophe came, the crisis in which he was tried so as by fire, sifted like as corn is shaken in a sieve. And in the lives of all men who have been conspicuous whether for holiness or for usefulness, we find a similar crisis occurring sooner or later, a crisis in which the fountains of the great deep seem to be broken up, and their whole being is agitated and driven as before huge waves and strong. Do not be surprised, therefore, if *your* course, however smoothly it may have run hitherto, should one day plunge as into a deep and sunless gulf, in which neither moon nor stars will for many days be visible to you, and all hope that you shall be saved is clean taken away from you. Do not let go your faith in God even when hope itself gives way. It is no strange thing which is happening to you, but such as is common to most of the true children of God. It is but the proof, or trial, of your faith; and your faith is tried because it is 'more precious than gold which perisheth:' it is tried that, unlike gold, it may be made imperishable.

Finally, there is still another lesson suggested by this passage, a lesson, too, very pertinent to the present time. For our Lord's words suggest how little they know of the true spirit of the Gospel who charge it with fostering selfishness, with only replacing the worldliness it condemns with an 'other-worldliness' equally reprehensible, because it teaches men to be so careful about 'saving their souls' and securing a heavenly reward. No more conclusive or impressive refutation of that charge could be given than the fact that our Lord Himself teaches us, as He taught Peter, to value our very 'conversion,' *i.e.* our very salvation, not for our own sake alone, but also because it enables us to save and strengthen our brethren. We, we of the Church, may have given too much ground for the charge by our coarse and inadequate presentations of the Gospel; but let any man take in the full significance of the words, '*When thou art converted, strengthen thy brethren,*' and he at least will see that the charge has no more foundation in the teaching than it has in the life of Him who loved not Himself, but freely gave Himself up for us all.

PRINTED AT THE CAXTON PRESS, BECCLES.

A LIST OF
C. KEGAN PAUL AND CO.'S
PUBLICATIONS.

10.79.

1, *Paternoster Square, London.*

A LIST OF
C. KEGAN PAUL AND CO.'S PUBLICATIONS.

ABDULLA (Hakayit).
Autobiography of a Malay Munshi. Translated by J. T. Thomson, F.R.G.S. With Photo-lithograph Page of Abdulla's MS. Post 8vo. Cloth, price 12s.

ADAMS (F. O.), F.R.G.S.
The History of Japan. From the Earliest Period to the Present Time. New Edition, revised. 2 volumes. With Maps and Plans. Demy 8vo. Cloth, price 21s. each.

ADAMS (W. D.).
Lyrics of Love, from Shakespeare to Tennyson. Selected and arranged by. Fcap. 8vo. Cloth extra, gilt edges, price 3s. 6d.
Also, a Cheap Edition. Fcap. 8vo. Cloth, price 2s. 6d.

ADAMS (John), M.A.
St. Malo's Quest, and other Poems. Fcap. 8vo. Cloth, 5s.

ADAMSON (H. T.), B.D.
The Truth as it is in Jesus. Crown 8vo. Cloth, price 8s. 6d.

ADON.
Through Storm & Sunshine. Illustrated by M. E. Edwards, A. T. H. Paterson, and the Author. Crown 8vo. Cloth, price 7s. 6d.

A. J. R.
Told at Twilight; Stories in Verse, Songs, &c. Fcap. 8vo. Cloth, price 3s. 6d.

A. K. H. B.
A Scotch Communion Sunday, to which are added Certain Discourses from a University City. By the Author of "The Recreations of a Country Parson." Second Edition. Crown 8vo. Cloth, price 5s.

From a Quiet Place. A New Volume of Sermons. Crown 8vo. Cloth, price 5s.

ALBERT (Mary).
Holland and her Heroes to the year 1585. An Adaptation from Motley's "Rise of the Dutch Republic." Small crown 8vo. Cloth, price, 4s. 6d.

ALLEN (Rev. R.), M.A.
Abraham; his Life, Times, and Travels, 3,800 years ago. Second Edition. With Map. Post 8vo. Cloth, price 6s.

ALLEN (Grant), B.A.
Physiological Æsthetics. Large post 8vo. 9s.

ALLIES (T. W.), M.A.
Per Crucem ad Lucem. The Result of a Life. 2 vols. Demy 8vo. Cloth, price 25s.

AMOS (Prof. Sheldon).
Science of Law. Third Edition. Crown 8vo. Cloth, price 5s. Volume X. of The International Scientific Series.

ANDERSON (Rev. C.), M.A.
New Readings of Old Parables. Demy 8vo. Cloth, price 4s. 6d.
Church Thought and Church Work. Edited by. Second Edition. Demy 8vo. Cloth, price 7s. 6d.
The Curate of Shyre. Second Edition. 8vo. Cloth, price 7s. 6d.

ANDERSON (Col. R. P.).
Victories and Defeats. An Attempt to explain the Causes which have led to them. An Officer's Manual. Demy 8vo. Cloth, price 14s.

ANDERSON (R. C.), C.E.
Tables for Facilitating the Calculation of every Detail in connection with Earthen and Masonry Dams. Royal 8vo. Cloth, price £2 2s.

ARCHER (Thomas).
About my Father's Business. Work amidst the Sick, the Sad, and the Sorrowing. Crown 8vo. Cloth, price 5s.

Army of the North German Confederation.
A Brief Description of its Organization, of the Different Branches of the Service and their *rôle* in War, of its Mode of Fighting, &c. &c. Translated from the Corrected Edition, by permission of the Author, by Colonel Edward Newdigate. Demy 8vo. Cloth, price 5s.

ARNOLD (Arthur).
Social Politics. Demy 8vo. Cloth, price 14s.

AUBERTIN (J. J.).
Camoens' Lusiads. Portuguese Text, with Translation by. With Map and Portraits. 2 vols. Demy 8vo. Price 30s.

Aunt Mary's Bran Pie.
By the author of "St. Olave's." Illustrated. Cloth, price 3s. 6d.

Aurora.
A Volume of Verse. Fcap. 8vo. Cloth, price 5s.

BAGEHOT (Walter).
Physics and Politics; or, Thoughts on the Application of the Principles of "Natural Selection" and "Inheritance" to Political Society. Fourth Edition. Crown 8vo. Cloth, price 4s.
Volume II. of The International Scientific Series.

Some Articles on the Depreciation of Silver, and Topics connected with it. Demy 8vo. Price 5s.

The English Constitution.
A New Edition, Revised and Corrected, with an Introductory Dissertation on Recent Changes and Events. Crown 8vo. Cloth, price 7s. 6d.

Lombard Street. A Description of the Money Market. Seventh Edition. Crown 8vo. Cloth, price 7s. 6d.

BAGOT (Alan).
Accidents in Mines: their Causes and Prevention. Crown 8vo. Cloth, price 6s.

BAIN (Alexander), LL.D.
Mind and Body: the Theories of their relation. Sixth Edition. Crown 8vo. Cloth, price 4s.
Volume IV. of The International Scientific Series.

Education as a Science.
Crown 8vo. Second Edition. Cloth, price 5s.
Volume XXV. of The International Scientific Series.

BAKER (Sir Sherston, Bart.).
Halleck's International Law; or Rules Regulating the Intercourse of States in Peace and War. A New Edition, Revised, with Notes and Cases. 2 vols. Demy 8vo. Cloth, price 38s.

The Laws relating to Quarantine. Crown 8vo. Cloth, price 12s. 6d.

BALDWIN (Capt. J. H.), F.Z.S.
The Large and Small Game of Bengal and the North-Western Provinces of India. 4to. With numerous Illustrations. Second Edition. Cloth, price 21s.

BANKS (Mrs. G. L.).
God's Providence House.
New Edition. Crown 8vo. Cloth, price 3s. 6d.

Ripples and Breakers.
Poems. Square 8vo. Cloth, price 5s.

BARING (T. C.), M.A., M.P.
Pindar in English Rhyme.
Being an Attempt to render the Epinikian Odes with the principal remaining Fragments of Pindar into English Rhymed Verse. Small Quarto. Cloth, price 7s.

BARLEE (Ellen).
Locked Out: a Tale of the Strike. With a Frontispiece. Royal 16mo. Cloth, price 1s. 6d.

BARNES (William).
An Outline of English Speechcraft. Crown 8vo. Cloth, price 4s.

Poems of Rural Life, in the Dorset Dialect. New Edition, complete in 1 vol. Crown 8vo. Cloth, price 8s. 6d.

BARTLEY (George C. T.).
Domestic Economy: Thrift in Every Day Life. Taught in Dialogues suitable for Children of all ages. Small crown 8vo. Cloth, limp, 2s.

BAUR (Ferdinand), Dr. Ph.
A Philological Introduction to Greek and Latin for Students. Translated and adapted from the German of. By C. KEGAN PAUL, M.A. Oxon., and the Rev. E. D. STONE, M.A., late Fellow of King's College, Cambridge, and Assistant Master at Eton. Second and revised edition. Crown 8vo. Cloth, price 6s.

BAYNES (Rev. Canon R. H.)
At the Communion Time. A Manual for Holy Communion. With a preface by the Right Rev. the Lord Bishop of Derry and Raphoe. Cloth, price 1s. 6d.
*** Can also be had bound in French morocco, price 2s. 6d.; Persian morocco, price 3s.; Calf, or Turkey morocco, price 3s. 6d.
Home Songs for Quiet Hours. Fourth and cheaper Edition. Fcap. 8vo. Cloth, price 2s. 6d.
This may also be had handsomely bound in morocco with gilt edges.

BECKER (Bernard H.).
The Scientific Societies of London. Crown 8vo. Cloth, price 5s.

BELLINGHAM (Henry), Barrister-at-Law.
Social Aspects of Catholicism and Protestantism in their Civil Bearing upon Nations. Translated and adapted from the French of M. le Baron de Haulleville. With a Preface by His Eminence Cardinal Manning. Crown 8vo. Cloth, price 6s.

BENNETT (Dr. W. C.).
Narrative Poems & Ballads. Fcap. 8vo. Sewed in Coloured Wrapper, price 1s.
Songs for Sailors. Dedicated by Special Request to H. R. H. the Duke of Edinburgh. With Steel Portrait and Illustrations. Crown 8vo. Cloth, price 3s. 6d.
An Edition in Illustrated Paper Covers, price 1s.

BENNETT (Dr. W. C.)—*continued.*
Songs of a Song Writer. Crown 8vo. Cloth, price 6s.

BENNIE (Rev. J. N.), M.A.
The Eternal Life. Sermons preached during the last twelve years. Crown 8vo. Cloth, price 6s.

BERNARD (Bayle).
Samuel Lover, the Life and Unpublished Works of. In 2 vols. With a Steel Portrait. Post 8vo. Cloth, price 21s.

BERNSTEIN (Prof.).
The Five Senses of Man. With 91 Illustrations. Second Edition. Crown 8vo. Cloth, price 5s.
Volume XXI. of The International Scientific Series.

BETHAM-EDWARDS (Miss M.).
Kitty. With a Frontispiece. Crown 8vo. Cloth, price 6s.

BEVINGTON (L. S.).
Key Notes. Small crown 8vo. Cloth, price 5s.

BISSET (A.)
History of the Struggle for Parliamentary Government in England. 2 vols. Demy 8vo. Cloth, price 24s.

BLASERNA (Prof. Pietro).
The Theory of Sound in its Relation to Music. With numerous Illustrations. Second Edition. Crown 8vo. Cloth, price 5s.
Volume XXII. of The International Scientific Series.

Blue Roses; or, Helen Malinofska's Marriage. By the Author of "Véra." 2 vols. Fifth Edition. Cloth, gilt tops, 12s.
*** Also a Cheaper Edition in 1 vol. With Frontispiece. Crown 8vo. Cloth, price 6s.

BLUME (Major W.).
The Operations of the German Armies in France, from Sedan to the end of the war of 1870-71. With Map. From the Journals of the Head-quarters Staff. Translated by the late E. M. Jones, Maj. 20th Foot, Prof. of Mil. Hist., Sandhurst. Demy 8vo. Cloth, price 9s.

BOGUSLAWSKI (Capt. A. von).
Tactical Deductions from the War of 1870-71. Translated by Colonel Sir Lumley Graham, Bart., late 18th (Royal Irish) Regiment. Third Edition, Revised and Corrected. Demy 8vo. Cloth, price 7s.

BONWICK (J.), F.R.G.S.
Egyptian Belief and Modern Thought. Large post 8vo. Cloth, price 10s. 6d.

Pyramid Facts and Fancies. Crown 8vo. Cloth, price 5s.

The Tasmanian Lily. With Frontispiece. Crown 8vo. Cloth, price 5s.

Mike Howe, the Bushranger of Van Diemen's Land. With Frontispiece. Crown 8vo. Cloth, price 5s.

BOSWELL (R. B.), M.A., Oxon.
Metrical Translations from the Greek and Latin Poets, and other Poems. Crown 8vo. Cloth, price 5s.

BOWEN (H. C.), M.A.
English Grammar for Beginners. Fcap. 8vo. Cloth, price 1s.

Studies in English, for the use of Modern Schools. Small crown 8vo. Cloth, price 1s. 6d.

Simple English Poems. English Literature for Junior Classes. In Four Parts. Parts I. and II., price 6d. each, now ready.

BOWRING (L.), C.S.I.
Eastern Experiences. Illustrated with Maps and Diagrams. Demy 8vo. Cloth, price 16s.

BOWRING (Sir John).
Autobiographical Recollections. With Memoir by Lewin B. Bowring. Demy 8vo. Price 14s.

BRADLEY (F. H.).
Ethical Studies. Critical Essays in Moral Philosophy. Large post 8vo. Cloth, price 9s.

Brave Men's Footsteps. By the Editor of "Men who have Risen." A Book of Example and Anecdote for Young People. With Four Illustrations by C. Doyle. Fifth Edition. Crown 8vo. Cloth, price 3s. 6d.

BRIALMONT (Col. A.).
Hasty Intrenchments. Translated by Lieut. Charles A. Empson, R.A. With Nine Plates. Demy 8vo. Cloth, price 6s.

BROOKE (Rev. S. A.), M.A.
The Late Rev. F. W. Robertson, M.A., Life and Letters of. Edited by.
I. Uniform with the Sermons. 2 vols. With Steel Portrait. Price 7s. 6d.
II. Library Edition. 8vo. With Two Steel Portraits. Price 12s.
III. A Popular Edition, in 1 vol. 8vo. Price 6s.

Theology in the English Poets. — COWPER, COLERIDGE, WORDSWORTH, and BURNS. Third Edition. Post 8vo. Cloth, price 9s.

Christ in Modern Life. Thirteenth Edition. Crown 8vo. Cloth, price 7s. 6d.

Sermons. First Series. Eleventh Edition. Crown 8vo. Cloth, price 6s.

Sermons. Second Series. Third Edition. Crown 8vo. Cloth, price 7s.

The Fight of Faith. Sermons preached on various occasions. Third Edition. Crown 8vo. Cloth, price 7s. 6d.

Frederick Denison Maurice: The Life and Work of. A Memorial Sermon. Crown 8vo. Sewed, price 1s.

BROOKE (W. G.), M.A.
The Public Worship Regulation Act. With a Classified Statement of its Provisions, Notes, and Index. Third Edition, Revised and Corrected. Crown 8vo. Cloth, price 3s. 6d.

BROOKE (W. G.)—*continued.*
Six Privy Council Judgments—1850-1872. Annotated by. Third Edition. Crown 8vo. Cloth, price 9s.

BROUN (J. A.).
Magnetic Observations at Trevandrum and Augustia Malley. Vol. I. 4to. Cloth, price 63s.
The Report from above, separately sewed, price 21s.

BROWN (Rev. J. Baldwin), B.A.
The Higher Life. Its Reality, Experience, and Destiny. Fifth and Cheaper Edition. Crown 8vo. Cloth, price 5s.
Doctrine of Annihilation in the Light of the Gospel of Love. Five Discourses. Third Edition. Crown 8vo. Cloth, price 2s. 6d.

BROWN (J. Croumbie), LL.D.
Reboisement in France; or, Records of the Replanting of the Alps, the Cevennes, and the Pyrenees with Trees, Herbage, and Bush. Demy 8vo. Cloth, price 12s. 6d.
The Hydrology of Southern Africa. Demy 8vo. Cloth, price 10s. 6d.

BRYANT (W. C.)
Poems. Red-line Edition. With 24 Illustrations and Portrait of the Author. Crown 8vo. Cloth extra, price 7s. 6d.
A Cheaper Edition, with Frontispiece. Small crown 8vo. Cloth, price 3s. 6d.

BUCHANAN (Robert).
Poetical Works. Collected Edition, in 3 vols., with Portrait. Crown 8vo. Cloth, price 6s. each.
Master-Spirits. Post 8vo. Cloth, price 10s. 6d.

BULKELEY (Rev. H. J.).
Walled in, and other Poems. Crown 8vo. Cloth, price 5s.

BURCKHARDT (Jacob).
The Civilization of the Period of the Renaissance in Italy. Authorized translation, by S. G. C. Middlemore. 2 vols. Demy 8vo. Cloth, price 24s.

BURTON (Mrs. Richard).
The Inner Life of Syria, Palestine, and the Holy Land. With Maps, Photographs, and Coloured Plates. 2 vols. Second Edition. Demy 8vo. Cloth, price 24s.
⁎ Also a Cheaper Edition in one volume. Large post 8vo. Cloth, price 10s. 6d.

BURTON (Capt. Richard F.).
The Gold Mines of Midian and the Ruined Midianite Cities. A Fortnight's Tour in North Western Arabia. With numerous Illustrations. Second Edition. Demy 8vo. Cloth, price 18s.
The Land of Midian Revisited. With numerous illustrations on wood and by Chromolithography. 2 vols. Demy 8vo. Cloth, price 32s.

CALDERON.
Calderon's Dramas: The Wonder-Working Magician—Life is a Dream—The Purgatory of St. Patrick. Translated by Denis Florence MacCarthy. Post 8vo. Cloth, price 10s.

CANDLER (H.).
The Groundwork of Belief. Crown 8vo. Cloth, price 7s.

CARLISLE (A. D.), B. A.
Round the World in 1870. A Volume of Travels, with Maps. New and Cheaper Edition. Demy 8vo. Cloth, price 6s.

CARNE (Miss E. T.).
The Realm of Truth. Crown 8vo. Cloth, price 5s. 6d.

CARPENTER (E.).
Narcissus and other Poems. Fcap. 8vo. Cloth, price 5s.

CARPENTER (W. B.), M.D.
The Principles of Mental Physiology. With their Applications to the Training and Discipline of the Mind, and the Study of its Morbid Conditions. Illustrated. Fifth Edition. 8vo. Cloth, price 12s.

CAVALRY OFFICER.
Notes on Cavalry Tactics, Organization, &c. With Diagrams. Demy 8vo. Cloth, price 12s.

CHAPMAN (Hon. Mrs. E. W.).
A Constant Heart. A Story.
2 vols. Cloth, gilt tops, price 12s.
Children's Toys, and some
Elementary Lessons in General Knowledge which they teach. Illustrated. Crown 8vo. Cloth, price 5s.

CHRISTOPHERSON (The late Rev. Henry), M.A.
Sermons. With an Introduction by John Rae, LL.D., F.S.A. Second Series. Crown 8vo. Cloth, price 6s.

CLERK (Mrs. Godfrey).
'Ilâm en Nâs. Historical Tales and Anecdotes of the Times of the Early Khalifahs. Translated from the Arabic Originals. Illustrated with Historical and Explanatory Notes. Crown 8vo. Cloth, price 7s.

CLERY (C.), Major.
Minor Tactics. With 26 Maps and Plans. Fourth and Revised Edition. Demy 8vo. Cloth, price 16s.

CLODD (Edward), F.R.A.S.
The Childhood of the World: a Simple Account of Man in Early Times. Sixth Edition. Crown 8vo. Cloth, price 3s.
A Special Edition for Schools. Price 1s.
The Childhood of Religions. Including a Simple Account of the Birth and Growth of Myths and Legends. Third Thousand. Crown 8vo. Cloth, price 5s.
A Special Edition for Schools. Price 1s. 6d.

COLERIDGE (Sara).
Pretty Lessons in Verse for Good Children, with some Lessons in Latin, in Easy Rhyme. A New Edition. Illustrated. Fcap. 8vo. Cloth, price 3s. 6d.
Phantasmion. A Fairy Tale. With an Introductory Preface by the Right Hon. Lord Coleridge, of Ottery St. Mary. A New Edition. Illustrated. Crown 8vo. Cloth, price 7s. 6d.
Memoir and Letters of Sara Coleridge. Edited by her Daughter. With Index. 2 vols. With Two Portraits. Third Edition, Revised and Corrected. Crown 8vo. Cloth, price 24s.
Cheap Edition. With one Portrait. Cloth, price 7s. 6d.

COLLINS (Mortimer).
The Secret of Long Life. Small crown 8vo. Cloth, price 3s. 6d.
Inn of Strange Meetings, and other Poems. Crown 8vo. Cloth, price 5s.

COLLINS (Rev. R.), M.A.
Missionary Enterprise in the East. With special reference to the Syrian Christians of Malabar, and the results of modern Missions. With Four Illustrations. Crown 8vo. Cloth, price 6s.

COOKE (M. C.), M.A., LL.D.
Fungi; their Nature, Influences, Uses, &c. Edited by the Rev. M. J. Berkeley, M.A., F.L.S. With Illustrations. Second Edition. Crown 8vo. Cloth, price 5s.
Volume XIV. of The International Scientific Series.

COOKE (Prof. J. P.)
The New Chemistry. With 31 Illustrations. Fourth Edition. Crown 8vo. Cloth, price 5s.
Volume IX. of The International Scientific Series.
Scientific Culture. Crown 8vo. Cloth, price 1s.

COOPER (T. T.), F.R.G.S.
The Mishmee Hills: an Account of a Journey made in an Attempt to Penetrate Thibet from Assam, to open New Routes for Commerce. Second Edition. With Four Illustrations and Map. Post 8vo. Cloth, price 10s. 6d.

COOPER (H. J.).
The Art of Furnishing on Rational and Æsthetic Principles. New and Cheaper Edition. Fcap. 8vo. Cloth, price 1s. 6d.

COPPÉE (François).
L'Exilée. Done into English Verse with the sanction of the Author by I. O. L. Crown 8vo. Cloth, price 5s.

Cornhill Library of Fiction (The). Crown 8vo. Cloth, price 3s. 6d. per volume.
Half-a-Dozen Daughters. By J. Masterman.
The House of Raby. By Mrs. G. Hooper.

Cornhill Library of Fiction—
continued.

A Fight for Life. By Moy Thomas.
Robin Gray. By Charles Gibbon.
One of Two; or, A Left-Handed Bride. By J. Hain Friswell.
God's Providence House. By Mrs. G. L. Banks.
For Lack of Gold. By Charles Gibbon.
Abel Drake's Wife. By John Saunders.
Hirell. By John Saunders.

CORY (Lieut. Col. Arthur).

The Eastern Menace; or, Shadows of Coming Events. Crown 8vo. Cloth, price 5s.

Ione. A Poem in Four Parts. Fcap. 8vo. Cloth, price 5s.

Cosmos.

A Poem. Fcap. 8vo. Cloth, price 3s. 6d.

COURTNEY (W. L.).

The Metaphysics of John Stuart Mill. Crown 8vo. Cloth, price 5s. 6d.

COWAN (Rev. William).

Poems: Chiefly Sacred, including Translations from some Ancient Latin Hymns. Fcap. 8vo. Cloth, price 5s.

COX (Rev. Sir G. W.), Bart.

A History of Greece from the Earliest Period to the end of the Persian War. New Edition. 2 vols. Demy 8vo. Cloth, price 36s.

The Mythology of the Aryan Nations. New Edition. 2 vols. Demy 8vo. Cloth, price 28s.

A General History of Greece from the Earliest Period to the Death of Alexander the Great, with a sketch of the subsequent History to the present time. New Edition. Crown 8vo. Cloth, price 7s. 6d.

Tales of Ancient Greece. New Edition. Small crown 8vo. Cloth, price 6s.

School History of Greece. With Maps. New Edition. Fcap. 8vo. Cloth, price 3s. 6d.

The Great Persian War from the Histories of Herodotus. New Edition. Fcap. 8vo. Cloth, price 3s. 6d.

COX (Rev. Sir G. W.), Bart.—*continued.*

A Manual of Mythology in the form of Question and Answer. New Edition. Fcap. 8vo. Cloth, price 3s.

COX (Rev. Samuel).

Salvator Mundi; or, Is Christ the Saviour of all Men? Sixth Edition. Crown 8vo. Cloth, price 5s.

CRAUFURD (A. H.).

Seeking for Light: Sermons. Crown 8vo. Cloth, price 5s.

CRESSWELL (Mrs. G.).

The King's Banner. Drama in Four Acts. Five Illustrations. 4to. Cloth, price 10s. 6d.

CROMPTON (Henry).

Industrial Conciliation. Fcap. 8vo. Cloth, price 2s. 6d.

D'ANVERS (N. R.).

The Suez Canal: Letters and Documents descriptive of its Rise and Progress in 1854-56. By Ferdinand de Lesseps. Translated by. Demy 8vo. Cloth, price 10s. 6d.

Parted. A Tale of Clouds and Sunshine. With 4 Illustrations. Extra Fcap 8vo. Cloth, price 3s. 6d.

Little Minnie's Troubles. An Every-day Chronicle. With Four Illustrations by W. H. Hughes. Fcap. Cloth, price 3s. 6d.

Pixie's Adventures; or, the Tale of a Terrier. With 21 Illustrations. 16mo. Cloth, price 4s. 6d.

Nanny's Adventures; or, the Tale of a Goat. With 12 Illustrations. 16mo. Cloth, price 4s. 6d.

DAVIDSON (Rev. Samuel), D.D., LL.D.

The New Testament, translated from the Latest Greek Text of Tischendorf. A New and thoroughly Revised Edition. Post 8vo. Cloth, price 10s. 6d.

Canon of the Bible: Its Formation, History, and Fluctuations. Second Edition. Small crown 8vo. Cloth, price 5s.

DAVIES (G. Christopher).

Mountain, Meadow, and Mere: a Series of Outdoor Sketches of Sport, Scenery, Adventures, and Natural History. With Sixteen Illustrations by Bosworth W. Harcourt. Crown 8vo. Cloth, price 6s.

DAVIES (G. Chris.)—*continued.*
Rambles and Adventures of Our School Field Club. With Four Illustrations. Crown 8vo. Cloth, price 5s.

DAVIES (Rev. J. L.), M.A.
Theology and Morality. Essays on Questions of Belief and Practice. Crown 8vo. Cloth, price 7s. 6d.

DAVIES (T. Hart.).
Catullus. Translated into English Verse. Crown 8vo. Cloth, price 6s.

DAWSON (George), M.A.
Prayers, with a Discourse on Prayer. Edited by his Wife. Fifth Edition. Crown 8vo. Price 6s.
Sermons on Disputed Points and Special Occasions. Edited by his Wife. Third Edition. Crown 8vo. Cloth, price 6s.
Sermons on Daily Life and Duty. Edited by his Wife. Second Edition. Crown 8vo. Cloth, price 6s.

DE L'HOSTE (Col. E. P.).
The Desert Pastor, Jean Jarousseau. Translated from the French of Eugène Pelletan. With a Frontispiece. New Edition. Fcap. 8vo. Cloth, price 3s. 6d.

DENNIS (J.).
English Sonnets. Collected and Arranged. Elegantly bound. Fcap. 8vo. Cloth, price 3s. 6d.

DE REDCLIFFE (Viscount Stratford), P.C., K.G., G.C.B.
Why am I a Christian? Fifth Edition. Crown 8vo. Cloth, price 3s.

DESPREZ (Philip S.).
Daniel and John; or, the Apocalypse of the Old and that of the New Testament. Demy 8vo. Cloth, price 12s.

DE TOCQUEVILLE (A.).
Correspondence and Conversations of, with Nassau William Senior, from 1834 to 1859. Edited by M. C. M. Simpson. 2 vols. Post 8vo. Cloth, price 21s.

DE VERE (Aubrey).
Legends of the Saxon Saints. Small crown 8vo. Cloth, price 6s.

A 2

DE VERE (Aubrey) *continued.*
Alexander the Great. A Dramatic Poem. Small crown 8vo. Cloth, price 5s.
The Infant Bridal, and Other Poems. A New and Enlarged Edition. Fcap. 8vo. Cloth, price 7s. 6d.
The Legends of St. Patrick, and other Poems. Small crown 8vo. Cloth, price 5s.
St. Thomas of Canterbury. A Dramatic Poem. Large fcap. 8vo. Cloth, price 5s.
Antar and Zara: an Eastern Romance. INISFAIL, and other Poems, Meditative and Lyrical. Fcap. 8vo. Price 6s.
The Fall of Rora, the Search after Proserpine, and other Poems, Meditative and Lyrical. Fcap. 8vo. Price 6s.

DOBSON (Austin).
Vignettes in Rhyme and Vers de Société. Third Edition. Fcap. 8vo. Cloth, price 5s.
Proverbs in Porcelain. By the Author of "Vignettes in Rhyme." Second Edition. Crown 8vo. 6s.

DOWDEN (Edward), LL.D.
Shakspere: a Critical Study of his Mind and Art. Fourth Edition. Large post 8vo. Cloth, price 12s.
Studies in Literature, 1789-1877. Large post 8vo. Cloth, price 12s.
Poems. Second Edition. Fcap. 8vo. Cloth, price 5s.

DOWNTON (Rev. H.), M.A.
Hymns and Verses. Original and Translated. Small crown 8vo. Cloth, price 3s. 6d.

DRAPER (J. W.), M.D., LL.D.
History of the Conflict between Religion and Science. Eleventh Edition. Crown 8vo. Cloth, price 5s.
Volume XIII. of The International Scientific Series.

DREW (Rev. G. S.), M.A.
Scripture Lands in connection with their History. Second Edition. 8vo. Cloth, price 10s. 6d.

DREW (Rev. G. S.), M.A. *continued.*
Nazareth: Its Life and Lessons. Third Edition. Crown 8vo. Cloth, price 5s.
The Divine Kingdom on Earth as it is in Heaven. 8vo. Cloth, price 10s. 6d.
The Son of Man: His Life and Ministry. Crown 8vo. Cloth, price 7s. 6d.

DREWRY (G. O.), M.D.
The Common-Sense Management of the Stomach. Fifth Edition. Fcap. 8vo. Cloth, price 2s. 6d.

DREWRY (G. O.), M.D., and BARTLETT (H. C.), Ph.D., F.C.S.
Cup and Platter: or, Notes on Food and its Effects. New and cheaper Edition. Small 8vo. Cloth, price 1s. 6d.

DRUMMOND (Miss).
Tripps Buildings. A Study from Life, with Frontispiece. Small crown 8vo. Cloth, price 3s. 6d.

DU MONCEL (Count).
The Telephone, the Microphone, and the Phonograph. With 74 Illustrations. Small crown 8vo. Cloth, price 5s.

DURAND (Lady).
Imitations from the German of Spitta and Terstegen. Fcap. 8vo. Cloth, price 4s.

DU VERNOIS (Col. von Verdy).
Studies in leading Troops. An authorized and accurate Translation by Lieutenant H. J. T. Hildyard, 71st Foot. Parts I. and II. Demy 8vo. Cloth, price 7s.

EDEN (Frederick).
The Nile without a Dragoman. Second Edition. Crown 8vo. Cloth, price 7s. 6d.

EDMONDS (Herbert).
Well Spent Lives: a Series of Modern Biographies. Crown 8vo. Price 5s.
The Educational Code of the Prussian Nation, in its Present Form. In accordance with the Decisions of the Common Provincial Law, and with those of Recent Legislation. Crown 8vo. Cloth, price 2s. 6d.

EDWARDS (Rev. Basil).
Minor Chords; or, Songs for the Suffering: a Volume of Verse. Fcap. 8vo. Cloth, price 3s. 6d.: paper, price 2s. 6d.

ELLIOT (Lady Charlotte).
Medusa and other Poems. Crown 8vo. Cloth, price 6s.

ELLIOTT (Ebenezer), The Corn Law Rhymer.
Poems. Edited by his Son, the Rev. Edwin Elliott, of St. John's, Antigua. 2 vols. Crown 8vo. Cloth, price 18s.

ELSDALE (Henry).
Studies in Tennyson's Idylls. Crown 8vo. Cloth, price 5s.

Epic of Hades (The).
By the author of "Songs of Two Worlds." Seventh and finally revised Edition. Fcap. 8vo. Cloth, price 7s. 6d.
*** Also an Illustrated Edition with seventeen full-page designs in photo-mezzotint by GEORGE R. CHAPMAN. 4to. Cloth, extra gilt leaves, price 25s.

Eros Agonistes.
Poems. By E. B. D. Fcap. 8vo. Cloth, price 3s. 6d.

Essays on the Endowment of Research.
By Various Writers. Square crown 8vo. Cloth, price 10s. 6d.

EVANS (Mark).
The Gospel of Home Life. Crown 8vo. Cloth, price 4s. 6d.
The Story of our Father's Love, told to Children. Fourth and Cheaper Edition. With Four Illustrations. Fcap. 8vo. Cloth, price 1s. 6d.
A Book of Common Prayer and Worship for Household Use, compiled exclusively from the Holy Scriptures. Fcap. 8vo. Cloth, price 2s. 6d.

EX-CIVILIAN.
Life in the Mofussil; or, Civilian Life in Lower Bengal. 2 vols. Large post 8vo. Price 14s.

EYRE (Maj.-Gen. Sir V.), C.B., K.C.S.I., &c.
Lays of a Knight-Errant in many Lands. Square crown 8vo. With Six Illustrations. Cloth, price 7s. 6d.

FARQUHARSON (M.).
 I. **Elsie Dinsmore.** Crown 8vo. Cloth, price 3s. 6d.
 II. **Elsie's Girlhood.** Crown 8vo. Cloth, price 3s. 6d.
 III. **Elsie's Holidays at Roselands.** Crown 8vo. Cloth, price 3s. 6d.

FERRIS (Henry Weybridge).
 Poems. Fcap. 8vo. Cloth, price 5s.

FIELD (Horace), B.A., Lond:
 The Ultimate Triumph of Christianity. Small crown 8vo. Cloth, price 3s. 6d.

FINN (the late James), M.R.A.S.
 Stirring Times; or, Records from Jerusalem Consular Chronicles of 1853 to 1856. Edited and Compiled by his Widow. With a Preface by the Viscountess STRANGFORD. 2 vols. Demy 8vo. Price 30s.

FLEMING (James), D.D.
 Early Christian Witnesses; or, Testimonies of the First Centuries to the Truth of Christianity. Small crown 8vo. Cloth, price 3s. 6d.

Folkestone Ritual Case (The). The Argument, Proceedings, Judgment, and Report, revised by the several Counsel engaged. Demy 8vo. Cloth, price 25s.

FOOTMAN (Rev. H.), M.A.
 From Home and Back; or, Some Aspects of Sin as seen in the Light of the Parable of the Prodigal. Crown 8vo. Cloth, price 5s.

FOWLE (Rev. Edmund).
 Latin Primer Rules made Easy. Crown 8vo. Cloth, price 3s.

FOWLE (Rev. T. W.), M.A.
 The Reconciliation of Religion and Science. Being Essays on Immortality, Inspiration, Miracles, and the Being of Christ. Demy 8vo. Cloth, price 10s. 6d.

 The Divine Legation of Christ. Crown 8vo. Cloth, price 7s.

FOX-BOURNE (H. R.).
 The Life of John Locke, 1632—1704. 2 vols. Demy 8vo. Cloth, price 28s.

FRASER (Donald).
 Exchange Tables of Sterling and Indian Rupee Currency, upon a new and extended system, embracing Values from One Farthing to One Hundred Thousand Pounds, and at Rates progressing, in Sixteenths of a Penny, from 1s. 9d. to 2s. 3d. per Rupee. Royal 8vo. Cloth, price 10s. 6d.

FRISWELL (J. Hain).
 The Better Self. Essays for Home Life. Crown 8vo. Cloth, price 6s.

 One of Two; or, A Left-Handed Bride. With a Frontispiece. Crown 8vo. Cloth, price 3s. 6d.

FYTCHE (Lieut.-Gen. Albert), C.S.I., late Chief Commissioner of British Burma.
 Burma Past and Present, with Personal Reminiscences of the Country. With Steel Portraits, Chromolithographs, Engravings on Wood, and Map. 2 vols. Demy 8vo. Cloth, price 30s.

GAMBIER (Capt. J. W.), R.N.
 Servia. Crown 8vo. Cloth, price 5s.

GARDNER (H.).
 Sunflowers. A Book of Verses. Fcap. 8vo. Cloth, price 5s.

GARDNER (J.), M.D.
 Longevity: The Means of Prolonging Life after Middle Age. Fourth Edition, Revised and Enlarged. Small crown 8vo. Cloth, price 4s.

GARRETT (E.).
 By Still Waters. A Story for Quiet Hours. With Seven Illustrations. Crown 8vo. Cloth, price 6s.

GEBLER (Karl Von).
 Galileo Galilei and the Roman Curia, from Authentic Sources. Translated with the sanction of the Author, by Mrs. GEORGE STURGE. Demy 8vo. Cloth, price 12s.

G. H. T.
 Verses, mostly written in India. Crown 8vo. Cloth, price 6s.

GILBERT (Mrs.).
 Autobiography and other Memorials. Edited by Josiah Gilbert. Third Edition. With Portrait and several Wood Engravings. Crown 8vo. Cloth, price 7s. 6d.

GILL (Rev. W. W.), B.A.
Myths and Songs from the South Pacific. With a Preface by F. Max Müller, M.A., Professor of Comparative Philology at Oxford. Post 8vo. Cloth, price 9s.

GLOVER (F.), M.A.
Exempla Latina. A First Construing Book with Short Notes, Lexicon, and an Introduction to the Analysis of Sentences. Fcap. 8vo. Cloth, price 2s.

GODKIN (James).
The Religious History of Ireland: Primitive, Papal, and Protestant. Including the Evangelical Missions, Catholic Agitations, and Church Progress of the last half Century. 8vo. Cloth, price 12s.

GODWIN (William).
William Godwin: His Friends and Contemporaries. With Portraits and Facsimiles of the handwriting of Godwin and his Wife. By C. Kegan Paul. 2 vols. Demy 8vo. Cloth, price 28s.
The Genius of Christianity Unveiled. Being Essays never before published. Edited, with a Preface, by C. Kegan Paul. Crown 8vo. Cloth, price 7s. 6d.

GOETZE (Capt. A. von).
Operations of the German Engineers during the War of 1870-1871. Published by Authority, and in accordance with Official Documents. Translated from the German by Colonel G. Graham, V.C., C.B., R.E. With 6 large Maps. Demy 8vo. Cloth, price 21s.

GOLDIE (Lieut. M. H. G.)
Hebe: a Tale. Fcap. 8vo. Cloth, price 5s.

GOLDSMID (Sir Francis Henry).
Memoir of. With Portrait. Crown 8vo. Cloth, price 5s.

GOODENOUGH (Commodore J. G.), R.N., C.B., C.M.G.
Memoir of, with Extracts from his Letters and Journals. Edited by his Widow. With Steel Engraved Portrait. Square 8vo. Cloth, 5s.
* Also a Library Edition with Maps, Woodcuts, and Steel Engraved Portrait. Square post 8vo. Cloth, price 14s.

GOSSE (Edmund W.).
Studies in the Literature of Northern Europe. With a Frontispiece designed and etched by Alma Tadema. Large post 8vo. Cloth, price 12s.
New Poems. Crown 8vo. Cloth, price 7s. 6d.

GOULD (Rev. S. Baring), M.A.
Germany, Present and Past. 2 Vols. Demy 8vo. Cloth, price 21s.
The Vicar of Morwenstow: a Memoir of the Rev. R. S. Hawker. With Portrait. Third Edition, revised. Square post 8vo. Cloth, 10s. 6d.

GRANVILLE (A. B.), M.D., F.R.S., &c.
Autobiography of A. B. Granville, F.R.S., &c. Edited, with a brief Account of the concluding Years of his Life, by his youngest Daughter, Paulina B. Granville. 2 vols. With a Portrait. Second Edition. Demy 8vo. Cloth, price 32s.

GREY (John), of Dilston.
John Grey (of Dilston): Memoirs. By Josephine E. Butler. New and Revised Edition. Crown 8vo. Cloth, price 3s. 6d.

GRIFFITH (Rev. T.), A.M.
Studies of the Divine Master. Demy 8vo. Cloth, price 12s.

GRIFFITHS (Capt. Arthur).
Memorials of Millbank, and Chapters in Prison History. With Illustrations by R. Goff and the Author. 2 vols. Post 8vo. Cloth, price 21s.

GRIMLEY (Rev. H. N.), M.A.
Tremadoc Sermons, chiefly on the SPIRITUAL BODY, the UNSEEN WORLD, and the DIVINE HUMANITY. Second Edition. Crown 8vo. Cloth, price 6s.

GRÜNER (M. L.).
Studies of Blast Furnace Phenomena. Translated by L. D. B. Gordon, F.R.S.E., F.G.S. Demy 8vo. Cloth, price 7s. 6d.

GURNEY (Rev. Archer).
Words of Faith and Cheer. A Mission of Instruction and Suggestion. Crown 8vo. Cloth, price 6s.

Gwen: A Drama in Monologue. By the Author of the "Epic of Hades." Second Edition. Fcap. 8vo. Cloth, price 5s.

HAECKEL (Prof. Ernst).
The History of Creation. Translation revised by Professor E. Ray Lankester, M.A., F.R.S. With Coloured Plates and Genealogical Trees of the various groups of both plants and animals. 2 vols. Second Edition. Post 8vo. Cloth, price 32s.

The History of the Evolution of Man. With numerous Illustrations. 2 vols. Large post 8vo. Cloth, price 32s.

Freedom in Science and Teaching. From the German of Ernst Haeckel, with a Prefatory Note by T. H. Huxley, F.R.S. Crown 8vo. Cloth, price 5s.

HAKE (A. Egmont).
Paris Originals, with twenty etchings, by Léon Richeton. Large post 8vo. Cloth, price 14s.

Halleck's International Law; or, Rules Regulating the Intercourse of States in Peace and War. A New Edition, revised, with Notes and Cases. By Sir Sherston Baker, Bart. 2 vols. Demy 8vo. Cloth, price 38s.

HARCOURT (Capt. A. F. P.).
The Shakespeare Argosy. Containing much of the wealth of Shakespeare's Wisdom and Wit, alphabetically arranged and classified. Crown 8vo. Cloth, price 6s.

HARDY (Thomas).
A Pair of Blue Eyes. New Edition. With Frontispiece. Crown 8vo. Cloth, price 6s.

The Return of the Native. New Edition. With Frontispiece. Crown 8vo. Cloth, price 6s.

HARRISON (Lieut.-Col. R.).
The Officer's Memorandum Book for Peace and War. Second Edition. Oblong 32mo. roan, elastic band and pencil, price 3s. 6d.; russia, 5s.

HAWEIS (Rev. H. R.), M.A.
Arrows in the Air. Crown 8vo. Second Edition. Cloth, price 6s.

HAWEIS (Rev. H. R.)—*continued*.
Current Coin. Materialism—The Devil—Crime—Drunkenness—Pauperism—Emotion—Recreation—The Sabbath. Third Edition. Crown 8vo. Cloth, price 6s.

Speech in Season. Fourth Edition. Crown 8vo. Cloth, price 9s.

Thoughts for the Times. Eleventh Edition. Crown 8vo. Cloth, price 7s. 6d.

Unsectarian Family Prayers, for Morning and Evening for a Week, with short selected passages from the Bible. Second Edition. Square crown 8vo. Cloth, price 3s. 6d.

HAWKER (Robert Stephen).
The Poetical Works of. Now first collected and arranged, with a prefatory notice by J. G. Godwin. With Portrait. Crown 8vo. Cloth, price 12s.

HELLWALD (Baron F. von).
The Russians in Central Asia. A Critical Examination, down to the present time, of the Geography and History of Central Asia. Translated by Lieut.-Col. Theodore Wirgman, LL.B. Large post 8vo. With Map. Cloth, price 12s.

HELVIG (Major H.).
The Operations of the Bavarian Army Corps. Translated by Captain G. S. Schwabe. With Five large Maps. In 2 vols. Demy 8vo. Cloth, price 24s.

Tactical Examples: Vol. I. The Battalion, price 15s. Vol. II. The Regiment and Brigade, price 10s. 6d. Translated from the German by Col. Sir Lumley Graham. With numerous Diagrams. Demy 8vo. Cloth.

HERFORD (Brooke).
The Story of Religion in England. A Book for Young Folk. Crown 8vo. Cloth, price 5s.

HEWLETT (Henry G.).
A Sheaf of Verse. Fcap. 8vo. Cloth, price 3s. 6d.

HINTON (James).
Life and Letters of. Edited by Ellice Hopkins, with an Introduction by Sir W. W. Gull, Bart., and Portrait engraved on Steel by C. H. Jeens. Second Edition. Crown 8vo. Cloth, 8s. 6d.

HINTON (James)—*continued*.
Chapters on the Art of Thinking, and other Essays. With an Introduction by Shadworth Hodgson. Edited by C. H. Hinton. Crown 8vo. Cloth, price 8s. 6d.

The Place of the Physician. To which is added ESSAYS ON THE LAW OF HUMAN LIFE, AND ON THE RELATION BETWEEN ORGANIC AND INORGANIC WORLDS. Second Edition. Crown 8vo. Cloth, price 3s. 6d.

Physiology for Practical Use. By various Writers. With 50 Illustrations. 2 vols. Second Edition. Crown 8vo. Cloth, price 12s. 6d.

An Atlas of Diseases of the Membrana Tympani. With Descriptive Text. Post 8vo. Price £6 6s.

The Questions of Aural Surgery. With Illustrations. 2 vols. Post 8vo. Cloth, price 12s. 6d.

The Mystery of Pain. New Edition. Fcap. 8vo. Cloth limp, 1s.

HOCKLEY (W. B.).
Tales of the Zenana; or, A Nuwab's Leisure Hours. By the Author of "Pandurang Hari." With a Preface by Lord Stanley of Alderley. 2 vols. Crown 8vo. Cloth, price 21s.

Pandurang Hari; or, Memoirs of a Hindoo. A Tale of Mahratta Life sixty years ago. With a Preface by Sir H. Bartle E. Frere, G. C. S. I., &c. New and Cheaper Edition. Crown 8vo. Cloth, price 6s.

HOFFBAUER (Capt.).
The German Artillery in the Battles near Metz. Based on the official reports of the German Artillery. Translated by Capt. E. O. Hollist. With Map and Plans. Demy 8vo. Cloth, price 21s.

HOLMES (E. G. A.).
Poems. First and Second Series. Fcap. 8vo. Cloth, price 5s. each.

HOLROYD (Major W. R. M.).
Tas-hil ul Kālām; or, Hindustani made Easy. Crown 8vo. Cloth, price 5s.

HOOPER (Mary).
Little Dinners: How to Serve them with Elegance and Economy. Thirteenth Edition. Crown 8vo. Cloth, price 5s.

Cookery for Invalids, Persons of Delicate Digestion, and Children. Crown 8vo. Cloth, price 3s. 6d.

Every-Day Meals. Being Economical and Wholesome Recipes for Breakfast, Luncheon, and Supper. Second Edition. Crown 8vo. Cloth, price 5s.

HOOPER (Mrs. G.).
The House of Raby. With a Frontispiece. Crown 8vo. Cloth, price 3s. 6d.

HOPKINS (Ellice).
Life and Letters of James Hinton, with an Introduction by Sir W. W. Gull, Bart., and Portrait engraved on Steel by C. H. Jeens. Second Edition. Crown 8vo. Cloth, price 8s. 6d.

HOPKINS (M.).
The Port of Refuge; or, Counsel and Aid to Shipmasters in Difficulty, Doubt, or Distress. Crown 8vo. Second and Revised Edition. Cloth, price 6s.

HORNE (William), M.A.
Reason and Revelation: an Examination into the Nature and Contents of Scripture Revelation, as compared with other Forms of Truth. Demy 8vo. Cloth, price 12s.

HORNER (The Misses).
Walks in Florence. A New and thoroughly Revised Edition. 2 vols. Crown 8vo. Cloth limp. With Illustrations.
Vol. I.—Churches, Streets, and Palaces. 10s. 6d. Vol. II.—Public Galleries and Museums. 5s.

HOWARD (Mary M.).
Beatrice Aylmer, and other Tales. Crown 8vo. Cloth, price 6s.

HOWELL (James).
A Tale of the Sea, Sonnets, and other Poems. Fcap. 8vo. Cloth, price 5s.

HUGHES (Allison).
Penelope and other Poems. Fcap. 8vo. Cloth, price 4s. 6d.

HULL (Edmund C. P.).
The European in India. With a MEDICAL GUIDE FOR ANGLO-INDIANS. By R. R. S. Mair, M.D., F.R.C.S.E. Third Edition, Revised and Corrected. Post 8vo. Cloth, price 6s.

HUTCHISON (Lieut. Col. F. J.), and Capt. G. H. MACGREGOR.
Military Sketching and Reconnaissance. With Fifteen Plates. Small 8vo. Cloth, price 6s.

The first Volume of Military Handbooks for Regimental Officers. Edited by Lieut.-Col. C. B. BRACKENBURY, R.A., A.A.G.

INCHBOLD (J. W.).
Annus Amoris. Sonnets. Fcap. 8vo. Cloth, price 4s. 6d.

INGELOW (Jean).
Off the Skelligs. A Novel. With Frontispiece. Second Edition. Crown 8vo. Cloth, price 6s.

The Little Wonder-horn. A Second Series of "Stories Told to a Child." With Fifteen Illustrations. Small 8vo. Cloth, price 2s. 6d.

Indian Bishoprics. By an Indian Churchman. Demy 8vo. 6d.

International Scientific Series (The).
I. Forms of Water: A Familiar Exposition of the Origin and Phenomena of Glaciers. By J. Tyndall, LL.D., F.R.S. With 25 Illustrations. Seventh Edition. Crown 8vo. Cloth, price 5s.
II. Physics and Politics; or, Thoughts on the Application of the Principles of "Natural Selection" and "Inheritance" to Political Society. By Walter Bagehot. Fourth Edition. Crown 8vo. Cloth, price 4s.
III. Foods. By Edward Smith, M.D., &c. With numerous Illustrations. Fifth Edition. Crown 8vo. Cloth, price 5s.
IV. Mind and Body: The Theories of their Relation. By Alexander Bain, LL.D. With Four Illustrations. Sixth Edition. Crown 8vo. Cloth, price 4s.
V. The Study of Sociology. By Herbert Spencer. Seventh Edition. Crown 8vo. Cloth, price 5s.

International Scientific Series (The)—*continued*.
VI. On the Conservation of Energy. By Balfour Stewart, LL.D., &c. With 14 Illustrations. Fifth Edition. Crown 8vo. Cloth, price 5s.
VII. Animal Locomotion; or, Walking, Swimming, and Flying. By J. B. Pettigrew, M.D., &c. With 130 Illustrations. Second Edition. Crown 8vo. Cloth, price 5s.
VIII. Responsibility in Mental Disease. By Henry Maudsley, M.D. Third Edition. Crown 8vo. Cloth, price 5s.
IX. The New Chemistry. By Professor J. P. Cooke. With 31 Illustrations. Fourth Edition. Crown 8vo. Cloth, price 5s.
X. The Science of Law. By Prof. Sheldon Amos. Third Edition. Crown 8vo. Cloth, price 5s.
XI. Animal Mechanism. A Treatise on Terrestrial and Aerial Locomotion. By Prof. E. J. Marey. With 117 Illustrations. Second Edition. Crown 8vo. Cloth, price 5s.
XII. The Doctrine of Descent and Darwinism. By Prof. Oscar Schmidt. With 26 Illustrations. Third Edition. Crown 8vo. Cloth, price 5s.
XIII. The History of the Conflict between Religion and Science. By J. W. Draper, M.D., LL.D. Eleventh Edition. Crown 8vo. Cloth, price 5s.
XIV. Fungi; their Nature, Influences, Uses, &c. By M. C. Cooke, LL.D. Edited by the Rev. M. J. Berkeley, F.L.S. With numerous Illustrations. Second Edition. Crown 8vo. Cloth, price 5s.
XV. The Chemical Effects of Light and Photography. By Dr. Hermann Vogel. With 100 Illustrations. Third and Revised Edition. Crown 8vo. Cloth, price 5s.
XVI. The Life and Growth of Language. By Prof. William Dwight Whitney. Second Edition. Crown 8vo. Cloth, price 5s.
XVII. Money and the Mechanism of Exchange. By W. Stanley Jevons, F.R.S. Fourth Edition. Crown 8vo. Cloth, price 5s.

International Scientific Series (The)—*continued.*

XVIII. The Nature of Light: With a General Account of Physical Optics. By Dr. Eugene Lommel. With 188 Illustrations and a table of Spectra in Chromo-lithography. Second Edition. Crown 8vo. Cloth, price 5s.

XIX. Animal Parasites and Messmates. By M. Van Beneden. With 83 Illustrations. Second Edition. Crown 8vo. Cloth, price 5s.

XX. Fermentation. By Prof. Schützenberger. With 28 Illustrations. Second Edition. Crown 8vo. Cloth, price 5s.

XXI. The Five Senses of Man. By Prof. Bernstein. With 91 Illustrations. Second Edition. Crown 8vo. Cloth, price 5s.

XXII. The Theory of Sound in its Relation to Music. By Prof. Pietro Blaserna. With numerous Illustrations. Second Edition. Crown 8vo. Cloth, price 5s.

XXIII. Studies in Spectrum Analysis. By J. Norman Lockyer. F.R.S. With six photographic Illustrations of Spectra, and numerous engravings on wood. Crown 8vo. Second Edition. Cloth, price 6s. 6d.

XXIV. A History of the Growth of the Steam Engine. By Prof. R. H. Thurston. With numerous Illustrations. Second Edition. Crown 8vo. Cloth, price 6s. 6d.

XXV. Education as a Science. By Alexander Bain, LL.D. Second Edition. Crown 8vo. Cloth, price 5s.

XXVI. The Human Species. By Prof. A. de Quatrefages. Second Edition. Crown 8vo. Cloth, price 5s.

XXVII. Modern Chromatics. With Applications to Art and Industry, by Ogden N. Rood. With 130 original Illustrations. Crown 8vo. Cloth, price 5s.

Forthcoming Volumes.

Prof. W. KINGDON CLIFFORD, M.A. The First Principles of the Exact Sciences explained to the Non-mathematical.

W. B. CARPENTER, LL.D., F.R.S. The Physical Geography of the Sea.

Sir JOHN LUBBOCK, Bart. F.R.S On Ants and Bees.

International Scientific Series (The)—*continued.*

Forthcoming Volumes— continued.

Prof. W. T. THISELTON DYER, B.A., B.Sc. Form and Habit in Flowering Plants.

Prof. MICHAEL FOSTER, M.D. Protoplasm and the Cell Theory.

H. CHARLTON BASTIAN, M.D., F.R.S. The Brain as an Organ of Mind.

Prof. A. C. RAMSAY, LL.D., F.R.S. Earth Sculpture: Hills, Valleys, Mountains, Plains, Rivers, Lakes; how they were Produced, and how they have been Destroyed.

P. BERT (Professor of Physiology, Paris). Forms of Life and other Cosmical Conditions.

Prof. T. H. HUXLEY. The Crayfish: an Introduction to the Study of Zoology.

The Rev. A SECCHI, D.J., late Director of the Observatory at Rome. The Stars.

Prof. J. ROSENTHAL, of the University of Erlangen. General Physiology of Muscles and Nerves.

FRANCIS GALTON, F.R.S. Psychometry.

J. W. JUDD, F.R.S. The Laws of Volcanic Action.

Prof. F. N. BALFOUR. The Embryonic Phases of Animal Life.

J. LUYS, Physician to the Hospice de la Salpêtrière. The Brain and its Functions. With Illustrations.

Dr. CARL SEMPER. Animals and their Conditions of Existence.

Prof. WURTZ. Atoms and the Atomic Theory.

GEORGE J. ROMANES, F.L.S. Animal Intelligence.

ALFRED W. BENNETT. A Handbook of Cryptogamic Botany.

JACKSON (T. G.). Modern Gothic Architecture. Crown 8vo. Cloth, price 5s.

JACOB (Maj.-Gen. Sir G. Le Grand), K.C.S.I., C.B. Western India before and during the Mutinies. Pictures drawn from life. Second Edition. Crown 8vo. Cloth, price 7s. 6d.

JENKINS (E.) and RAYMOND (J.), Esqs.
A Legal Handbook for Architects, Builders, and Building Owners. Second Edition Revised. Crown 8vo. Cloth, price 6s.

JENKINS (Rev. R. C.), M.A.
The Privilege of Peter and the Claims of the Roman Church confronted with the Scriptures, the Councils, and the Testimony of the Popes themselves. Fcap. 8vo. Cloth, price 3s. 6d.

JENNINGS (Mrs. Vaughan).
Rahel: Her Life and Letters. With a Portrait from the Painting by Daffinger. Square post 8vo. Cloth, price 7s. 6d.

Jeroveam's Wife and other Poems. Fcap. 8vo. Cloth, price 3s. 6d.

JEVONS (W. Stanley), M.A., F.R.S.
Money and the Mechanism of Exchange. Fourth Edition. Crown 8vo. Cloth, price 5s.

Volume XVII. of The International Scientific Series.

JONES (Lucy).
Puddings and Sweets. Being Three Hundred and Sixty-Five Receipts approved by Experience. Crown 8vo., price 2s. 6d.

KAUFMANN (Rev. M.), B.A.
Utopias; or, Schemes of Social Improvement, from Sir Thomas More to Karl Marx. Crown 8vo. Cloth, price 5s.

Socialism: Its Nature, its Dangers, and its Remedies considered. Crown 8vo. Cloth, price 7s. 6d.

KAY (Joseph), M.A., Q.C.
Free Trade in Land. Edited by his Widow. With Preface by the Right Hon. John Bright, M.P. Third Edition. Crown 8vo. Cloth, price 5s.

KER (David).
The Boy Slave in Bokhara. A Tale of Central Asia. With Illustrations. Crown 8vo. Cloth, price 5s.

The Wild Horseman of the Pampas. Illustrated. Crown 8vo. Cloth, price 5s.

KERNER (Dr. A.), Professor of Botany in the University of Innsbruck.
Flowers and their Unbidden Guests. Translation edited by W. Ogle, M.A., M.D., and a prefatory letter by C. Darwin, F.R.S. With Illustrations. Sq. 8vo. Cloth, price 9s.

KIDD (Joseph), M.D.
The Laws of Therapeutics, or, the Science and Art of Medicine. Crown 8vo. Cloth, price 6s.

KINAHAN (G. Henry), M.R.I.A., &c., of her Majesty's Geological Survey.
Manual of the Geology of Ireland. With 8 Plates, 26 Woodcuts, and a Map of Ireland, geologically coloured. Square 8vo. Cloth, price 15s.

KING (Alice).
A Cluster of Lives. Crown 8vo. Cloth, price 7s. 6d.

KING (Mrs. Hamilton).
The Disciples. A Poem. Third Edition, with some Notes. Crown 8vo. Cloth, price 7s. 6d.

Aspromonte, and other Poems. Second Edition. Fcap. 8vo. Cloth, price 4s. 6d.

KINGSLEY (Charles), M.A.
Letters and Memories of his Life. Edited by his Wife. With 2 Steel engraved Portraits and numerous Illustrations on Wood, and a Facsimile of his Handwriting. Thirteenth Edition. 2 vols. Demy 8vo. Cloth, price 36s.

*** Also a Cabinet Edition in 2 vols. Crown 8vo. Cloth, price 12s.

All Saints' Day and other Sermons. Second Edition. Crown 8vo. Cloth, 7s. 6d.

True Words for Brave Men: a Book for Soldiers' and Sailors' Libraries. Fifth Edition. Crown 8vo. Cloth, price 2s. 6d.

KNIGHT (A. F. C.).
Poems. Fcap. 8vo. Cloth, price 5s.

KNIGHT (Professor W.).
Studies in Philosophy and Literature. Large post 8vo. Cloth, price 7s. 6d.

LACORDAIRE (Rev. Père).
Life: Conferences delivered at Toulouse. A New and Cheaper Edition. Crown 8vo. Cloth, price 3s. 6d.

Lady of Lipari (The).
A Poem in Three Cantos. Fcap. 8vo. Cloth, price 5s.

LAIRD-CLOWES (W.).
Love's Rebellion: a Poem.
Fcap. 8vo. Cloth, price 3s. 6d.

LAMBERT (Cowley), F.R.G.S.
A Trip to Cashmere and Ladâk. With numerous Illustrations. Crown 8vo. Cloth, 7s. 6d.

LAMONT (Martha MacDonald).
The Gladiator: A Life under the Roman Empire in the beginning of the Third Century. With four Illustrations by H. M. Paget. Extra fcap. 8vo. Cloth, price 3s. 6d.

LAYMANN (Capt.).
The Frontal Attack of Infantry. Translated by Colonel Edward Newdigate. Crown 8vo. Cloth, price 2s. 6d.

LEANDER (Richard).
Fantastic Stories. Translated from the German by Paulina B. Granville. With Eight full-page Illustrations by M. E. Fraser-Tytler. Crown 8vo. Cloth, price 5s.

LEE (Rev. F. G.), D.C.L.
The Other World; or, Glimpses of the Supernatural. 2 vols. A New Edition. Crown 8vo. Cloth, price 15s.

LEE (Holme).
Her Title of Honour. A Book for Girls. New Edition. With a Frontispiece. Crown 8vo. Cloth, price 5s.

LENOIR (J.).
Fayoum; or, Artists in Egypt.
A Tour with M. Gérome and others. With 13 Illustrations. A New and Cheaper Edition. Crown 8vo. Cloth, price 3s. 6d.

LEWIS (Edward Dillon).
A Draft Code of Criminal Law and Procedure. Demy 8vo. Cloth, price 21s.

LEWIS (Mary A.).
A Rat with Three Tales.
With Four Illustrations by Catherine F. Frere. Crown 8vo. Cloth, price 5s.

LINDSAY (W. Lauder), M.D., &c.
Mind in the Lower Animals in Health and Disease. 2 vols. Demy 8vo. Cloth, price 32s.

LOCKER (F.).
London Lyrics. A New and Revised Edition, with Additions and a Portrait of the Author. Crown 8vo. Cloth, elegant, price 6s.
Also, a Cheaper Edition. Fcap. 8vo. Cloth, price 2s. 6d.

LOCKYER (J. Norman), F.R.S.
Studies in Spectrum Analysis; with six photographic illustrations of Spectra, and numerous engravings on wood. Second Edition. Crown 8vo. Cloth, price 6s. 6d.
Vol. XXIII. of The International Scientific Series.

LOMMEL (Dr. E.).
The Nature of Light: With a General Account of Physical Optics. Second Edition. With 188 Illustrations and a Table of Spectra in Chromo-lithography. Second Edition. Crown 8vo. Cloth, price 5s.
Volume XVIII. of The International Scientific Series.

LORIMER (Peter), D.D.
John Knox and the Church of England: His Work in her Pulpit, and his Influence upon her Liturgy, Articles, and Parties. Demy 8vo. Cloth, price 12s.

John Wiclif and his English Precursors, by Gerhard Victor Lechler. Translated from the German, with additional Notes. 2 vols. Demy 8vo. Cloth, price 21s.

LOTHIAN (Roxburghe).
Dante and Beatrice from 1282 to 1290. A Romance. 2 vols. Post 8vo. Cloth, price 24s.

LUCAS (Alice).
Translations from the Works of German Poets of the 18th and 19th Centuries. Fcap. 8vo. Cloth, price 5s.

MACAULAY (J.), M.A., M.D., Edin.
The Truth about Ireland: Tours of Observation in 1872 and 1875. With Remarks on Irish Public Questions. Being a Second Edition of "Ireland in 1872," with a New and Supplementary Preface. Crown 8vo. Cloth, price 3s. 6d.

MAC CLINTOCK (L.).
Sir Spangle and the Dingy Hen. Illustrated. Square crown 8vo., price 2s. 6d.

MAC DONALD (G.).
Malcolm. With Portrait of the Author engraved on Steel. Fourth Edition. Crown 8vo. Price 6s.
The Marquis of Lossie. Second Edition. Crown 8vo. Cloth, price 6s.
St. George and St. Michael. Second Edition. Crown 8vo. Cloth, 6s.

MAC KENNA (S. J.).
Plucky Fellows. A Book for Boys. With Six Illustrations. Second Edition. Crown 8vo. Cloth, price 3s. 6d.
At School with an Old Dragoon. With Six Illustrations. Second Edition. Crown 8vo. Cloth, price 5s.

MACLACHLAN (A. N. C.), M.A.
William Augustus, Duke of Cumberland: being a Sketch of his Military Life and Character, chiefly as exhibited in the General Orders of His Royal Highness, 1745—1747. With Illustrations. Post 8vo. Cloth, price 15s.

MACLACHLAN (Mrs.).
Notes and Extracts on Everlasting Punishment and Eternal Life, according to Literal Interpretation. Small crown 8vo. Cloth, price 3s. 6d.

MACNAUGHT (Rev. John).
Cœna Domini: An Essay on the Lord's Supper, its Primitive Institution, Apostolic Uses, and Subsequent History. Demy 8vo. Cloth, price 14s.

MAGNUSSON (Eirikr), M.A., and PALMER (E. H.), M.A.
Johan Ludvig Runeberg's Lyrical Songs, Idylls and Epigrams. Fcap. 8vo. Cloth, price 5s.

MAIR (R. S.), M.D., F.R.C.S.E.
The Medical Guide for Anglo-Indians. Being a Compendium of Advice to Europeans in India, relating to the Preservation and Regulation of Health. With a Supplement on the Management of Children in India. Second Edition. Crown 8vo. Limp cloth, price 3s. 6d.

MALDEN (H. E. and E. E.)
Princes and Princesses. Illustrated. Small crown 8vo. Cloth, price 2s. 6d.

MANNING (His Eminence Cardinal).
Essays on Religion and Literature. By various Writers. Third Series. Demy 8vo. Cloth, price 10s. 6d.
The Independence of the Holy See, with an Appendix containing the Papal Allocution and a translation. Cr. 8vo. Cloth, price 5s.
The True Story of the Vatican Council. Crown 8vo. Cloth, price 5s.

MAREY (E. J.).
Animal Mechanics. A Treatise on Terrestrial and Aerial Locomotion. With 117 Illustrations. Second Edition. Crown 8vo. Cloth, price 5s.
Volume XI. of The International Scientific Series.

MARRIOTT (Maj.-Gen. W. F.), C.S.I.
A Grammar of Political Economy. Crown 8vo. Cloth, price 6s.

Master Bobby: a Tale. By the Author of "Christina North." With Illustrations by E. H. BELL. Extra fcap. 8vo. Cloth, price 3s. 6d.

MASTERMAN (J.).
Worth Waiting for. A New Novel. 3 vols. Crown 8vo. Cloth.
Half-a-dozen Daughters. With a Frontispiece. Crown 8vo. Cloth, price 3s. 6d.

MAUDSLEY (Dr. H.).
Responsibility in Mental Disease. Third Edition. Crown 8vo. Cloth, price 5s.
Volume VIII. of The International Scientific Series.

MAUGHAN (W. C.).
The Alps of Arabia; or, Travels through Egypt, Sinai, Arabia, and the Holy Land. With Map. Second Edition. Demy 8vo. Cloth, price 5s.

MAURICE (C. E.).
Lives of English Popular Leaders. No. 1.—STEPHEN LANGTON. Crown 8vo. Cloth, price 7s. 6d. No. 2.—TYLER, BALL, and OLDCASTLE. Crown 8vo. Cloth, price 7s. 6d.

MEDLEY (Lieut.-Col. J. G.), R.E.
An Autumn Tour in the United States and Canada. Crown 8vo. Cloth, price 5s.

MEREDITH (George).
The Egoist. A Comedy in Narrative. 3 vols. Crown 8vo. Cloth.
The Ordeal of Richard Feverel. A History of Father and Son. In one vol. with Frontispiece. Crown 8vo. Cloth, price 6s.

MERRITT (Henry).
Art - Criticism and Romance. With Recollections, and Twenty-three Illustrations in *eau-forte*, by Anna Lea Merritt. Two vols. Large post 8vo. Cloth, 25s.

MICKLETHWAITE (J. T.), F.S.A.
Modern Parish Churches: Their Plan, Design, and Furniture. Crown 8vo. Cloth, price 7s. 6d.

MIDDLETON (The Lady).
Ballads. Square 16mo. Cloth, price 3s. 6d.

MILLER (Edward).
The History and Doctrines of Irvingism; or, the so-called Catholic and Apostolic Church. 2 vols. Large post 8vo. Cloth, price 25s.

MILLER (Robert).
The Romance of Love. Fcap. 8vo. Cloth, price 5s.

MILNE (James).
Tables of Exchange for the Conversion of Sterling Money into Indian and Ceylon Currency, at Rates from 1s. 8d. to 2s. 3d. per Rupee. Second Edition. Demy 8vo. Cloth, price £2 2s.

MIVART (St. George), F.R.S.
Contemporary Evolution: An Essay on some recent Social Changes. Post 8vo. Cloth, price 7s. 6d.

MOCKLER (E.).
A Grammar of the Baloochee Language, as it is spoken in Makran (Ancient Gedrosia), in the Persia-Arabic and Roman characters. Fcap. 8vo. Cloth, price 5s.

MOFFAT (Robert Scott).
The Economy of Consumption; an Omitted Chapter in Political Economy, with special reference to the Questions of Commercial Crises and the Policy of Trades Unions; and with Reviews of the Theories of Adam Smith, Ricardo, J. S. Mill, Fawcett, &c. Demy 8vo. Cloth, price 18s.
The Principles of a Time Policy: being an Exposition of a Method of Settling Disputes between Employers and Employed in regard to Time and Wages, by a simple Process of Mercantile Barter, without recourse to Strikes or Locks-out. Reprinted from "The Economy of Consumption," with a Preface and Appendix containing Observations on some Reviews of that book, and a Re-criticism of the Theories of Ricardo and J. S. Mill on Rent, Value, and Cost of Production. Demy 8vo. Cloth, price 3s. 6d.

MOLTKE (Field-Marshal Von).
Letters from Russia. Translated by Robina Napier. Crown 8vo. Cloth, price 6s.

MOORE (Rev. D.), M.A.
Christ and His Church. By the Author of "The Age and the Gospel," &c. Crown 8vo. Cloth, price 3s. 6d.

MORE (R. Jasper).
Under the Balkans. Notes of a Visit to the District of Philippopolis in 1876. With a Map and Illustrations from Photographs. Crown 8vo. Cloth, price 6s.

MORELL (J. R.).
Euclid Simplified in Method and Language. Being a Manual of Geometry. Compiled from the most important French Works, approved by the University of Paris and the Minister of Public Instruction. Fcap. 8vo. Cloth, price 2s. 6d.

MORICE (Rev. F. D.), M.A.
The Olympian and Pythian Odes of Pindar. A New Translation in English Verse. Crown 8vo. Cloth, price 7s. 6d.

MORLEY (Susan).
Margaret Chetwynd. A Novel. 3 vols. Crown 8vo. Cloth.

MORSE (E. S.), Ph.D.
First Book of Zoology.
With numerous Illustrations. Crown 8vo. Cloth, price 5s.

MORSHEAD (E. D. A.)
The Agamemnon of Æschylus. Translated into English verse. With an Introductory Essay. Crown 8vo. Cloth, price 5s.

MUSGRAVE (Anthony).
Studies in Political Economy. Crown 8vo. Cloth, price 6s.

Mystery of Miracles, The.
By the Author of "The Supernatural in Nature." Crown 8vo. Cloth, price 6s.

NAAKE (J. T.).
Slavonic Fairy Tales. From Russian, Servian, Polish, and Bohemian Sources. With Four Illustrations. Crown 8vo. Cloth, price 5s.

NEWMAN (J. H.), D.D.
Characteristics from the Writings of. Being Selections from his various Works. Arranged with the Author's personal approval. Third Edition. With Portrait. Crown 8vo. Cloth, price 6s.
** A Portrait of the Rev. Dr. J. H. Newman, mounted for framing, can be had, price 2s. 6d.

NEW WRITER (A).
Songs of Two Worlds. Fourth Edition. Complete in one volume with Portrait. Fcap. 8vo. Cloth, price 7s. 6d.

The Epic of Hades. Seventh and finally revised Edition. Fcap. 8vo. Cloth, price 7s. 6d.

NICHOLAS (Thomas), Ph.D., F.G.S.
The Pedigree of the English People: an Argument, Historical and Scientific, on the Formation and Growth of the Nation, tracing Race-admixture in Britain from the earliest times, with especial reference to the incorporation of the Celtic Aborigines. Fifth Edition. Demy 8vo. Cloth, price 16s.

NICHOLSON (Edward B.).
The Christ Child, and other Poems. Crown 8vo. Cloth, price 4s. 6d.

The Rights of an Animal. Crown 8vo. Cloth, price 3s. 6d.

NICHOLSON (Edward B.)—*continued.*
The Gospel according to the Hebrews. Its Fragments translated and annotated with a critical Analysis of the External and Internal Evidence relating to it. Demy 8vo. Cloth, price 9s. 6d.

NOAKE (Major R. Compton).
The Bivouac ; or, Martial Lyrist, with an Appendix—Advice to the Soldier. Fcap. 8vo. Price 5s. 6d.

NORMAN PEOPLE (The).
The Norman People, and their Existing Descendants in the British Dominions and the United States of America. Demy 8vo. Cloth, price 21s.

NORRIS (Rev. Alfred).
The Inner and Outer Life Poems. Fcap. 8vo. Cloth, price 6s.

Notes on Cavalry Tactics, Organization, &c. By a Cavalry Officer. With Diagrams. Demy 8vo. Cloth, price 12s.

Nuces : Exercises on the Syntax of the Public School Latin Primer. New Edition in Three Parts. Crown 8vo. Each 1s.
** The Three Parts can also be had bound together in cloth, price 3s.

O'BRIEN (Charlotte G.).
Light and Shade. 2 vols. Crown 8vo. Cloth, gilt tops, price 12s.

O'MEARA (Kathleen).
Frederic Ozanam, Professor of the Sorbonne ; His Life and Works. Second Edition. Crown 8vo. Cloth, price 7s. 6d.

Oriental Sporting Magazine (The).
A Reprint of the first 5 Volumes, in 2 Volumes. Demy 8vo. Cloth, price 28s.

PALGRAVE (W. Gifford).
Hermann Agha ; An Eastern Narrative. Third and Cheaper Edition. Crown 8vo. Cloth, price 6s.

PANDURANG HARI ;
Or, Memoirs of a Hindoo. With an Introductory Preface by Sir H. Bartle E. Frere, G.C.S.I., C.B. Crown 8vo. Price 6s.

PARKER (Joseph), D.D.
The Paraclete: An Essay on the Personality and Ministry of the Holy Ghost, with some reference to current discussions. Second Edition. Demy 8vo. Cloth, price 12s.

PARR (Harriet).
Echoes of a Famous Year. Crown 8vo. Cloth, price 8s. 6d.

PARSLOE (Joseph).
Our Railways: Sketches, Historical and Descriptive. With Practical Information as to Fares, Rates, &c., and a Chapter on Railway Reform. Crown 8vo. Cloth, price 6s.

PATTISON (Mrs. Mark).
The Renaissance of Art in France. With Nineteen Steel Engravings. 2 vols. Demy 8vo. Cloth, price 32s.

PAUL (C. Kegan).
Mary Wollstonecraft. Letters to Imlay. With Prefatory Memoir by, and Two Portraits in *eau forte*, by Anna Lea Merritt. Crown 8vo. Cloth, price 6s.
Goethe's Faust. A New Translation in Rime. Crown 8vo. Cloth, price 6s.
William Godwin: His Friends and Contemporaries. With Portraits and Facsimiles of the Handwriting of Godwin and his Wife. 2 vols. Square post 8vo. Cloth, price 28s.
The Genius of Christianity Unveiled. Being Essays by William Godwin never before published. Edited, with a Preface, by C. Kegan Paul. Crown 8vo. Cloth, price 7s. 6d.

PAUL (Margaret Agnes).
Gentle and Simple: A Story. 2 vols. Crown 8vo. Cloth, gilt tops, price 12s.
** Also a Cheaper Edition in one vol. with Frontispiece. Crown 8vo. Cloth, price 6s.

PAYNE (John).
Songs of Life and Death. Crown 8vo. Cloth, price 5s.

PAYNE (Prof. J. F.).
Lectures on Education. Price 6d.
II. Fröbel and the Kindergarten system. Second Edition.

PAYNE (Prof. J. F.)—*continued*.
A Visit to German Schools: Elementary Schools in Germany. Notes of a Professional Tour to inspect some of the Kindergartens, Primary Schools, Public Girls' Schools, and Schools for Technical Instruction in Hamburgh, Berlin, Dresden, Weimar, Gotha, Eisenach, in the autumn of 1874. With Critical Discussions of the General Principles and Practice of Kindergartens and other Schemes of Elementary Education. Crown 8vo. Cloth, price 4s. 6d.

PEACOCKE (Georgiana).
Rays from the Southern Cross: Poems. Crown 8vo. With Sixteen Full-page Illustrations by the Rev. P. Walsh. Cloth elegant, price 10s. 6d.

PELLETAN (E.).
The Desert Pastor, Jean Jarousseau. Translated from the French. By Colonel E. P. De L'Hoste. With a Frontispiece. New Edition. Fcap. 8vo. Cloth, price 3s. 6d.

PENNELL (H. Cholmondeley).
Pegasus Resaddled. By the Author of "Puck on Pegasus," &c. &c. With Ten Full-page Illustrations by George Du Maurier. Second Edition. Fcap. 4to. Cloth elegant, price 12s. 6d.

PENRICE (Maj. J.), B.A.
A Dictionary and Glossary of the Ko-ran. With copious Grammatical References and Explanations of the Text. 4to. Cloth, price 21s.

PERCIVAL (Rev. P.).
Tamil Proverbs, with their English Translation. Containing upwards of Six Thousand Proverbs. Third Edition. Demy 8vo. Sewed, price 9s.

PESCHEL (Dr. Oscar).
The Races of Man and their Geographical Distribution. Large crown 8vo. Cloth, price 9s.

PETTIGREW (J. Bell), M.D., F.R.S.
Animal Locomotion; or, Walking, Swimming, and Flying. With 130 Illustrations. Second Edition. Crown 8vo. Cloth, price 5s.
Volume VII. of The International Scientific Series.

PFEIFFER (Emily).
Quarterman's Grace, and other Poems. Crown 8vo. Cloth, price 5s.
Glan Alarch: His Silence and Song. A Poem. Second Edition. Crown 8vo. price 6s.
Gerard's Monument, and other Poems. Second Edition. Crown 8vo. Cloth, price 6s.
Poems. Second Edition. Crown 8vo. Cloth, price 6s.

PIGGOT (J.), F.S.A., F.R.G.S.
Persia—Ancient and Modern. Post 8vo. Cloth, price 10s. 6d.

PINCHES (Thomas), M.A.
Samuel Wilberforce: Faith —Service—Recompense. Three Sermons. With a Portrait of Bishop Wilberforce (after a Photograph by Charles Watkins). Crown 8vo. Cloth, price 4s. 6d.

PLAYFAIR (Lieut.-Col.), Her Britannic Majesty's Consul-General in Algiers.
Travels in the Footsteps of Bruce in Algeria and Tunis. Illustrated by facsimiles of Bruce's original Drawings, Photographs, Maps, &c. Royal 4to. Cloth, bevelled boards, gilt leaves, price £3 3s.

POLLOCK (W. H.).
Lectures on French Poets. Delivered at the Royal Institution. Small crown 8vo. Cloth, price 5s.

POOR (Henry V.).
Money and its Laws, embracing a History of Monetary Theories and a History of the Currencies of the United States. Demy 8vo. Cloth, price 21s.

POUSHKIN (A. S.).
Russian Romance. Translated from the Tales of Belkin, &c. By Mrs. J. Buchan Telfer (née Mouravieff). Crown 8vo. Cloth, price 7s. 6d.

POWER (H.).
Our Invalids: How shall we Employ and Amuse Them? Fcap. 8vo. Cloth, price 2s. 6d.

POWLETT (Lieut. N.), R.A.
Eastern Legends and Stories in English Verse. Crown 8vo. Cloth, price 5s.

PRESBYTER.
Unfoldings of Christian Hope. An Essay showing that the Doctrine contained in the Damnatory Clauses of the Creed commonly called Athanasian is unscriptural. Small crown 8vo. Cloth, price 4s. 6d.

PRICE (Prof. Bonamy).
Currency and Banking. Crown 8vo. Cloth, price 6s.
Chapters on Practical Political Economy. Being the Substance of Lectures delivered before the University of Oxford. Large post 8vo. Cloth, price 12s.

PROCTOR (Richard A.), B.A.
Our Place among Infinities. A Series of Essays contrasting our little abode in space and time with the Infinities around us. To which are added Essays on "Astrology," and "The Jewish Sabbath." Third Edition. Crown 8vo. Cloth, price 6s.
The Expanse of Heaven. A Series of Essays on the Wonders of the Firmament. With a Frontispiece. Fourth Edition. Crown 8vo. Cloth, price 6s.

Proteus and Amadeus. A Correspondence. Edited by Aubrey De Vere. Crown 8vo. Cloth, price 5s.

PUBLIC SCHOOLBOY.
The Volunteer, the Militiaman, and the Regular Soldier. Crown 8vo. Cloth, price 5s.

Punjaub (The) and North Western Frontier of India. By an old Punjaubee. Crown 8vo. Cloth, price 5s.

QUATREFAGES (Prof. A. de).
The Human Species. Second Edition. Crown 8vo. Cloth, price 5s.
Vol. XXVI. of The International Scientific Series.

RAM (James).
The Philosophy of War. Small crown 8vo. Cloth, price 3s. 6d.

RAVENSHAW (John Henry), B.C.S.
Gaur: Its Ruins and Inscriptions. Edited with considerable additions and alterations by his Widow. With forty-four photographic illustrations and twenty-five fac-similes of Inscriptions. Super royal 4to. Cloth, 3*l*. 13*s*. 6*d*.

READ (Carveth).
On the Theory of Logic: An Essay. Crown 8vo. Cloth, price 6*s*.

REANEY (Mrs. G. S.).
Blessing and Blessed; a Sketch of Girl Life. With a frontispiece. Crown 8vo. Cloth, price 5*s*.

Waking and Working; or, from Girlhood to Womanhood. With a Frontispiece. Crown 8vo. Cloth, price 5*s*.

English Girls: their Place and Power. With a Preface by R. W. Dale, M.A., of Birmingham. Second Edition. Fcap. 8vo. Cloth, price 2*s*. 6*d*.

Just Anyone, and other Stories. Three Illustrations. Royal 16mo. Cloth, price 1*s*. 6*d*.

Sunshine Jenny and other Stories. Three Illustrations. Royal 16mo. Cloth, price 1*s*. 6*d*.

Sunbeam Willie, and other Stories. Three Illustrations. Royal 16mo. Cloth, price 1*s*. 6*d*.

RHOADES (James).
Timoleon. A Dramatic Poem. Fcap. 8vo. Cloth, price 5*s*.

RIBOT (Prof. Th.).
English Psychology. Second Edition. A Revised and Corrected Translation from the latest French Edition. Large post 8vo. Cloth, price 9*s*.

Heredity: A Psychological Study on its Phenomena, its Laws, its Causes, and its Consequences. Large crown 8vo. Cloth, price 9*s*.

RINK (Chevalier Dr. Henry).
Greenland: Its People and its Products. By the Chevalier Dr. HENRY RINK, President of the Greenland Board of Trade. With sixteen Illustrations, drawn by the Eskimo, and a Map. Edited by Dr. ROBERT BROWN. Crown 8vo. Price 10*s*. 6*d*.

ROBERTSON (The Late Rev. F. W.), M.A., of Brighton.
Notes on Genesis. New and cheaper Edition. Crown 8vo., price 3*s*. 6*d*.

Sermons. Four Series. Small crown 8vo. Cloth, price 3*s*. 6*d*. each.

Expository Lectures on St. Paul's Epistles to the Corinthians. A New Edition. Small crown 8vo. Cloth, price 5*s*.

Lectures and Addresses, with other literary remains. A New Edition. Crown 8vo. Cloth, price 5*s*.

An Analysis of Mr. Tennyson's "In Memoriam." (Dedicated by Permission to the Poet-Laureate.) Fcap. 8vo. Cloth, price 2*s*.

The Education of the Human Race. Translated from the German of Gotthold Ephraim Lessing. Fcap. 8vo. Cloth, price 2*s*. 6*d*.

Life and Letters. Edited by the Rev. Stopford Brooke, M.A., Chaplain in Ordinary to the Queen.

I. 2 vols., uniform with the Sermons. With Steel Portrait. Crown 8vo. Cloth, price 7*s*. 6*d*.

II. Library Edition, in Demy 8vo., with Two Steel Portraits. Cloth, price 12*s*.

III. A Popular Edition, in one vol. Crown 8vo. Cloth, price 6*s*.

The above Works can also be had half-bound in morocco.

*** A Portrait of the late Rev. F. W. Robertson, mounted for framing, can be had, price 2*s*. 6*d*.

ROBINSON (A. Mary F.).
A Handful of Honeysuckle. Fcap. 8vo. Cloth, price 3*s*. 6*d*.

RODWELL (G. F.), F.R.A.S., F.C.S.
Etna: a History of the Mountain and its Eruptions. With Maps and Illustrations. Square 8vo. Cloth, price 9s.

ROOD (Ogden N.).
Modern Chromatics, with Applications to Art and Industry. With 130 Original Illustrations. Crown 8vo. Cloth, price 5s.
Vol. XXVII. of The International Scientific Series.

ROSS (Mrs. E.), ("Nelsie Brook").
Daddy's Pet. A Sketch from Humble Life. With Six Illustrations. Royal 16mo. Cloth, price 1s.

ROSS (Alexander), D.D.
Memoir of Alexander Ewing, Bishop of Argyll and the Isles. Second and Cheaper Edition. Demy 8vo. Cloth, price 10s. 6d.

RUSSELL (Major Frank S.).
Russian Wars with Turkey, Past and Present. With Two Maps. Second Edition. Crown 8vo., price 6s.

RUTHERFORD (John).
The Secret History of the Fenian Conspiracy; its Origin, Objects, and Ramifications. 2 vols. Post 8vo. Cloth, price 18s.

SADLER (S. W.), R.N.
The African Cruiser. A Midshipman's Adventures on the West Coast. With Three Illustrations. Second Edition. Crown 8vo. Cloth, price 3s. 6d.

SAMAROW (G.).
For Sceptre and Crown. A Romance of the Present Time. Translated by Fanny Wormald. 2 vols. Crown 8vo. Cloth, price 15s.

SAUNDERS (Katherine).
Gideon's Rock, and other Stories. Crown 8vo. Cloth, price 6s.
Joan Merryweather, and other Stories. Crown 8vo. Cloth, price 6s.
Margaret and Elizabeth. A Story of the Sea. Crown 8vo. Cloth, price 6s.

SAUNDERS (John).
Israel Mort, Overman: A Story of the Mine. Cr. 8vo. Price 6s.
Hirell. With Frontispiece. Crown 8vo. Cloth, price 3s. 6d.
Abel Drake's Wife. With Frontispiece. Crown 8vo. Cloth, price 3s. 6d.

SCHELL (Maj. von).
The Operations of the First Army under Gen. von Goeben. Translated by Col. C. H. von Wright. Four Maps. Demy 8vo. Cloth, price 9s.
The Operations of the First Army under Gen. von Steinmetz. Translated by Captain E. O. Hollist. Demy 8vo. Cloth, price 10s. 6d.

SCHELLENDORF (Maj.-Gen. B. von).
The Duties of the General Staff. Translated from the German by Lieutenant Hare. Vol. I. Demy 8vo. Cloth, 10s. 6d.

SCHERFF (Maj. W. von).
Studies in the New Infantry Tactics. Parts I. and II. Translated from the German by Colonel Lumley Graham. Demy 8vo. Cloth, price 7s. 6d.

SCHMIDT (Prof. Oscar).
The Doctrine of Descent and Darwinism. With 26 Illustrations. Third Edition. Crown 8vo. Cloth, price 5s.
Volume XII. of The International Scientific Series.

SCHÜTZENBERGER (Prof. F.).
Fermentation. With Numerous Illustrations. Second Edition. Crown 8vo. Cloth, price 5s.
Volume XX. of The International Scientific Series.

SCOTT (Leader).
A Nook in the Apennines: A Summer beneath the Chestnuts. With Frontispiece, and 27 Illustrations in the Text, chiefly from Original Sketches. Crown 8vo. Cloth, price 7s. 6d.

SCOTT (Patrick).
The Dream and the Deed, and other Poems. Fcap. 8vo. Cloth, price 5s.

SCOTT (W. T.).
Antiquities of an Essex Parish; or, Pages from the History of Great Dunmow. Crown 8vo. Cloth, price 5s. Sewed, 4s.

SCOTT (Robert H.).
Weather Charts and Storm Warnings. Illustrated. Second Edition. Crown 8vo. Cloth, price 3s. 6d.
Seeking his Fortune, and other Stories. With Four Illustrations. Crown 8vo. Cloth, price 3s. 6d.

SENIOR (N. W.).
Alexis De Tocqueville. Correspondence and Conversations with Nassau W. Senior, from 1833 to 1859. Edited by M. C. M. Simpson. 2 vols. Large post 8vo. Cloth, price 21s.

Journals Kept in France and Italy. From 1848 to 1852. With a Sketch of the Revolution of 1848. Edited by his Daughter, M. C. M. Simpson. 2 vols. Post 8vo. Cloth, price 24s.

Seven Autumn Leaves from Fairyland. Illustrated with Nine Etchings. Square crown 8vo. Cloth, price 3s. 6d.

SHADWELL (Maj.-Gen.), C.B.
Mountain Warfare. Illustrated by the Campaign of 1799 in Switzerland. Being a Translation of the Swiss Narrative compiled from the Works of the Archduke Charles, Jomini, and others. Also of Notes by General H. Dufour on the Campaign of the Valtelline in 1635. With Appendix, Maps, and Introductory Remarks. Demy 8vo. Cloth, price 16s.

SHAKSPEARE (Charles).
Saint Paul at Athens: Spiritual Christianity in Relation to some Aspects of Modern Thought. Nine Sermons preached at St. Stephen's Church, Westbourne Park. With Preface by the Rev. Canon FARRAR. Crown 8vo. Cloth, price 5s.

SHAW (Major Wilkinson).
The Elements of Modern Tactics. Practically applied to English Formations. With Twenty-five Plates and Maps. Small crown 8vo. Cloth, price 12s.
*** The Second Volume of "Military Handbooks for Officers and Non-commissioned Officers." Edited by Lieut.-Col. C. B. Brackenbury, R.A., A.A.G.

SHAW (Flora L.).
Castle Blair: a Story of Youthful Lives. 2 vols. Crown 8vo. Cloth, gilt tops, price 12s. Also, an edition in one vol. Crown 8vo. 6s.

SHELLEY (Lady).
Shelley Memorials from Authentic Sources. With (now first printed) an Essay on Christianity by Percy Bysshe Shelley. With Portrait. Third Edition. Crown 8vo. Cloth, price 5s.

SHERMAN (Gen. W. T.).
Memoirs of General W. T. Sherman, Commander of the Federal Forces in the American Civil War. By Himself. 2 vols. With Map. Demy 8vo Cloth, price 24s. *Copyright English Edition.*

SHILLITO (Rev. Joseph).
Womanhood: its Duties, Temptations, and Privileges. A Book for Young Women. Second Edition. Crown 8vo. Price 3s. 6d.

SHIPLEY (Rev. Orby), M.A.
Principles of the Faith in Relation to Sin. Topics for Thought in Times of Retreat. Eleven Addresses. With an Introduction on the neglect of Dogmatic Theology in the Church of England, and a Postscript on his leaving the Church of England. Demy 8vo. Cloth, price 12s.

Church Tracts, or Studies in Modern Problems. By various Writers. 2 vols. Crown 8vo. Cloth, price 5s. each.

SHUTE (Richard), M.A.
A Discourse on Truth. Large Post 8vo. Cloth, price 9s.

SMEDLEY (M. B.).
Boarding-out and Pauper Schools for Girls. Crown 8vo. Cloth, price 3s. 6d.

SMITH (Edward), M.D., LL.B., F.R.S.
Health and Disease, as Influenced by the Daily, Seasonal, and other Cyclical Changes in the Human System. A New Edition. Post 8vo. Cloth, price 7s. 6d.

Foods. Profusely Illustrated. Fifth Edition. Crown 8vo. Cloth, price 5s.
Volume III. of The International Scientific Series.

Practical Dietary for Families, Schools, and the Labouring Classes. A New Edition. Post 8vo. Cloth, price 3s. 6d.

Tubercular Consumption in its Early and Remediable Stages. Second Edition. Crown 8vo. Cloth, price 6s.

SMITH (Hubert).
Tent Life with English Gipsies in Norway. With Five full-page Engravings and Thirty-one smaller Illustrations by Whymper and others, and Map of the Country showing Routes. Third Edition. Revised and Corrected. Post 8vo. Cloth, price 21s.

Songs of Two Worlds. By the Author of "The Epic of Hades." Fourth Edition. Complete in one Volume, with Portrait. Fcap. 8vo. Cloth, price 7s. 6d.

Songs for Music.
By Four Friends. Square crown 8vo. Cloth, price 5s.
Containing songs by Reginald A. Gatty, Stephen H. Gatty, Greville J. Chester, and Juliana Ewing.

SPEDDING (James).
Reviews and Discussions, Literary, Political, and Historical not relating to Bacon. Demy 8vo. Cloth, price 12s. 6d.

SPENCER (Herbert).
The Study of Sociology. Seventh Edition. Crown 8vo. Cloth, price 5s.
Volume V. of The International Scientific Series.

SPICER (H.).
Otho's Death Wager. A Dark Page of History Illustrated. In Five Acts. Fcap. 8vo. Cloth, price 5s.

STAPLETON (John).
The Thames: A Poem. Crown 8vo. Cloth, price 6s.

STEPHENS (Archibald John), LL.D.
The Folkestone Ritual Case. The Substance of the Argument delivered before the Judicial Committee of the Privy Council. On behalf of the Respondents. Demy 8vo. Cloth, price 6s.

STEVENSON (Robert Louis).
An Inland Voyage. With Frontispiece by Walter Crane. Crown 8vo. Cloth, price 7s. 6d.
Travels with a Donkey in the Cevennes. With Frontispiece by Walter Crane. Crown 8vo. Cloth, price 7s. 6d.

STEVENSON (Rev. W. F.).
Hymns for the Church and Home. Selected and Edited by the Rev. W. Fleming Stevenson.
The most complete Hymn Book published.
The Hymn Book consists of Three Parts:—I. For Public Worship.—II. For Family and Private Worship.—III. For Children.
₊ *Published in various forms and prices, the latter ranging from 8d. to 6s. Lists and full particulars will be furnished on application to the Publishers.*

STEWART (Prof. Balfour), M.A., LL.D., F.R.S.
On the Conservation of Energy. Fifth Edition. With Fourteen Engravings. Crown 8vo. Cloth, price 5s.
Volume VI. of The International Scientific Series.

STONEHEWER (Agnes).
Monacella: A Legend of North Wales. A Poem. Fcap. 8vo. Cloth, price 3s. 6d.

STORR (Francis), and TURNER (Hawes).
Canterbury Chimes; or, Chaucer Tales retold to Children. With Illustrations from the Ellesmere MS. Extra Fcap. 8vo. Cloth, price 3s. 6d.

STRETTON (Hesba). Author of "Jessica's First Prayer."
Michel Lorio's Cross, and other Stories. With Two Illustrations. Royal 16mo. Cloth, price 1s. 6d.
The Storm of Life. With Ten Illustrations. Twenty-first Thousand. Royal 16mo. Cloth, price 1s. 6d.
The Crew of the Dolphin. Illustrated. Fourteenth Thousand. Royal 16mo. Cloth, price 1s. 6d.
Cassy. Thirty-eighth Thousand. With Six Illustrations. Royal 16mo. Cloth, price 1s. 6d.
The King's Servants. Forty-third Thousand. With Eight Illustrations. Royal 16mo. Cloth, price 1s. 6d.
Lost Gip. Fifty-ninth Thousand. With Six Illustrations. Royal 16mo. Cloth, price 1s. 6d.
₊ *Also a handsomely bound Edition, with Twelve Illustrations, price 2s. 6d.*

STRETTON (Hesba)—*continued.*
David Lloyd's Last Will. With Four Illustrations. Royal 16mo., price 2s. 6d.

The Wonderful Life. Thirteenth Thousand. Fcap. 8vo. Cloth, price 2s. 6d.

A Man of His Word. With Frontispiece. Royal 16mo. Limp cloth, price 6d.

A Night and a Day. With Frontispiece. Twelfth Thousand. Royal 16mo. Limp cloth, price 6d.

Friends till Death. With Illustrations and Frontispiece. Twenty-fourth Thousand. Royal 16mo. Cloth, price 1s. 6d.; limp cloth, price 6d.

Two Christmas Stories. With Frontispiece. Twenty-first Thousand. Royal 16mo. Limp cloth, price 6d.

Michel Lorio's Cross, and Left Alone. With Frontispiece. Fifteenth Thousand. Royal 16mo. Limp cloth, price 6d.

Old Transome. With Frontispiece. Sixteenth Thousand. Royal 16mo. Limp cloth, price 6d.
⁎ Taken from "The King's Servants."

The Worth of a Baby, and how Apple-Tree Court was won. With Frontispiece. Nineteenth Thousand. Royal 16mo. Limp cloth, price 6d.

Through a Needle's Eye: a Story. 2 vols. Crown 8vo. Cloth, gilt top, price 12s.

STUBBS (Lieut.-Colonel F. W.)
The Regiment of Bengal Artillery. The History of its Organization, Equipment, and War Services. Compiled from Published Works, Official Records, and various Private Sources. With numerous Maps and Illustrations. 2 vols. Demy 8vo. Cloth, price 32s.

STUMM (Lieut. Hugo), German Military Attaché to the Khivan Expedition.
Russia's advance Eastward. Based on the Official Reports of. Translated by Capt. C. E. H. VINCENT. With Map. Crown 8vo. Cloth, price 6s.

SULLY (James), M.A.
Sensation and Intuition. Demy 8vo. Cloth, price 10s. 6d.
Pessimism: a History and a Criticism. Demy 8vo. Price 14s.

Sunnyland Stories. By the Author of "Aunt Mary's Bran Pie." Illustrated. Small 8vo. Cloth, price 3s. 6d.

Supernatural in Nature, The. A Verification by Free Use of Science. Demy 8vo. Cloth, price 14s.

Sweet Silvery Sayings of Shakespeare. Crown 8vo. Cloth gilt, price 7s. 6d.

SYME (David).
Outlines of an Industrial Science. Second Edition. Crown 8vo. Cloth, price 6s.

Tales of the Zenana. By the Author of "Pandurang Hari." 2 vols. Crown 8vo. Cloth, price 21s.

TAYLOR (Algernon).
Guienne. Notes of an Autumn Tour. Crown 8vo. Cloth, price 4s. 6d.

TAYLOR (Rev. J. W. A.), M.A.
Poems. Fcap. 8vo. Cloth, price 5s.

TAYLOR (Sir H.).
Works Complete. Author's Edition, in 5 vols. Crown 8vo. Cloth, price 6s. each.
Vols. I. to III. containing the Poetical Works, Vols. IV. and V. the Prose Works.

TAYLOR (Col. Meadows), C.S.I., M.R.I.A.
A Noble Queen: a Romance of Indian History. 3 vols. Crown 8vo. Cloth.

Seeta. 3 vols. Crown 8vo. Cloth.

Tippoo Sultaun: a Tale of the Mysore War. New Edition with Frontispiece. Crown 8vo. Cloth price 6s.

Ralph Darnell. New and Cheaper Edition. With Frontispiece. Crown 8vo. Cloth, price 6s.

The Confessions of a Thug. New Edition. Crown 8vo. Cloth, price 6s.

Tara: a Mahratta Tale. New Edition. Crown 8vo. Cloth, price 6s.

TELFER (J. Buchan), F.R.G.S., Commander, R.N.
The Crimea and Trans-Caucasia. With numerous Illustrations and Maps. 2 vols. Medium 8vo. Second Edition. Cloth, price 36s.

TENNYSON (Alfred).
The Imperial Library Edition. Complete in 7 vols. Demy 8vo. Cloth, price £3 13s. 6d.; in Roxburgh binding, £4 7s. 6d.

Author's Edition. Complete in 6 Volumes. Post 8vo. Cloth gilt; or half-morocco, Roxburgh style :—

VOL. I. Early Poems, and English Idylls. Price 6s.; Roxburgh, 7s. 6d.

VOL. II. Locksley Hall, Lucretius, and other Poems. Price 6s.; Roxburgh, 7s. 6d.

VOL. III. The Idylls of the King (*Complete*). Price 7s. 6d.; Roxburgh, 9s.

VOL. IV. The Princess, and Maud. Price 6s.; Roxburgh, 7s. 6d.

VOL. V. Enoch Arden, and In Memoriam. Price 6s.; Roxburgh, 7s. 6d.

VOL. VI. Dramas. Price 7s.; Roxburgh, 8s. 6d.

Cabinet Edition. 12 vols. Each with Frontispiece. Fcap. 8vo. Cloth, price 2s. 6d. each.
CABINET EDITION. 12 vols. Complete in handsome Ornamental Case. 32s.

Pocket Volume Edition. 13 vols. In neat case, 36s. Ditto, ditto. Extra cloth gilt, in case, 42s.

The Royal Edition. Complete in one vol. Cloth, 16s. Cloth extra, 18s. Roxburgh, half morocco, price 20s.

The Guinea Edition. Complete in 12 vols., neatly bound and enclosed in box. Cloth, price 21s. French morocco, price 31s. 6d.

The Shilling Edition of the Poetical and Dramatic Works, in 12 vols., pocket size. Price 1s. each.

The Crown Edition. Complete in one vol., strongly bound in cloth, price 6s. Cloth, extra gilt leaves, price 7s. 6d. Roxburgh, half morocco, price 8s. 6d.

*** Can also be had in a variety of other bindings.

TENNYSON (Alfred)—*continued*.
Original Editions :

The Lover's Tale. (Now for the first time published.) Fcap. 8vo. Cloth, 3s. 6d.

Poems. Small 8vo. Cloth, price 6s.

Maud, and other Poems. Small 8vo. Cloth, price 3s. 6d.

The Princess. Small 8vo. Cloth, price 3s. 6d.

Idylls of the King. Small 8vo. Cloth, price 5s.

Idylls of the King. Complete. Small 8vo. Cloth, price 6s.

The Holy Grail, and other Poems. Small 8vo. Cloth, price 4s. 6d.

Gareth and Lynette. Small 8vo. Cloth, price 3s.

Enoch Arden, &c. Small 8vo. Cloth, price 3s. 6d.

In Memoriam. Small 8vo. Cloth, price 4s.

Queen Mary. A Drama. New Edition. Crown 8vo. Cloth, price 6s.

Harold. A Drama. Crown 8vo. Cloth, price 6s.

Selections from Tennyson's Works. Super royal 16mo. Cloth, price 3s. 6d. Cloth gilt extra, price 4s.

Songs from Tennyson's Works. Super royal 16mo. Cloth extra, price 3s. 6d.
Also a cheap edition. 16mo. Cloth, price 2s. 6d.

Idylls of the King, and other Poems. Illustrated by Julia Margaret Cameron. 2 vols. Folio. Half-bound morocco, cloth sides, price £6 6s. each.

Tennyson for the Young and for Recitation. Specially arranged. Fcap. 8vo. Price 1s. 6d.

Tennyson Birthday Book. Edited by Emily Shakespear. 32mo. Cloth limp, 2s.; cloth extra, 3s.

*** A superior edition, printed in red and black, on antique paper, specially prepared. Small crown 8vo. Cloth, extra gilt leaves, price 5s.; and in various calf and morocco bindings.

THOMAS (Moy).
A Fight for Life. With Frontispiece. Crown 8vo. Cloth, price 3s. 6d.

THOMPSON (Alice C.).
Preludes. A Volume of Poems. Illustrated by Elizabeth Thompson (Painter of "The Roll Call"). 8vo. Cloth, price 7s. 6d.

THOMPSON (Rev. A. S.).
Home Words for Wanderers. A Volume of Sermons. Crown 8vo. Cloth, price 6s.

THOMSON (J. Turnbull).
Social Problems; or, an Inquiry into the Law of Influences. With Diagrams. Demy 8vo. Cloth, price 10s. 6d.

Thoughts in Verse.
Small Crown 8vo. Cloth, price 1s. 6d.

THRING (Rev. Godfrey), B.A.
Hymns and Sacred Lyrics. Fcap. 8vo. Cloth, price 5s.

THURSTON (Prof. R. H.).
A History of the Growth of the Steam Engine. With numerous Illustrations. Second Edition. Crown 8vo. Cloth, price 6s. 6d.

TODHUNTER (Dr. J.)
Alcestis: A Dramatic Poem. Extra fcap. 8vo. Cloth, price 5s.
Laurella; and other Poems. Crown 8vo. Cloth, price 6s. 6d.

TOLINGSBY (Frere).
Elnora. An Indian Mythological Poem. Fcap. 8vo. Cloth, price 6s.

TRAHERNE (Mrs. A.).
The Romantic Annals of a Naval Family. A New and Cheaper Edition. Crown 8vo. Cloth, price 5s.

Translations from Dante, Petrarch, Michael Angelo, and Vittoria Colonna. Fcap. 8vo. Cloth, price 7s. 6d.

TURNER (Rev. C. Tennyson).
Sonnets, Lyrics, and Translations. Crown 8vo. Cloth, price 4s. 6d.

TYNDALL (John), LL.D., F.R.S.
Forms of Water. A Familiar Exposition of the Origin and Phenomena of Glaciers. With Twenty-five Illustrations. Seventh Edition. Crown 8vo. Cloth, price 5s.
Volume I. of The International Scientific Series.

VAN BENEDEN (Mons.).
Animal Parasites and Messmates. With 83 Illustrations. Second Edition. Cloth, price 5s.
Volume XIX. of The International Scientific Series.

VAUGHAN (H. Halford), sometime Regius Professor of Modern History in Oxford University.
New Readings and Renderings of Shakespeare's Tragedies. Vol. I. Demy 8vo. Cloth, price 15s.

VILLARI (Prof.).
Niccolo Machiavelli and His Times. Translated by Linda Villari. 2 vols. Large post 8vo. Cloth, price 24s.

VINCENT (Capt. C. E. H.).
Elementary Military Geography, Reconnoitring, and Sketching. Compiled for Non-Commissioned Officers and Soldiers of all Arms. Square crown 8vo. Cloth, price 2s. 6d.

VOGEL (Dr. Hermann).
The Chemical effects of Light and Photography, in their application to Art, Science, and Industry. The translation thoroughly revised. With 100 Illustrations, including some beautiful specimens of Photography. Third Edition. Crown 8vo. Cloth, price 5s.
Volume XV. of The International Scientific Series.

VYNER (Lady Mary).
Every day a Portion. Adapted from the Bible and the Prayer Book, for the Private Devotions of those living in Widowhood. Collected and edited by Lady Mary Vyner. Square crown 8vo. Cloth extra, price 5s.

WALDSTEIN (Charles), Ph.D.
The Balance of Emotion and Intellect: An Essay Introductory to the Study of Philosophy. Crown 8vo. Cloth, price 6s.

WALLER (Rev. C. B.)
The Apocalypse, Reviewed under the Light of the Doctrine of the Unfolding Ages and the Restitution of all Things. Demy 8vo. Cloth, price 12s.

WALTERS (Sophia Lydia).
The Brook: A Poem. Small crown 8vo. Cloth, price 3s. 6d.
A Dreamer's Sketch Book. With Twenty-one Illustrations by Percival Skelton, R. P. Leitch, W. H. J. Boot, and T. R. Pritchett. Engraved by J. D. Cooper. Fcap. 4to. Cloth, price 12s. 6d.

WARTENSLEBEN (Count H. von).
The Operations of the South Army in January and February, 1871. Compiled from the Official War Documents of the Head-quarters of the Southern Army. Translated by Colonel C. H. von Wright. With Maps. Demy 8vo. Cloth, price 6s.
The Operations of the First Army under Gen. von Manteuffel. Translated by Colonel C. H. von Wright. Uniform with the above. Demy 8vo. Cloth, price 9s.

WATERFIELD, W.
Hymns for Holy Days and Seasons. 32mo. Cloth, price 1s. 6d.

WATSON (Sir Thomas), Bart., M.D.
The Abolition of Zymotic Diseases, and of other similar enemies of Mankind. Small crown 8vo. Cloth, price 3s. 6d.

WAY (A.), M.A.
The Odes of Horace Literally Translated in Metre. Fcap. 8vo. Cloth, price 2s.

WELLS (Capt. John C.), R.N.
Spitzbergen—The Gateway to the Polynia; or, A Voyage to Spitzbergen. With numerous Illustrations by Whymper and others, and Map. New and Cheaper Edition. Demy 8vo. Cloth, price 6s.

Wet Days, by a Farmer. Small crown 8vo. Cloth, price 6s.

WETMORE (W. S.).
Commercial Telegraphic Code. Second Edition. Post 4to. Boards, price 42s.

WHITAKER (Florence).
Christy's Inheritance. A London Story. Illustrated. Royal 16mo. Cloth, price 1s. 6d.

WHITE (A. D.), LL.D.
Warfare of Science. With Prefatory Note by Professor Tyndall. Second Edition. Crown 8vo. Cloth, price 3s. 6d.

WHITNEY (Prof. W. D.)
The Life and Growth of Language. Second Edition. Crown 8vo. Cloth, price 5s. *Copyright Edition.*
Volume XVI. of The International Scientific Series.
Essentials of English Grammar for the Use of Schools. Crown 8vo. Cloth, price 3s. 6d.

WICKHAM (Capt. E. H., R.A.)
Influence of Firearms upon Tactics: Historical and Critical Investigations. By an OFFICER OF SUPERIOR RANK (in the German Army). Translated by Captain E. H. Wickham, R.A. Demy 8vo. Cloth, price 7s. 6d.

WICKSTEED (P. H.).
Dante: Six Sermons. Crown 8vo. Cloth, price 5s.

WILLIAMS (A. Lukyn).
Famines in India; their Causes and Possible Prevention. The Essay for the Le Bas Prize, 1875. Demy 8vo. Cloth, price 5s.

WILLIAMS (Charles), one of the Special Correspondents attached to the Staff of Ghazi Ahmed Mouktar Pasha.
The Armenian Campaign: Diary of the Campaign of 1877 in Armenia and Koordistan. With Two Special Maps. Large post 8vo. Cloth, price 10s. 6d.

WILLIAMS (Rowland), D.D.
Life and Letters of, with Extracts from his Note-Books. Edited by Mrs. Rowland Williams. With a Photographic Portrait. 2 vols. Large post 8vo. Cloth, price 24s.
Stray Thoughts from the Note-Books of the Late Rowland Williams, D.D. Edited by his Widow. Crown 8vo. Cloth, price 3s. 6d.

WILLIAMS (Rowland), D.D.— *continued.*
Psalms, Litanies, Counsels and Collects for Devout Persons. Edited by his Widow. New and Popular Edition. Crown 8vo. Cloth, price 3s. 6d.

WILLIS (R.), M.D.
Servetus and Calvin: a Study of an Important Epoch in the Early History of the Reformation. 8vo. Cloth, price 16s.

William Harvey. A History of the Discovery of the Circulation of the Blood. With a Portrait of Harvey, after Faithorne. Demy 8vo. Cloth, price 14s.

WILLOUGHBY (The Hon. Mrs.).
On the North Wind— Thistledown. A Volume of Poems. Elegantly bound. Small crown 8vo. Cloth, price 7s. 6d.

WILSON (H. Schütz).
Studies and Romances. Crown 8vo. Cloth, price 7s. 6d.
The Tower and Scaffold. A Miniature Monograph. Large fcap. 8vo. Price 1s.

WILSON (Lieut.-Col. C. T.).
James the Second and the Duke of Berwick. Demy 8vo. Cloth, price 12s. 6d.

WINTERBOTHAM (Rev. R.), M.A., B.Sc.
Sermons and Expositions. Crown 8vo. Cloth, price 7s. 6d.

WINTERFELD (A. Von).
A Distinguished Man. A Humorous Romance. Translated by W. Laird-Clowes. 3 vols. Crown 8vo. Cloth.

Within Sound of the Sea. By the Author of "Blue Roses," "Vera," &c. Third Edition. 2 vols. Crown 8vo. Cloth, gilt tops, price 12s.
*** Also a cheaper edition in one Vol. with frontispiece. Crown 8vo. Cloth, price 6s.

WOINOVITS (Capt. I.).
Austrian Cavalry Exercise. Translated by Captain W. S. Cooke. Crown 8vo. Cloth, price 7s.

WOLLSTONECRAFT (Mary).
Letters to Imlay. With a Preparatory Memoir by C. Kegan Paul, and two Portraits in *eau forte* by Anna Lea Merritt. Crown 8vo. Cloth, price 6s.

WOOD (C. F.).
A Yachting Cruise in the South Seas. With Six Photographic Illustrations. Demy 8vo. Cloth, price 7s. 6d.

WOODS (James Chapman).
A Child of the People, and other poems. Small crown 8vo. Cloth, price 5s.

WRIGHT (Rev. David), M.A.
Waiting for the Light, and other Sermons. Crown 8vo. Cloth, price 6s.

WYLD (R. S.), F.R.S.E.
The Physics and the Philosophy of the Senses; or, The Mental and the Physical in their Mutual Relation. Illustrated by several Plates. Demy 8vo. Cloth, price 16s.

YOUMANS (Eliza A.).
An Essay on the Culture of the Observing Powers of Children, especially in connection with the Study of Botany. Edited, with Notes and a Supplement, by Joseph Payne, F.C.P., Author of "Lectures on the Science and Art of Education," &c. Crown 8vo. Cloth, price 2s. 6d.

First Book of Botany. Designed to Cultivate the Observing Powers of Children. With 300 Engravings. New and Cheaper Edition. Crown 8vo. Cloth, price 2s. 6d.

YOUMANS (Edward L.), M.D.
A Class Book of Chemistry, on the Basis of the New System. With 200 Illustrations. Crown 8vo. Cloth, price 5s.

YOUNG (William).
Gottlob, etcetera. Small crown 8vo. Cloth, price 3s. 6d.

ZIMMERN (H.).
Stories in Precious Stones. With Six Illustrations. Third Edition. Crown 8vo. Cloth, price 5s.

LONDON:—C. KEGAN PAUL & CO., 1, PATERNOSTER SQUARE.